J.R.J. HAIGHT lives in Australia.

It has been suggested that the great works of seventeenth-century literature were written despite rather than because of the contemporary reverence for reason. Nineteenth-century scholars associated classical reason with the rules of art and with adherence to the precepts of the ancients. They attributed the rigidity of seventeenth-century literature to those restrictive influences – a view of classical reason that has survived into the twentieth century in spite of more sympathetic interpretations of classical literature.

For those who believe that the concept of reason in French classical drama and prose is narrow and technical, J.R.J. Haight's book will be a revelation. She demonstrates, through an analysis of theological, philosophical, political, moral, and aesthetic implications of *raison*, that the literature of the period displays a wide range of uses of the word. She concludes that, in its most general form, *raison* conveyed in French classicist doctrine a profound if not original metaphysical insight into the nature of the universe.

JEANNE HAIGHT

The concept of reason
in French classical literature
1635–1690

UNIVERSITY OF TORONTO PRESS
Toronto Buffalo London

University of Toronto Romance Series 45

© University of Toronto Press 1982
Toronto Buffalo London
Printed in Canada

ISBN 0-8020-2384-3

Canadian Cataloguing in Publication Data

Haight, Jeanne, 1946-
The concept of reason in French classical literature
1635-1690

Includes index.
ISBN 0-8020-2384-3

1. Reason in literature – History – 17th century.
2. French literature – 17th century – History and
criticism. I. Title.

PQ245.H34   840'.9'384   C82-094546-3

TO MY MOTHER AND FATHER

Le Vulgaire sçait bien qu'il parle et qu'il se fait entendre aux autres ;
Mais les Esprits esclairez veulent connoistre les differentes Idées sur
lesquelles nos Paroles se forment.

Préface *Dictionnaire de l'Académie*

Contents

Acknowledgments

This study is based upon a doctoral dissertation at Oxford University. I owe a great debt to my supervisor, Dr R.A. Sayce of Worcester College, for his guidance and concern. His faith in my work was an inspiration to me and I deeply regret that he has not lived to see the publication of this work.

I wish to thank my husband, Peter Abelson, and all those relatives and friends who, in different ways, have helped to make this work possible. I also remember with pleasure illuminating talks with Dr D.C. Potts, Professor Anthony Levi, the late Dr Will Moore, and, once, briefly in Paris, with Professor Jules Brody.

I am grateful to the Canada Council for its financial assistance in the preparation of the original thesis. This book has been published with the help of grants from the Canadian Federation for the Humanities, using funds provided by the Social Sciences and Humanities Research Council of Canada, and from the Publications Fund of University of Toronto Press.

THE CONCEPT OF REASON IN
FRENCH CLASSICAL LITERATURE
1635–1690

Introduction

A man that seeketh precise truth had need to remember what every name he
uses stands for, and to place it accordingly, or else he will find himself entangled
in words, as a bird in lime twiggs: the more he struggles the more belimed.

Hobbes *Leviathan* I 4

Art and language are virtually our only means of access to the thought of
earlier times. Yet they can be deceptive. Both require interpretation and to
this task we inevitably tend to bring our own conceptions and our own meanings. In literature it is all too easy to assume that we understand the thought
of earlier periods because the words used are still employed today. But words
do not have fixed meanings and, like colours, their meanings can be entirely
changed by the background in which they are set. Definition and redefinition
of words are a necessary part of thinking, of conceiving, and of grappling
with reality. If this is true today it was no less true for those who lived before
us and, in any period of European history, words, especially key words
descriptive of reality, must be affected by the changing conception of man
and of the universe of which he is a part.

The seventeenth century saw an important shift in man's conception of the
world, a change which in its broadest terms can be described as a move away
from the religious to a more scientific outlook. Inevitably this change is
reflected in the use and definition of central concepts such as *reason, truth,*
and *nature*. Thus Bush sees a narrowing in the concept of reason,[1] Bethell
points to a fragmentation of the human mind,[2] and Hoopes concludes: 'The
intellectual history of the seventeenth century is marked by the gradual dis-
association of knowledge and virtue ... a shift from the tradition of right
reason to the new tradition of scientific reasoning.'[3] A similar view is
expressed by C.S. Lewis.[4]

The questions raised by these broad perspectives have begun to have an impact on our understanding of reason in French classical literature. Reason has generally been regarded as a key concept in that literature and almost any discussion of classical literature includes some reference to reason – its meaning, role, or significance. Yet, except for two short essays – by Fidao-Justiniani[5] – and by Michéa[6] – no general or comparative study has been made of the concept or of the uses and senses of the word. *Raison* in French classical literature has been fairly consistently interpreted as narrow and restrictive and it has been suggested that the great works were written despite rather than because of the contemporary reverence for reason. Nineteenth-century scholars, especially Taine,[7] associated classical reason with the rules of art and with adherence to the precepts of the ancients and they attributed the rigidity which they saw in seventeenth-century literature to these restrictive influences. This view of classical reason has survived into the twentieth century[8] despite more sympathetic interpretations of the literature of the period. In 1927, Bray stressed the doctrinaire aspect of classical theory and of classical reason.[9] Other critics from Lanson and Mornet to Peyre and Borgerhoff have demonstrated the inspired quality of much seventeenth-century French literature, but on the whole they also attribute this inspiration either to defiance of reason and precept or to the influence of non-rational principles such as *l'art de plaire*, *le sublime*, and *le je ne sais quoi*.[10] Only a few, particularly Michéa and Brody, have considered the possibility that in the seventeenth century reason may not have been indissolubly linked with rules and restrictive principles and that it may have had associations and connotations which it no longer possesses today.[11] It is largely in response to their call for further exploration of this question that the present study was undertaken.

An attitude which may be partly Platonic and partly Christian is clearly apparent in classical literature. Many critics have noted the belief in a universal truth which transcends the vicissitudes of history and of custom.[12] But the consequences of this belief for the concept of reason have not been fully explored. Those who question Bray's emphasis on the dogmatic aspects of classicism stress the importance of this belief and consider that it counters the dogmatism of reason and of the rules of art. They see it as the source of those rules and as the denial of their adequacy and ultimate authority. Mornet holds that the great classical writers freed themselves from the inhibiting influence of classical doctrine[13] and Brody thinks the Platonic belief in a metaphysical world of ultimate truth was essential to the flowering of classicism.[14] Borgerhoff sees the notion of the *je ne sais quoi* as evidence of a Platonic awareness of a higher reality and he concludes that 'terms which express the indefinable' save classicism from 'the killing finality of applied reason.'[15] If there is such a hidden impulse inspiring classical literature, there seems little cause to assume that it would not be reflected in the concept of reason as well as in the *je ne sais quoi*. *Raison*, in some uses, may also capture and express this striving for the ideal.

In attempting to discover the meaning of *raison* in seventeenth-century French literature I have chosen the years 1635–90 so as not to prejudice the question whether there is a *classicisme* or a classical doctrine as usually conceived. The classical period has often been given a narrower definition and has been confined to the years 1660–80, the earlier part of the century being regarded as pre-classical or baroque. This derives from the view that classical reason is dogmatic and that classicism reaches its apogee with Boileau, the great exponent of the supremacy of reason. No one will doubt Boileau's devotion to reason, but the narrowness of his conception has been contested[16] and his influence on Molière, Racine, La Fontaine, and Bossuet has also been questioned.[17] If Boileau and his contemporaries are regarded as distinctive rather than as forming a school, there is no good cause for separating them from earlier important and, in this sense, classical writers. The years from 1635 to 1690 span roughly the period between the appearance of Descartes's *Discours de la méthode* and La Bruyère's *Les caractères*. They thus allow consideration of the much disputed connection between the reason of Descartes and that of Boileau and his contemporaries.[18] They also allow comparison of the concepts of reason in Boileau, Molière, Racine, La Fontaine, and Bossuet with those of earlier writers such as Balzac, Corneille, and Pascal. This book concentrates on these and on other well-known writers such as Chapelain, Bouhours, La Bruyère, La Rochefoucauld, Mme de La Fayette, Malebranche, and Fontenelle. It draws on the commentaries of important painters and architects such as Poussin, Blondel, and Perrault, but it ignores less well-known dramatists, poets, and theologians such as Thomas Corneille, Colletet, and Bourdaloue. Thus the term *classical literature* is here intended to designate the works of authors of some high repute during a century which may loosely, but conveniently, be called the period of classicism.

The method used in this book is essentially pragmatic. The concept of reason in the various authors is approached through their use of the word *raison* and the meaning of this word is sought in moral and political commentary as well as in aesthetic theory. *Raison* in the seventeenth century possessed a great variety of acceptations and these are examined in some detail in seventeenth-century dictionary definitions at the start of this study. However, in literature, the collection and tabulation of individual uses, while interesting as an adjunct to dictionary definitions, are insufficient if we are to arrive at an understanding of the concept and if we are to comment on the relative restrictiveness or freedom of reason as an aesthetic principle. For these purposes individual uses need to be seen in relation to each other and to be examined within a framework which makes it possible to distil the underlying conception to which they relate. Studies touching on the sense of *raison* in the seventeenth century have generally been concerned to find a predominant or central meaning for this word. Wright suggests that the *raison* of classicism refers above all to 'common sense'[19] and Fidao-Justiniani virtually identifies it with 'prudence.'[20] But the meaning of these definitions, like all other senses of the word, is likely to be altered by an author's conceptual framework. *Raison* as a principle, as an ideal, and in its adjectival form *raisonnable* contains some form of evaluation and it may also represent an idea which the author himself seeks to discover and to define. Inevitably, we are led to look beyond the word to the context in which it is used and hence to the parameters against which it is measured and from which it may draw meaning.

These parameters may have little to do with the professed beliefs of an author and in many instances they may cut across partisan divisions and individual attitudes and philosophies. Michéa has observed that reason in the seventeenth century represented a collective concern approachable from many points of view and expressing many different attitudes.[21] Similarly, Bayet points out that there can be as many rationalisms as there are definitions of reason[22] and Hazard, in his chapter 'Les rationaux,' shows the diverse origins and forms of faith in reason in the seventeenth century.[23] The great complexity of seventeenth-century thought may in many instances conceal shared assumptions and these may emerge most clearly in an analysis of the meaning of words. Consequently, this book makes no attempt to classify authors except in terms of their use of the word *raison*. Indeed, some classifications such as epicurean or stoic can be misleading because they imply notions of reason which encourage twentieth-century preconceptions. Thus the view that reason can control the passions has a very different meaning if reason is held to involve feeling elements and is not regarded as a purely cerebral faculty. Nevertheless, discussion of the senses and meaning of *raison* in the seventeenth century is bound to lead to some assessment of the relative importance of these and other influences, particularly perhaps of the Augustinian influence since this most closely resembles the Platonic. As Borgerhoff says, 'To understand how much of the seventeenth century was the extension of Scholasticism and how much of it was an Augustinian reaction against Scholasticism is perhaps to understand the true nature of its classicism.'[24]

In seventeenth-century literature the use of the word *raison* itself suggests a framework through which to discover the broader connotations and associations of the concept. *Raison* was used to refer to an object of intellection as well as to a human faculty for cognition.[25] One might say that it is sometimes the star and sometimes the telescope. In such uses, *raison* is hypostatized, it is treated as something which exists in reality itself irrespective of our knowledge about it. The conception of the reasonable and the conception of human reason may be related in different ways and in different degrees to this object of intellection. Thus the concept of reason emerges as having a number of different levels and these can be discussed separately. While such divisions within the concept are in a sense artificial and while they tend to splinter the individual author's conception, they are also valuable because they allow a comparison between authors and make it possible to discover and to analyse those shared assumptions which may underlie different attitudes and philosophies. Indeed, the failure to distinguish between different levels in the concept of reason may be largely responsible for the tendency to label classical reason as 'desséchée et froide.'[26] An author may conceive of the ideal of reason as not in the least restrictive while he sees the faculty of reasoning as limiting and restraining. Bénichou expresses just such a paradoxical contrast when, referring to Racine, he speaks of 'la déraison raisonnante.'[27]

Accordingly, when, after discussing dictionary definitions, I move on to the use of *raison* in literature, I have organized my material so as to separate as far as possible reason as an object of intellection and as standard from discussion of the faculty reason. The second chapter is concerned with the definition of *raison* as predicated of God, the third with three different standards of the reasonable, and the fourth and fifth with two distinct conceptions of human reason. In the sixth chapter, the conclusions of earlier chapters are brought to bear on the conception of reason as an aesthetic principle.

Within this framework, I discuss at some length the use of the word by the philosophers – particularly Descartes, Pascal, Malebranche, Bayle, and Fontenelle – in order to provide a background against which the variations of usage may be explored. When philosophers refer to reason they often define their meaning more clearly than do other writers. In the obviously literary authors, such as the dramatists Corneille, Molière, and Racine, the conception of reason is more difficult to pinpoint. The relative clarity of the philosophers' definition is valuable since an abstract word such as *raison* does not refer to an identifiable phenomenon and consequently there is frequently no common ground for comparison. Since there is no fixed anatomy of the human mind, one author may speak of reason where another speaks of the heart: their ideas will sound very different to the modern reader who may conclude that the first is a rationalist while the second is a partisan of the irrational. Yet they may be striving to express something essentially similar. Taking literature in its broader sense, the work of the philosophers is of course a part of literature and it may be, as Allonnes suggests, that 'Le classicisme peut se définir par des traits communs à l'art et à la philosophie.'[28]

Analysis within this framework reveals a sliding movement in the concept of reason during the seventeenth century. Reason is throughout associated with order and proportion, but the nature of this order and proportion changes as the religious aspiration gives way to the scientific. This study does not agree with Brody that *raison* is equivalent, either in Boileau or in classical literature as a whole, to the modern 'intuition.'[29] But, in line with the thrust of Brody's thought, it argues that the concept of reason expands to meet the needs of the classical writer and that it contracts in response to the more pragmatic aspirations of the sceptic and the empiricist. Through the greater part of the century *raison* can represent a point of balance which may be achieved both in discursive logical thought and in intense feeling. In such uses, *raison* is not opposed to the art of pleasing, or to the *je ne sais quoi*; on the contrary, it represents an order and a sense of judgment which are necessary prerequisites for the achievement of these qualities. This broad conception of reason and of the *raisonnable* accompanies the flowering of the great works of seventeenth-century French literature and consequently can be regarded as distinctively classical. For a time it coexists with and overlays a narrower notion predominant in early *libertin* writers and, again, in a more positive and progressive form, in empirical writers towards the end of the period. This narrow view of reason is that which survives the seventeenth century. It is this conception, always present but not always predominant in seventeenth-century literature, which has been largely responsible for the modern interpretation of classical reason as narrow and restrictive.

I

Raison and related words

Quand notre langue sera changée, il [le Dictionnaire de l'Académie] servira à
faire entendre les livres dignes de la postérité qui sont écrits en notre temps.
Fénelon *Lettre à l'Académie* 24

Although in the seventeenth century lexicography was still a science in
embryo, the dictionaries of the period contain a wealth of information about
senses and uses and they raise important questions concerning possible
meanings. Of course the full connotations and associations of an abstract
word such as *raison* are almost certainly beyond the scope of dictionary
definitions which cannot be expected to give the many contexts in which a
word is used. Nevertheless, the definitions of *raison*, particularly in the
monolingual dictionaries, are surprisingly detailed and reveal an astonishing
complexity and variety of meanings contained in this single word or concept.
The main body of lexicographical work in the seventeenth century con-
sisted in bilingual and multilingual dictionaries intended principally to serve
as aids to translators and to readers of Latin and foreign texts. These dictionaries tended to plagiarize and there is no guarantee that their definitions or
translations are contemporary.[1] Only the all-French dictionaries published
in the second half of the century – Richelet's *Dictionnaire françois* (1680),
Furetière's *Dictionnaire universel* (1690), and the *Dictionnaire de l'Académie* (1694) – made the recording of contemporary language their principal
concern. Consequently these three dictionaries can be expected to contribute
most to our understanding of seventeenth-century meanings. The *Dictionnaire de l'Académie* deserves particular attention since it was the official lexicographical work compiled by some of the leading writers of the period and
since its compilation, 1638–94, spanned the greater part of the century. Its
concern with good usage does not appear to affect its definitions of *raison*
which are quite as varied and numerous as those of Richelet and Furetière.

There seems little to be gained from a chronological treatment of these dictionaries. The main purpose of such an approach would be to ascertain changes in the meaning of *raison* during our period. But this is rendered impossible by the tendency of the Latin dictionaries to plagiarize and, more particularly, by the frequent time-lag between the compilation of a dictionary and its publication. The *Dictionnaire de l'Académie* is, of course, notable in this respect, 56 years passing between its commencement and its appearance. This difficulty would perhaps be overcome if the dictionaries recorded the sources from which their definitions and examples are drawn. However, although the monolingual dictionaries, especially Richelet, sometimes give quotations with references, these do not provide sufficient material to trace possible changes in meaning or emphasis.

The definitions of *raison* (given in full in the Appendix) in the three monolingual dictionaries often complement each other. They emphasize different aspects of meaning and introduce synonyms or antonyms suggesting a variety of paths of investigation. The Latin and bilingual dictionaries may be used to supplement these definitions: translations from the French can show the common idea lying behind two French words or indicate a distinction between words which in the monolingual dictionaries are presented as synonymous. The Academy gives 7 main senses of *raison*, Richelet 9, and Furetière 12. All three deal initially with the faculty reason. They go on to define *raison* variously as argument, explanation, proof, cause, and motive; as duty, equity, satisfaction, and vengeance; and as proportion. What might be called the technical senses of *raison* – terme de marchant, terme de logique, terme de mathématique, terme de marine – appear in the Academy and in Furetière, while the supplement to the Academy dictionary, the *Dictionnaire des arts et des sciences*, provides further detail. Finally, all three dictionaries give definitions of *raisonnable*, *raisonnement*, and *raisonner*.

A FACULTY OF MIND

Beginning then with the definitions of reason as a mental faculty, the *Dictionnaire de l'Académie* defines *raison* as 'puissance de l'ame, par laquelle l'homme discourt, et est distingué des bestes.'[2] The examples which follow considerably extend this definition and suggest that *raison* has attributes or functions other than discursive speech and thought[3]: reason makes man responsible for his actions, it is a guide to conduct, it should control the passions, it is capable of understanding. The Academy goes on to say: '*Raison*, se prend aussi quelquefois pour le bon sens, le droit usage de la raison.'

Raison in this definition refers not simply to a formal faculty but to a rightful or correct use of this faculty. The Academy relates it to sense, good sense, or sanity. 'Le droit usage de la raison' is presented in the context of these meanings rather than in the context of a discursive function.

In contrast with the Academy, Richelet and Furetière give as their primary definition the capacity to distinguish truth from falsehood, good from evil. According to Richelet, *raison* has the same meaning as 'la droite raison' and it refers specifically to the capacity for a true knowledge or judgment.[4] Furetière identifies *raison* with *entendement*[5] which he defines as understanding and judgment. Like Richelet, he uses *raison* in his examples to refer to the capacity for correct judgment, linking it with sanity and responsible action.[6] He associates 'la droite raison' with a natural capacity – 'la lumiere naturelle' – and also with the divine – 'selon Dieu et raison.' However, he indicates also that reason is not necessarily associated with truth since it can be a false and misleading guide – 'La raison est perduë et égarée.'

While neither Richelet nor Furetière mentions discourse, Furetière relates *entendement* to sound reasoning[7] and he defines *raisonnement* as an 'action de l'entendement par laquelle on connoist le bien ou le mal, la verité ou la fausseté des choses.' The capacity for discursive thought is thus presented as an intimate part of judgment and understanding, just as the Academy's examples imply that good judgment is an aspect of *raison qui discourt*. Taken together, the definitions of the three dictionaries thus present two main aspects of reason that are at least artificially distinguishable; reason is a capacity for discursive thought and speech, not necessarily correct or right, and it is a capacity for understanding and judgment, more particularly for good or true judgment.

The translations of *raison* in the Latin dictionaries reflect the distinction between discourse and judgment or understanding and indicate that to some extent this distinction may be contained in the words *esprit* and *entendement*. *Raison* is translated as 'ratio' and as 'iudicium,' and 'ratio' is used, along with 'ratiocinari,' most consistently in translations of *raisonner* and of *esprit*.[8] *Esprit* and *entendement* are sometimes used interchangeably and can be synonyms for *raison*; their definition illustrates the difficulty of making clear distinctions in the activities and faculties of the mind.[9] However, despite a considerable overlap in meanings, *esprit* and *entendement* can also be opposed. In this event, *esprit* tends to refer to inventiveness and cleverness, qualities necessary to impressive discourse and argument, while *entendement* is related rather to sound judgment. The Academy gives: 'Il a beaucoup d'esprit, mais il n'a point de jugement.' It would seem that *raison* can be used to designate either element in this equation but that where this sort of contrast is intended *raison* would be more likely to be used to refer to *jugement-entendement* owing to its predominant association with true or correct mental function.

The association of *raison* with rightness and truth tends to blur the definition of the faculty of reason by confusing the faculty with a standard. The phrase *droite raison* can refer to the capacity for both correct thought or argument and correct judgment or understanding. The *Glossarium ad scriptores* by Du Cange gives examples where *recta ratio* is used to mean reaching the right judgment or conclusion. In Latin translations of *raison*, *recta* is often used without *ratio* to mean 'it is right,' 'what is right,' as in 'C'est raison qu'il l'ait, Rectè datur.'[10] In this sense, *droite raison* can mean simply that which is true or right as is suggested by the Academy's example 'Cela est contraire à la droite raison.' In this use *raison* is a standard as well as a faculty; it may be both the object of perception and the consciousness which perceives. The Academy says also that 'droit' can be used to qualify man himself ('un homme droit et incorruptible'); his intentions, soul, or heart; or his 'sens' and 'esprit.'[11] In so far as *raison* represents the element which distinguishes man from animal and endows him with a capacity for truth, it can perhaps be used loosely as the equivalent of any of these apparently distinct faculties.

The connection drawn between *raison* and *sens* or *bon sens* also suggests a broader meaning for *raison* than either discourse or judgment and understanding. All three monolingual dictionaries relate *raison-bon sens* to sanity. The Latin dictionaries show that *sens* can be used like *esprit*, *entendement*, and *raison* simply to refer to 'the mind' but it can also mean to be in one's right mind: 'apud se esse, redire ad se.' The Latin words used in translation of 'être hors du sens' and of 'qui n'est pas de sens rassis' are *furere*, *insanire*, *mente alienari*, *amens*, *demens*, and *insanus*. In addition, *sens* can refer to wisdom. Pomey connects it with *sagesse*. Estienne, Jacques du Puys, and Ranconnet translate both 'homme de bon sens naturel' and 'homme de raison et de bon cerveau' as 'homo cordatus.' To this they add that *bon sens* can be translated by forms of *sapientia* and *intelligentia* and they describe a man with *bon sens* as *sobrius*, *sanus* (opposites of *fanaticus*). Thus *sens* and *bon sens* may refer to mental and emotional stability and not just to the power of thought. Cotgrave translates *sens* as 'sense, wit, conceit, apprehension, understanding, judgment, reason, knowledge, opinion, thought,' and he adds that it can refer to 'natural sense, or feeling.' If *raison* can mean wisdom and natural sense or feeling and if it can, like *sens* and *bon sens*, refer to mental and emotional stability, it may be that its judging and discerning aspect is not always considered as purely cerebral or intellectual. Something more immediate may be involved which ensures the correctness or rightness of thought and judgment.

Furetière identifies *droite raison* with *lumière naturelle*. This phrase does not appear in the Latin dictionaries but they give *raison naturelle* which may have the same meaning. Following Estienne's example, Nicot and his editors say *raison naturelle* is a law or set of rules which is unwritten and inborn ('lex non scripta, sed nata'). The Academy defines *lumière* as knowledge ('connoissance'), as the capacity to acquire knowledge ('intelligence,' 'clarté d'esprit'), and as that which enables man to see truth ('Tout ce qui esclaire l'ame... la lumiere de la foy... la lumiere des sciences'). If, as seems likely, *raison* in the phrase *raison naturelle* is equivalent to *lumière*, then *lumière naturelle* and *droite raison* can refer to a law or light which is inborn and which enables man to see truth. Confirmation of this supposition is provided by the account in the Trévoux dictionary of *droite raison* which presents this phrase in the context of moral truth. God in creating man, it says, gave him knowledge of good and evil and this knowledge is what is meant by *droite raison*. *Droite raison* is a light with which man is born and it acts as a law commanding right and forbidding evil. Its principles are the source of all the rules of *honnôteté* and *justice*, used for the guidance of individuals and society, and it enables man to be almost independent of God. The account ends by relating *droite raison*, *lumière naturelle*, and *raison* to *conscience*. *Conscience* (in the sense of conscience and not just consciousness) may be what the Latin dictionaries mean by 'lex non scripta, sed nata' and it may be related to the sense or feeling involved in the capacity of reason for right judgment and right thinking.

In their definitions of *conscience*, the monolingual dictionaries do indeed connect *conscience* with *droite raison*. Making no clear distinction between consciousness and conscience Richelet claims that *conscience* is dictated by *droite raison*. The definition reads: 'Connoissance qu'on a de soi-même, et que dicte la droite raison dont les lumieres nous font connoitre ce que nous faisons de bien ou de mal. Intérieur éclairé par les lumieres de la droite raison qui est notre juge.' Richelet adds that *conscience* is 'scrupule et difficulté qu'on sent à faire, ou à dire quelque chose, parce que la raison et le bon sens y sont contraires.' Thus *raison* in the form of *droite raison* operates like *conscience* and gives a sense or feeling of right and wrong. Furetière links *conscience* with *cœur*: 'Scrupule, doute et incertitude qu'on a de ce qui est bon ou mauvais... secret du cœur.' And the Academy also stresses the element of feeling: 'Lumiere interieure, sentiment interieur, par lequel l'homme se rend tesmoignage à luy-mesme du bien et du mal qu'il fait.' The connection of *droite raison* and *raison* with *conscience* does not exclude the possibility that *droite raison*, like *recta ratio*, can refer to the correct conduct of thought or argument. Nevertheless the connection with *conscience*, like the association of *raison* with *sens* and *bon sens*, blurs the distinction between cognitive judgment and sentiment.

Because the dictionaries show a clear involvement of feeling in the function of reason and relate the awareness and judgment of reason to conscience, one is led to inquire whether there is any connection between reason and intuition and indeed between reason and imagination. According to modern French dictionaries[12] *intuition* now means a direct and specific knowledge, independent of reasoned proof or argument, of the relationship between things, of their existence or essence; it can also mean a more or less precise feeling about things which cannot be verified. Both these meanings pertain to *raison* in so far as it refers to *bon sens*, *droite raison*, and *conscience*. Although Block and Wartburg's *Dictionnaire étymologique de la langue française* gives 1542 as a first instance of *intuition*, this word is not included in any seventeenth-century French dictionary. Furetière and the Academy give only the adjective *intuitif* which they describe as a purely theological term – 'Il n'a guere d'usage qu'en cette phrase, La vision intuitive de Dieu' (Académie). According to Lalande only the Latin form *intuitio* was used in a non-theological context in seventeenth-century France, appearing first in Descartes's *Regulae*. He says that Descartes uses it to mean a 'connaissance d'une vérité évidente' acting as the foundation on which discursive reasoning is based.[13] Interestingly, in seventeenth-century English the adjective 'intuitive' was apparently used to mean 'of the mind or reason' and was also often contrasted with discursive mental faculties[14] and Lalande maintains that Locke in fact borrowed his use of intuition from Descartes.

Since *intuition* is not mentioned in seventeenth-century French dictionaries, it may be that its meaning, both in its specialized and in its wider form, was incorporated in the word *raison* and that a function of *raison* is the immediate and intuitive grasp of truth. An intuitive quality in the seventeenth-century conception of reason has frequently been claimed by modern critics. Bethel sees such a quality in the English use of 'reason' before Locke and Newton,[15] and Brody takes the Academy's remark 'On dit fig[urative-ment] voir les choses par les yeux de l'esprit, pour dire les examiner par la raison'[16] as evidence for his contention that *raison* is sometimes equivalent to *intuition*. While this metaphorical use is not in itself sufficient evidence for such an equivalence, it may be that *raison* could refer, as Brody maintains, to 'a sensitivity to nuance, a flair for rightness.'[17] However, the evidence provided by the dictionaries is inconclusive.[18]

A possible connection between *raison* and *imagination* is actually implied by the Academy dictionary which, in its definition of the faculty of reason, introduces the phrase *estre de raison*, described as a *Terme de Logique*. The Academy describes *estre de raison*: 'Un Estre qui n'est point réel, et qui ne subsiste que dans l'imagination. Les universels sont des estres de raison.' Furetière makes the connection between *raison* and *imagination* quite explicit, saying that *raison* is sometimes used to refer to *imagination* and that this is its meaning in the phrase *estre de raison*: '*Raison*, se dit quelquefois de la seule faculté imaginative. Les chimeres sont des estres de raison, qui ne subsistent que dans nostre imagination.' The dictionaries attribute a double function to the imagination: it can produce false inventions and it can present the mind with concrete images and ideas. For example, the Academy says that *imagination* can be used of a 'creance, opinion... fantaisie erronnée et bizarre' or of a 'pensée... conception.' It remains unclear whether *raison* is identified with *imagination* only when the latter has true conceptions or also when it produces *chimères*.[19]

A primitive form of the modern French meaning of *imagination* – 'création, inspiration artistique ou littéraire'[20] – is glimpsed in Furetière's definitions. He defines the verb *imaginer* as 'penser, assembler plusieurs idées dans son esprit, dans son imagination' and he remarks that this capacity for forming a clear image in the mind is essential to the artist and poet. However, even in his definition, the imagination is not presented as the artist's source of inspiration. Richelet and the Academy make only passing reference to an association between imagination and art. According to Castor, in the sixteenth century, imagination was on the whole regarded with suspicion while invention, meaning a 'coming into, a finding' ('*in rem venire*'), was 'solidly founded upon the faculty reason.'[21] Perhaps this unfavourable attitude towards the imagination lingers on into the seventeenth century. Given that *raison* involves more than purely cerebral and intellectual functions, it may be that some aesthetically creative or inspirational capacities are included in the attributes of human reason.

Although the faculty of reason is not presented in the dictionaries as consistently reliable, its potential for truth and rightness receives considerable emphasis. Reason is described as referring to the mind or soul of man, as that which elevates man above animal, renders him sane, capable of knowing truth from falsehood and of living according to that knowledge. Reason is an inner light or law, a conscience, perhaps an intuition; it is a capacity for understanding, for judgment, and for thought and speech. Only the last of these is specifically described as fallible. Also, the faculty is not always clearly distinguished from the truth that is perceived and both *raison* and *droite raison* can refer to a standard as well as to the faculty.

A strong connection with truth is apparent in the etymology of *raison*. According to Yon the antecedents of *ratio* are the verb *reor*, meaning 'to say,' and its adjectival participle *ratus* refers to the fixed and reliable.[22] Bayet has investigated possible connections between these meanings and concludes that in primitive culture, owing to the power of the word, speech was associated with injunction and with the making of law. Accordingly, *ratio* (which Lachelier defines as 'système d'idées liées entre elles, compte, raisonnement')[23] came to refer to reliable, or at least potentially reliable, mental processes of various kinds including counting, computing, argument, reasoning, and perception. In all cases, the notion of something fixed and true represents an underlying thread of meaning.[24]

The association of reason with truth provides a link between *raison* as a faculty of the mind and the other senses of *raison*. The definitions of *raison* in Richelet, Furetière, and the Academy, which follow those of the faculty *raison*, fall roughly into two types: those where *raison* is a principle of explanation and those where it is an ideal or standard. In the first of these types, *raison* refers to *preuve par argument*, *preuve par discours*, *sujet*, *cause*, *motif*, *considération*, and *fondement*. In the second type, *raison* is equated with *devoir*, *droit*, *justice*, *équité*, and *titre* and, related to these, it is defined as *satisfaction* and *vengeance*. *Raison* as a principle of explanation and as a standard is in the first instance, like the faculty reason, associated with the true and the reliable. But explanations can be excuses or false justifications, and they can be misleading. Equally, *raison* as a standard can be unjust, answering to personal and selfish needs. Thus it can be used in a negative and derogatory sense. Derogatory senses may however confirm rather than deny the primary association of reason with truth. That a culture may revile what it also reveres is well known to modern anthropologists. Commenting on the derogatory uses of *raison*, Bayet has remarked: 'Non seulement ces acceptations ironiques n'altèrent pas le sens favorable du mot employé, mais elles s'y réfèrent, l'impliquent, et, en fin de compte, n'existent que par lui.'[25]

Another link between the various meanings of *raison* is the notion of relationship between things. Both explanation and justice, in their different ways, establish relationships and this is of course also a function of thought, speech, understanding, and judgment. The idiomatic *livre de raison* and the mathematical uses of *raison* stress this aspect which is central to both the French *raison* and the Latin *ratio*. *Raison* refers to measure and to proportion and these meanings are seen in the adjectival form *raisonnable* suggesting that measure and proportion may underlie the diverse senses of *raison* as if orderly relationship, proportion, measure were themselves features of truth.

A PRINCIPLE OF EXPLANATION

Raisonnement

According to the *Dictionnaire des arts et des sciences*, *raison* was at one time used to mean 'harangue' as in: 'Et il commença orgüeilleusement sa raison, et dit... ' In the sense of proof by argument or discourse, *raison* is akin to the verb *raisonner* and to the noun *raisonnement* and all three can convey an unspoken evaluative good or they can be used derogatorily. Furetière defines *raisonner* in three ways. It can mean to exercise one's understanding, to examine and discuss a question, or to make excuses. Similarly, *raisonnement* can mean the action which seeks knowledge by drawing a formerly unknown conclusion from a known principle, the understanding which distinguishes good from bad and true from false, or it can mean false arguments and excuses. An opposition is thus set up which reflects the distinction between *bon sens* and *raison discursive*. The latter is portrayed as having an ambiguous relationship with the personality as a whole and is always in danger of falling into sophistry. Richelet expresses these two positions as 'discourir de bon sens' and 'aporter ou aléguer des raisons.' A *raisonnement* is a 'discours raisonné,' a 'raison qu'on aporte pour persüader,' but it need not be honest or in search of truth. Furetière gives both meanings: '*Raisonnement*, se dit... de l'argumentation formée par la puissance qui raisonne. Voilà un *raisonnement* démonstratif ; un *raisonnement* captieux, un *raisonnement* sophistique... *Raisonnement* se dit aussi des repliques, des excuses, des difficultez qu'on apporte à faire quelque chose.' While *raison-bon sens* refers to true understanding, *raisonner* and *raisonnement* may or may not be founded on good judgment. Used derogatorily they may designate false arguments and explanations and may be intended to mislead or to cloak the distinction between true and false, good and bad. In so far as *raison-argument* implies a logical development, a link between cause and effect, it is closely associated with *raison-sujet-cause-motif*.

Sujet-cause-motif

Raison as *sujet*, *cause*, *motif* can be neutral and does not necessarily imply an evaluation: 'Les philosophes ignorent la *raison*, la cause de la plus-part des effets de la nature'; 'Avez-vous raison [cause, sujet] de vous plaindre ? '; 'La raison [sujet] de douter est que... '; 'Conter ses raisons [motifs] à quelqu'un.' However, in such uses *raison* may refer to that which gives sense, meaning, or purpose to a thought or action. Furetière illustrates his definition with: 'Ce prince a eu des *raisons* secrettes, de bons motifs pour faire une telle entreprise. Quand on veut croire une chose, il faut voir s'il y a de la *raison*, du fondement, de l'apparence.' In this sense of *fondement*, *raison-cause* is related to *bon sens*, to uses such as 'Il n'y a point de raison à ce qu'il fait, à ce qu'il dit,' which the Academy interprets 'Il n'y a point de bon sens à ce qu'il fait, à ce qu'il dit.' In so far as *raison*, in this definition, may refer to self-justification or to spurious motive, it can have the derogatory sense of false excuses and reasonings. The Academy's examples show the slight but significant variations in meaning: 'On dit *conter ses raisons à quelqu'un*, pour dire, L'entretenir de ses affaires, de ses interests, du sujet qu'on a eu d'en user comme on a fait, luy justifier la conduite qu'on a tenuë. *Je luy ay conté mes raisons*, et il a approuvé tout ce que j'avois fait. On dit aussi d'Un homme qui s'attache auprés d'une femme, et qui l'entretient de sa passion, qu'*Il luy conte ses raisons*.'

The phrases *raison d'état* and *raison de famille* are included under *cause*, *motif* and are defined by the Academy as 'les considérations d'interest par lesquelles on se conduit dans un estat, dans une famille.' Furetière indicates that these may conflict: 'La *raison* d'Estat prevaut souvent sur les *raisons* de famille, l'emporte sur l'interest des particuliers.' *Raison* in this sense refers to interest, purpose, or aim which may explain behaviour but which may also justify it in terms of expedience or of duty. Clearly, the idea of 'being in the right' can be introduced subtly in such uses, and they can refer to a subjective rather than an absolute right.

AN IDEAL OR STANDARD

Justice-équité

As duty, right, equity, and justice *raison* is on the whole a standard beyond individual motive and interest. It may be used as a yardstick to assess persons or actions, as in 'il a raison,' or it may represent an authority which commands submission and obedience as in the Academy's examples: 'se rendre à la raison, se mettre à la raison, réduire, ranger, amener à la raison, cela est contre tout droit et raison, la droite raison veut.' In these uses, *raison* achieves a static absolute with an imperative force and is often associated with God as in 'selon Dieu et raison' (Furetière and the Academy). The Academy also gives examples which link *raison* in the sense of duty, right, justice with *raison* meaning motive; and here the negative or derogatory use is again possible: *raison* can mean claims – *pretentions* – and, in contract law, the individual's titles and rights: 'On dit, *Faire valoir ses raisons*, pour dire, Faire valoir ses pretentions.' Furetière classifies these under *raison d'état* and *raison de famille*, and in a sense the meanings overlap: in so far as the claims of the individual are felt by him to be his rights, they are associated in his mind with justice and equity. In some of these uses *raison* as standard is not clearly distinguishable from *raison* as faculty: 'La droite raison veut' suggests that the dictates of human reason may themselves be a law or authority commanding obedience.

Satisfaction-vengeance

Raison can also mean justice in the sense of an eye for an eye. Richelet and Furetière define it as *réparation* and the Academy as *satisfaction*. It can mean to return a toast, to humour one's companions by drinking as much as they do, to make an apology, or to give a satisfactory account of oneself. In other words, both the ideas of justification and of explanation are involved in the use of *raison* to mean reparation and satisfaction. Littré lists consecutively, 'se rendre raison d'une chose, se l'expliquer' and 'raison, satisfaction, contentement sur quelque chose qu'on demande.'[26] However, the principal seventeenth-century meaning would seem to be revenge, 'to satisfy oneself... with retaliation.'[27] Richelet says: 'Ce mot [raison] sert a marquer le ressentiment qu'on a d'une injure reçüe, et il signifie une sorte de vengeance, une sorte de reparation et de satisfaction à cause de l'injure qu'on a reçüe.' He gives the example of Pascal: 'Les lois du monde défendent de soufrir les injures sans en *tirer raison* soi-même et souvent par la mort de ses ennemis' and of Molière: 'Venez me *faire raison* de l'insolence la plus grande du monde.' The Academy gives other examples: 'il a tiré raison de cet affront,' 'je luy ferai raison par les voyes d'honneur,' and 'se faire raison,' meaning to obtain justice and satisfaction by force or authority. *Raison* meaning reparation and satisfaction still appears in modern French dictionaries but Robert classifies 'faire raison de quelqu'un, s'en venger' as archaic, and according to Littré this phrase is no longer in use.

Bayet makes an interesting observation on the use of *raison* to mean vengeance. He links this use with both *raison* meaning measure and *raison* meaning justice. The connection with measure is apparent from the interchangeability of the phrases 'vous m'en rendrez raison' and 'vous m'en rendrez compte.' Both expressions require that the compensation be in proportion to the offence. The connection with justice and justification is that vengeance was often regarded as a form of ad hoc execution of justice. For example, the winner of a duel was perceived as vindicated and as having proved 'qu'il avait raison.' Hence, such surprising expressions as 'Il a eu raison de l'armée ennemie.'[28] Of course, measure, proportion, and justice are themselves closely interconnected, referring as they do to a balancing of the parts, and this is implied by the unexpected listing in the Academy dictionary of *livre de raison* under *raison-satisfaction*.

RELATIONSHIP

Livre de raison

According to Block and Wartburg's *Dictionnaire étymologique*, the expression *livre de raison* was in use only until the sixteenth century. If this is so, it serves as a reminder that uses given in seventeenth-century dictionaries cannot necessarily be assumed to have been current at that time. This phrase is of peculiar interest and it has been suggested by Maurice Blondel that it may contain the original meaning of the Latin *ratio*, that is, a system of linked ideas, an account, a reasoning.[29] The *livre de raison*, of which Montaigne's is no doubt the most widely known example, was more than a book of daily accounts and was used to record important family events, births, marriages, and deaths, changes in life-style or activity, all of which could have financial repercussions. Owing to this broad use of the *livre de raison*, Lalande has suggested that the phrase may be connected with the expression 'se rendre compte, voir d'un coup d'œil.'[30] Certainly, the *livre de raison* provided an opportunity to review one's situation and, as it were, to take a mental hold on it. This suggests a way in which the function of perceiving may be etymologically linked with the ideas of measuring and accounting.

Ratio

The original sense of *ratio* (a system of linked ideas, an account, a reasoning) is most clearly seen in the mathematical and technical uses of *raison* just as it is in the English ratio or rate and the Italian *ragioniere*. The Academy says that in mathematics *raison* means 'rapport d'une quantité, soit estendüe, soit numérique à une autre' and that the adjective *rationnel* (confined to mathematical usage) refers to all those quantities which can be expressed by a number – 'Le nombre de six est la racine rationnelle quarrée de trente-six.' *Raison*, in this use, refers directly to the relationship between parts or between a part and the whole.

In the same sense, *raison* comes to refer to a portion or ration of food or materials. For example, Furetière says: '*Raison*, en termes de Marine est la mesure de biscuit, pitance et boisson qui se distribüe à chacun dans le vaisseau. A Dieppe on l'appelle l'*ordinaire*, dans les armées de terre, *ration*.' The Academy gives *à raison* meaning *à proportion*, or *sur le pié*, a use which is still current today. Some examples are: 'Je vous payeray cette estoffe à raison de dix livres l'aune ; il luy doit le change de dix mille livres à raison de dix pour cent.' To these meanings, the *Dictionnaire des arts et des sciences* adds a 'Terme de Charpenterie' where *raison* means the right or appropriate arrangement of materials: 'On dit... *Mettre les pièces de bois en leur raison*, pour dire, Disposer les pieces... mettre chaque morceau en sa place.' Furetière implies that *raison* can have the meaning of proportion or correct arrangement in other contexts: 'il y a raison partout' means, he says, 'qu'il faut qu'il y ait une certaine égalité ou proportion entre les choses.' Littré relates this phrase 'il y a raison partout' to the notion that there must be no excess. He says it means 'la raison doit mettre une borne, c'est un excès qu'il faut empêcher' and he cites the words of Madame de La Fayette: 'Il n'y a pas de raison à toutes les louanges que vous me donnez.' While these words here serve as an example of the use of *raison* to mean proportion and measure, they could also be quoted to illustrate *raison* in the sense of 'fondement,' 'justification,' or 'bon sens.' Clearly the notion of proportion is present in many of the diverse meanings of *raison*. One is inevitably led to wonder whether these senses of *raison* could have a bearing on the use of *raison* as an aesthetic principle in the literature of the period. Indeed, the idea of right measure and disposition may underlie uses of *raison* in many contexts, moral and physical as well as aesthetic.

Raisonnable

The adjectival form *raisonnable* is defined by the dictionaries first in relation to the faculty reason. Man is by definition the reasonable creature; he possesses a faculty called reason and this endowment differentiates him from animals. Furetière says: 'L'homme est defini, animal *raisonnable* ; il a une ame *raisonnable* et immaterielle.' *Raisonnable* can indicate, more specifically, that a man is capable of discourse or of judgment and it can mean that he is equitable and lives according to some ideal of reason. As in the definitions of the faculty *raison*, these meanings are so interlocked that they become barely distinguishable. Richelet defines *raisonnable*: 'Qui a de la raison, du sens, du jugement. Qui peut raisonner. (L'homme est né raisonnable) ... Sage, judicieux ... Juste.' And the Academy defines it: 'Qui est doüé de raison, qui a la faculté de raisonner... Equitable, qui agit, qui se gouverne suivant la raison, selon le droit et l'équité ; qui est conforme a l'équité, à la raison.' While these definitions show that *raisonnable* can refer simply to the possession of a formal faculty called *raison*, they also indicate that *raisonnable* tends to distil the element of rightness in *raison* and to imply the possession of a capacity for sound logic, true judgment, or moral uprightness.

In so far as it refers to a standard, *raisonnable* can point to an ideal or to the adequate. In both cases the notion of proportion and measure is implied. Thus the Academy says *raisonnable* can mean 'Qui est au dessus du médiocre.' Richelet describes it thus: 'Qui est fait comme il faut. Bien fait. Bien proportionné,' and Furetière gives: 'Ce qui est mediocre, convenable, suffisant... Cet appartement n'est pas magnifique, mais il est raisonnable.' The last usage given by the Academy under *raison* is the idiomatic *hors de raison* used in connection with the price of goods to mean excessive, exorbitant, and unjustified. *Raisonnable* is used in the same context to mean not excessive, justified, as in 'un prix raisonnable.' An author's style can also be said to be 'fort raisonnable' and in this use *raisonnable* may mean 'comme il faut' or 'au dessus du médiocre.'

The translations of *raisonnable* in the Latin dictionaries introduce a variety of notions related to the idea of right measure. Estienne, Nicot, Ranconnet, Pajot, and Pomey associate *raisonnable* with *decet* (that which is seemly, comely, becoming),[31] *honestus* (honourable, respectable, reputable), *rectus* (straight, upright), *merere* (to be worthy, to deserve, to merit), and with *iustus* and *aequus*. Guy Miège translates *raisonnable* as 'ce qui est dans le juste milieu.' In these senses *raisonnable* is reminiscent of *bon sens* and, like *bon sens*, may be contrasted with the capacity to reason or argue as in Trévoux's example: 'Combien de Sçavans qui sçavent raisonner sans être plus raisonnables.' Thus applied to human thought and behaviour, *raisonnable* can indicate a well-balanced disposition, sanity, uprightness, truthfulness, or simply rightness, and these may or may not be reflected in discourse.

Indeed, since *raisonnable* refers to that which is right and true it may in some uses represent the adjectival form of *droite raison* and not just of *raison*. *Raisonnable* often implies *droit* and, like *droite raison* and *conscience*, is linked with *honnêteté*. Furetière defines *honnête* in terms of the *raisonnable*: 'Conforme à l'honneur et à la vertu... Ce qui merite de l'estime, de la loüange, à cause qu'il est raisonnable, selon les bonnes mœurs.' The Academy defines *honnête* as 'conforme à la raison.' In these definitions, *raison* and *raisonnable* refer to a standard which may be known and attained by means of right reason. The *raisonnable*, like the *honnête*, is associated with honour and virtue and is dependent on a rightness in man's being, his disposition or general outlook. In this sense, man is distinguished from animal by his potential for virtue as well as by his capacity for thought and judgment. Thus in the notion of the *raisonnable* the various definitions of the faculty *raison* are united in a common origin, the reasonable soul, and in a common goal, the ideal of reason and of reasonableness. And this in turn is linked with notions of justice and proportion.

CONCLUSION

The meaning of the word *raison*, as it emerges from seventeenth-century dictionaries, is highly complex. As Bayet has commented, *raison* presents a semantic nebula: while the lexicographer like the astronomer can pinpoint and examine some of the elements, no definition can be given which is at once brief and precise and which takes account of both the diversity and the interconnections of the parts.[32] The numerous definitions and the ramifications which these suggest make it possible to describe some of this complexity and so to outline possible links between uses which at first sight appear unrelated. An intriguing aspect of this complexity is the immense possibility for word-play. While *raison* is usually associated with the reliable, it can be used to refer to the false and spurious; while it calls for justice, it can also mean vengeance and false justifications; while it implies a moral conscience, it can designate a fallible and discursive faculty which is the tool of the sophist as well as of the logician and scientist. In many uses of the word, several meanings may be present and some of these will be evident only from the context. Underlying the diverse definitions of *raison* is a persistent association of this word with the notion of measure and proportion. The uses of *raison* in the literature of the period simplify and colour the meaning of this association for the seventeenth-century thinker and writer. Above all, the value given to *raison* in the seventeenth century and the significance of its association with God, truth, morality, and aesthetics are beyond the capacity of dictionary definitions and must be sought in the literature of the period.

2

Reason, God, and nature

Et qu'est-ce qui saurait exclure, réduire ou, ce qui revient au même, *comprendre absolument* la folie, sinon la raison en général, la raison absolue et sans détermination, dont l'autre nom est Dieu pour les rationalistes classiques ?
Derrida 'A propos de "Cogito et histoire de la folie"'[1]

When uses of *raison* in the literature of the seventeenth century are collected and tabulated, it becomes apparent that the concept of reason can be broken down, at least artificially, into three broad categories: reason as it refers to the godhead, reason as a norm or standard, reason as a human faculty. Looked at in this way, there is a striking change at what might be called the highest level of the concept: reason as related to God and to nature. In some authors, especially those interested in theological and philosophical discussion, phrases such as *raison éternelle* and *raison supérieure* are used to refer to God. Bossuet, Malebranche, and Fénelon use them most frequently, but a connection between reason and God is also drawn earlier by Descartes and by Pascal. By contrast, these phrases are entirely absent from the work of Fontenelle and Bayle. In their writings, the word *nature* is partly substituted for *raison éternelle* in that *nature* is personified and is associated with some of the ideas (most notably with order) which in other authors are connected with *raison éternelle*. This change is foreshadowed in different ways in the work of Descartes and of Pascal and it poses important questions: what is the significance for the concept of reason of hypostatizing *raison* and treating it as the origin of all things and, conversely, in what way is the concept of reason affected by the disappearance of the notion of *raison éternelle*?

Since *nature* as used by Bayle and Fontenelle does not refer to an absolute that is external to the physical world, only some of the attributes and functions of *raison éternelle* devolve upon *nature* and the latter never fully replaces the former. Consequently, the use of different words expresses a deeper difference in outlook which is reflected at all levels of the concept of reason – in the conceptions of reason as a standard of perfection and as a human faculty.

In the sixteenth and seventeenth centuries belief in God or in a universal truth extends the meaning both of *raison* and of *nature* so that these words acquire considerable imperative force. Reason and nature are often called upon to confirm or to deny the rightness of an assertion as if they represent moral tribunals. In a single phrase, Rabelais appeals to reason, nature, and God: 'comme raison le veut, nature l'ordonne, et Dieu le commande' (quoted by H. Vernay *Les divers sens du mot 'raison'* [1962] 63). Poussin calls upon 'la nature et la raison' (lettre à Sublet de Noyer, n.d, *Lettres et propos sur l'art* 64) and Pascal says that suicide is 'contraire à Dieu, à la raison et à la nature tout ensemble' (*Pensées* §148). Malebranche speaks of God as 'la raison supérieure' and in the same passage describes divine injunctions as issuing from 'la voix de la nature' (*Recherche de la vérité* I 14). While the separate emphasis given to *raison*, *nature*, and *Dieu* indicates that they are in some degree disjunctive, they nevertheless endorse the same affirmations and consequently must have something in common.

All three terms refer the reader to a belief in universal laws or values. Vernay claims that, in uses such as that cited from Rabelais, *raison* designates a natural law which provides man with rules of conduct: 'Surtout lié à Dieu, parfois à nature, le mot *raison* désigne la loi naturelle servant à l'homme de règle de conduite.'[2] Numerous critics have suggested a link between the use of reason to represent a static absolute and the natural law tradition. Crocker remarks that the notion of right reason tends to accompany belief in a natural law whereby there is held to be 'an objective right and wrong in the very nature of things.' Although natural law is essentially unprovable, it is dependent on man's reason – his 'right reason,' not his logical powers.[3] Hoopes points out that before Locke and Newton 'to follow nature' meant 'the effort on the part of men to realize their true potentialities.' 'Nature' referred to a universal moral law, and reason likewise was 'not just a subjective faculty of the mind' but 'a principle inherent in reality.'[4] The notion of natural law is thus dependent on belief in a constant reality behind created things and if *nature* and *raison* can both refer to this intangible and unprovable truth then *nature* is not equivalent to the physical world and *raison* is not identical with the human faculty.

The notion of two realities, one eternal and immutable, the other inconstant and changing, is common in the seventeenth century. Bossuet says: 'Le monde passe, la concupiscence passe... mais celuy [le monde] qui fait la volonté du Seigneur demeure eternellement, rien ne passe plus, tout est fixe, tout est immuable' (*Traité de la concupiscence* 90). While this notion is not usually so clearly formulated, it would seem to underlie much of the language of seventeenth-century literature and explains the frequent ambiguity in the use of words and particularly of abstract words. *Raison* and *nature* are used to refer to a true reason and nature issuing from God and to a fallen reason and nature present only in man and his surroundings. Thus, while Malebranche uses both *raison* and *nature* to refer to something emanating from God, he also describes human reason as 'la voie naturelle' and uses 'nature' or 'l'ordre de la nature' to mean the physical and mutable world in contrast to the eternal and constant (*Recherche* I 357 and 464, II 453–4). Sometimes it is unclear to which of these realities *raison* and *nature* refer. This difficulty arises partly because qualifiers (such as *droite* and *vraie*) are not always provided, but more significantly because the immutable is regarded as present in varying degrees within the mutable.

Through most of European history, the orthodox Christian view of an absolute being is accompanied by what might be called a second religion: a belief in the presence of the divine spirit within the temporal world.[5] *Nature* can be used to designate this spirit. The *Dictionnaire de l'Académie* says that *nature*, in one of its senses, signifies the universal spirit which is diffused throughout all created things and by which everything has its beginning and its end. In such uses, *nature* refers to a moral law existing outside created things and to what Spink calls 'the Spirit of Nature,' 'the Soul of the World.'[6] This possible permeation of the mutable by the immutable means that *raison* may refer simultaneously to the human faculty and to the universal natural law. In Fénelon, the faculty reason is explicitly described as partly human and partly divine.

The predication of reason for God adds yet a further dimension to the meaning of *raison*. There is always something indefinable, something ineffable in the idea of God. Busson and Borgerhoff have pointed out that Balzac, Bouhours, and Bossuet use the phrase *je ne sais quoi* to refer to God and to his effects.[7] It may be that when God is called *raison* something of this indefinable quality is transferred to *raison*. Ramsey says that to call God 'wise' and 'good' caps all stories of wisdom and goodness and that these predicates preside over and 'complete' the language of created things. He compares these predicates with infinite number which is both the sum of and more than the sum of all numbers.[8] Thus when *raison* is used of the godhead, the lines of demarcation between *raison* and other attributes of God are unclear. The absolute is one and distinctions made in reference to it are only artificial. Thomas Aquinas says: 'The perfections which in creatures are many and various pre-exist in God as one' (quoted in I.T. Ramsey ed *Words about God* [1971] 43–4). Pascal speaks of God as 'cet etre infini et sans parties' (*Pensées* §418). God is truth, justice, reason, and all other perfections: he can be spoken of as any of these but, in him, they are inseparable and each implies the other. Thus, if God is spoken of as *raison*, then in its highest and most perfect form *raison* is one with all perfections. The ideal of reason expands to embrace all truth and the reader is required to look beyond the word itself and to attempt to probe the unseen and unknowable.

To the extent that reason, justice, and truth are separate in man but united in God, these concepts form a pyramid. The paths to justice, truth, and reason lead upward and inward toward a point of convergence. This type of schema is suggested by passages from La Bruyère and Bossuet. La Bruyère connects justice, reason, and truth in man with sovereign reason and truth in God. Moving as it were upwards on a scale, he says: 'Toute justice est une conformité à une souveraine raison... or toute conformité à la raison est une vérité : cette conformité... a toujours été ; elle est donc de celles que l'on appelle des eternelles vérités. Cette vérité, d'ailleurs, ou n'est point et ne peut être, ou elle est l'objet d'une connaissance ; elle est donc éternelle, cette connaissance, et c'est Dieu' (*Des esprits forts* §47). Bossuet also presents the diverse qualities in man, his virtues and 'honnêteté,' as effects of God. 'Sans doute il y a au dedans de nous une divine clarté : "Un rayon de votre face, ô Seigneur, c'est imprimé en nos ames... " C'est là que nous découvrons, comme dans un globe de lumière, un agrément immortel dans l'honnêteté et la vertu : c'est la première Raison, qui se montre à nous par son image ; c'est la Vérité elle-même, qui nous parle' (*Sermon sur la mort* 275). In their most perfect form all ideals are united and, because the immutable is sometimes regarded as present within the mutable, the distinction in man himself between reason and other godlike qualities may be blurred. Sometimes man's capacity for perfection is attributed to his 'reasonable nature' and this, rather than simply his reason, is linked with the unity of truth in God. For example, Bossuet says: 'Il y a donc premierement le bien supreme, qui est Dieu, autour duquel sont occupées toutes les vertus et où se trouve la felicité de la nature raisonnable' (*Traité* 46). In so far as *raison* can refer to this 'reasonable nature,' *raison* may designate more than a discursive and rational faculty; it may refer to moral capacities.

If the faculty reason is extended in this way to include moral capacities, *raison* is not necessarily contrary to passion or in conflict with deeply felt emotion. Usually the predication of reason for God has been regarded as associated with a stoical attitude. Busson points out that Senault, who describes Christ as 'la Raison primitive,' also stresses that Christ is able to control 'la partie inférieure de son âme.' However, if *raison* in the phrase 'la Raison primitive' refers to eternal truth and law, its effects may not be confined to Christ's reasoning faculty; they may spring from his 'reasonable nature' and possibly permeate his emotional and instinctual self, giving rise to a virtuousness which does not depend on reflective thought or on effort of will. Consequently, it may be misleading to say that reason controls: Christ's lower nature and his reasoning faculty may both reflect the same reasonableness. Busson implies as much when he says, quoting Senault: 'Les passions "naissaient de la Raison" du Christ.'[9]

The use of *raison* to refer to God is thus accompanied by a linguistic ambiguity due to an awareness of two types of reality and by broad associations of *raison* as an ideal and as a human faculty. In the seventeenth century, this conception of reason gives way to a narrower conception when *nature* and not *raison éternelle* is used of the personified power behind or within created things. The scientific and pragmatic viewpoint calls forth a reaction from those who uphold religion and consequently two strongly differentiated presentations of the relationship of reason with nature and God are found contemporaneously at the end of the period, notably in Fénelon and Fontenelle. Fontenelle's conception is, however, the newer of the two and in this sense a change can be said to occur. In its simplest terms the change is one of emphasis. When God's presence is emphasized, as in Fénelon, *nature* and *raison* in all forms are subsidiary to God: they are effects dependent on a higher source or cause and, because usually *raison* and not *nature* is predicated of God, *raison* can be said to be a key concept to which *nature* is secondary. When, as in Fontenelle, the divine element is removed or given less emphasis, *raison* becomes, as it were, the product and creation of *nature*. Vereker claims that in the eighteenth century the key concept is nature rather than reason and a gradual shift in that direction is already apparent during the seventeenth century.[10] In Fontenelle, the notion of two realities is almost entirely absent; *nature* refers to the physical world or to the laws of the physical world and *raison* is a purely human faculty having no immediate access to immutable and unchanging values.

This second view, of *nature* and *raison* not linked to an immutable realm, is foreshadowed in different ways in the work of Descartes and of Pascal. Both these authors associate God with reason. But in Descartes's work the laws of God are established in nature once and for all and consequently appear as laws of nature as well as laws issuing from a transcendent being. In Pascal, human reason is in large measure divorced from God and so has many of the characteristics of *raison* as understood by Fontenelle.

In considering the use of *raison éternelle* it must be borne in mind that the associations of this phrase may tell us something about the central meaning of *raison* generally. In other words, if Ramsey is right, *raison* as used of God may provide a clue to the predominant associations of that word in the seventeenth century. The associations of *nature* in Fontenelle and Bayle in contrast are interesting only in so far as they are similar to those of *raison éternelle* and thus suggest that *nature*, in some respects, replaces *raison éternelle*.

Descartes's conception of nature is in some ways similar to that of Fontenelle and Bayle. He uses *nature* to refer to the physical world or to the laws of the physical world and he is rightly regarded as contributing to the mechanistic conception of nature prevalent in the late seventeenth and in the eighteenth century.[11] Yet Descartes's conception of nature and more particularly of reason still owes much to the natural law tradition: both reason and nature are, in his view, effects dependent on a higher source or cause and in some degree they reflect or manifest ultimate truth.

Descartes does not call God *raison* but he says that in God are contained 'tous les trésors de la science et de la sagesse' (*Méditations* 42), and he presents human reason as the exact replica in miniature of this eternal truth. Knowledge of the perfect being is innate, 'elle est née et produite avec moy dés lors que j'ay esté creé' (ibid 41) and by following the true method, 'qui apprend à bien conduire sa raison' (*Principes* 13–14) man may attain 'la connoissance de la verité et de la Sagesse' (ibid 9). The fulfilment of reason is a unified knowledge reflecting the indivisible truth of God, and Descartes gives considerable emphasis both to this unity of truth in God and to the dependence of the human intellect on the divine:

L'unité, la simplicité, ou l'inseparabilité de toutes les choses qui sont en Dieu, est une des principales perfections que je conçoy estre en luy ; et certes l'idée de cette unité et assemblage de toutes les perfections de Dieu, n'a peu estre mise en moi par aucune cause, de qui je n'aye point aussi reçue les idées de toutes les autres perfections. Car elle ne peut pas me les avoir fait comprendre ensemblement jointes et inseparables, sans avoir fait en sorte en mesme temps que je sceusse ce qu'elles estoient, et que je les connusse toutes en quelque façon. (*Méditations* 40)

The unity and simplicity of divine truth are the guarantee that a single method applied to diverse disciplines will culminate in man's possession of a complete and unified knowledge and Descartes describes this final knowledge as 'la parfaite morale, qui, presupposant une entiere connoissance des autres sciences, est le dernier degré de la Sagesse' (*Principes* 14). Since Descartes maintains that all human knowledge or potential knowledge depends on an awareness of God, his conception of God must resemble the goal which he sets for human reason. As Keefe remarks, it is only because all knowledge is indivisible in God that Descartes can propose 'to deduce an ethic from non-ethical branches of knowledge' and to treat all knowledge as welded to a single trunk which reaches upward through science to morality.[12] Consequently, by the description of God as encompassing 'tous les trésors de la science et de la sagesse,' Descartes would seem to mean that God represents a moral truth which encompasses within itself all other forms of truth.

Gilson suggests that the notion of innate ideas permits Descartes to separate man's intellect from the natural world and that this in turn enables him to develop an entirely mechanistic physics.[13] However, while the laws of nature do not in any obvious sense appear to be moral laws, it would seem that in the Creator there is no distinction between moral and other forms of truth or law. Quite as important to Descartes's philosophy as the separation of mind and matter is the parallel which he draws between the seeds of truth implanted in man and the laws instilled in nature. It is this parallel which renders the external world directly accessible to the human intellect. Descartes more than once relates innate knowledge to the laws of nature. In the *Discours de la méthode*, he refers to innate ideas as 'certaines semences de Veritez qui sont naturellement en nos ames' (64), and, speaking of nature, he says that he seeks to describe the physical world, 'en demonstrant les effets par les causes, et faisant voir de quelles semences, et en quelles façons, la Nature les doit produire' (45). Owing to innate ideas, man possesses an actual knowledge of the laws of nature: 'aussy... j'ai remarqué certaines loix, que Dieu a tellement establies en la nature, et dont il a imprimé de telles notions en nos ames, qu'aprés y avoir fait assez de reflexion, nous ne sçaurions douter qu'elles ne soient exactement observées, en tout ce qui est fait dans le monde' (41). And, in the *Méditations*, he indicates that this knowledge results initially from the contemplation of God: 'Et desia il me semble que je découvre un chemin qui nous conduira de cette contemplation du vray Dieu... à la connoissance des autres choses de l'Univers' (42). Thus the mutual dependence of the laws of nature and of innate ideas on a higher unified truth is of fundamental importance to Descartes's philosophy: both man and nature reflect the truths or laws of God and, because of this divine imprint, man can hope to understand nature.

In general terms this shared or common property of divine origin would seem to be a tendency toward order. Clearly a form of order may be manifest in physical laws, in thought, and in morality and the notion of a perfect order, best expressed in mathematics, may thus provide the clue to the unity of all truth in God and of all knowledge in man. By virtue of his reason, man is able to establish an order among the diverse thoughts which pass through his mind (*Principes* 59–60) and to develop a method suitable to the examination of anything which has order, for, Descartes says, 'Toutes les choses où l'on étudie l'ordre et la mesure se rattachent à la Mathématique' (*Regulae ad directionem ingenii* 39). Order in nature also receives considerable emphasis. Nothing in the universe is made at random: everything is 'tel qu'il devoit estre' (*Discours* 45). The laws of nature are mechanical – 'la nature agit en tout suivant les lois des mécaniques' (lettre à Mersenne, 20 février 1639, *Oeuvres* II 525) – and the functions of the human body can be compared to the movement of a clock: 'Ce mouvement... suit aussy necessairement de la seule disposition des organes... que fait celuy d'un horloge, de la force, de la situation, et de la figure de ses contrepois et de ses roües' (*Discours* 50). In nature the order imparted by God is necessary and automatic, in man it can be developed by means of conscious effort. Consciousness with its corollary – the possibility of development toward ever increasing order – would consequently seem to represent the main distinction between thought and matter, between reason and nature.

Descartes's conception of reason and of nature has some of the characteristics which accompany the notion of natural law and yet his use of *raison* and of *nature* also prefigures Fontenelle's use. The laws imprinted in nature issue from a transcendent being but they function automatically and to this extent they are autonomous. Human reason reflects eternal truth and contains the seed of that truth, but it is capable of developing that knowledge by human effort and without further aid from above. Thus the way is opened to a notion of man's reason as a purely human faculty, as the manifestation or product of nature itself.

In some ways, Pascal's idea of God is similar to that of Descartes and the views expressed in Pascal's *Pensées* complement those of his earlier scientific work. He sees the natural world and the principles of mathematics as reflections of divine law: 'Je vois bien qu'il y a dans la nature un être nécessaire, éternel et infini' (§135). In his commentary on the letters of le père Noël, he denounces those who speak of nature as capricious, as loving this and hating that: the laws of the physical world are constant and nature does not have sentiment (*Oeuvres* 213). He considers that there is a perfect model or design in natural things (*Pensées* §§582 and 199) and that the principles of mathematics are eternal and God-given: 'Les proportions des nombres sont des vérités immatérielles, éternelles et dépendantes d'une première vérité en qui elles subsistent, et qu'on appelle Dieu'

(§449). Chance is a sign of human frailty: 'Hasard donne les pensées, et hasard les ôte' (§542).

However, on the whole Pascal is concerned with God as saviour and not as architect. A vivid awareness of two realities pervades the *Pensées* and the words *nature* and *raison* are used to refer to both. *Nature* is not only the physical world, it is also moral truth and human nature. It may be significant that these uses of the word accompany a concern with human salvation. Lenoble remarks that in François de Sales (who shares Pascal's concern) *nature* has nothing to do with the nature of the biologist and physicist.[14] In fragment 33 of the *Pensées* Pascal uses *naturelle* first of man's corrupt or fallen nature and then of true wisdom: 'L'homme est bien capable des plus extravagantes opinions, puisqu'il est capable de croire qu'il n'est pas dans cette faiblesse naturelle et inévitable, et de croire, qu'il est au contraire dans la sagesse naturelle.' This dual use of *nature* or *naturelle* is accompanied by a similar ambivalence in Pascal's conception of reason. If *nature*, in the sense of human nature, is corrupt (§471), *raison* partakes of this corruption (§60); if *nature* can refer to a true moral law, *raison* can also designate the true reason of God and religion or the reliable reason which would have been man's but for the fall.

Pascal's use of *raison* in the *Pensées* provides a good example of the pyramid structure in the concept of reason. Occasionally human reason is referred to as a potentially reliable guide, as in 'L'homme n'agit point par la raison qui fait sont être' (§491; cf §§505 and 768). But on the whole Pascal separates human reason from eternal truth. Perhaps in order to preserve the mystery of religion (§173) he rarely uses predicates to refer to the godhead and an idea of God is conveyed to the reader mainly by means of contrast. Thus, God's truth and constancy are emphasized through a description of human inconstancy: 'Chaque chose est ici vraie en partie, fausse en partie. La vérité essentielle n'est point ainsi, elle est toute pure et toute vraie. Ce mélange la détruit et l'anéantit. Rien n'est purement vrai et ainsi rien n'est vrai en l'entendant du pur vrai' (§905). This 'vérité essentielle' is probably intended to refer to a divine truth: 'Il faut se tenir en silence autant qu'on peut et ne s'entretenir que de Dieu qu'on sait être la vérité' (§99). Man behaves as if he knew true justice and reason – 'comme si chacun savait certainement où est la raison et la justice' (§33) – and yet he is incapable of good, of truth (§28), or of moral perspective (§21). Again these are provided only by God who is 'le Souverain Bien' (§147). In other passages, Pascal speaks of 'la véritable justice' (§44), of 'la véritable équité (§60), and, in each case, he appears to be referring the reader to the idea of God: 'Le saint des saints amènerait la justice éternelle, non la légale, mais l'éternelle' (§269). Thus reason, justice, and truth are all presented as whole and united in God but as incomplete and separate in man.

Pascal's conception of eternal reason clearly contains an element of the ineffable. God's reason and wisdom, as known through religion, appear to be madness and folly unless, through grace, man understands them with his heart. Again Pascal's language in the *Pensées* plays on contrast: 'Cette folie [de la religion] est plus sage que toute la sagesse des hommes' (§695). In experiencing Christ, man understands the reason behind all things: 'Jésus-Christ est l'objet de tout, et le centre où tout tend. Qui le connaît connaît la raison de toutes choses' (§449). But this understanding is not within the grasp of reason (§§308 and 424). Christianity, which alone possesses reason and truth, requires 'inspiration': 'La religion chrétienne qui seule a la raison n'admet point pour ses vrais enfants ceux qui croient sans inspiration' (§808). Thus the reasonableness of religion and the wisdom of God have only a tangential relationship with human reason which, unaided, remains ensnared by the flux and movement of this world. True reason is constant and perfect and is also undemonstrable.

In so far as Pascal presents human reason as a fallible faculty, his conception of this faculty bears a stronger resemblance to that of Fontenelle than does Descartes's. The extreme emphasis given in the *Pensées* to the separation of the eternal from the mutable links human reason in a horizontal bond with imperfect nature – a bond which Descartes denies.

In broad outline the different relationships of eternal reason to human reason seen in Descartes and in Pascal are found in authors who explicitly describe God as *raison*. The predication of reason for God does not necessarily accompany a belief in the reliability of human reason as Busson would seem to imply.[15] On the contrary, the presence of a sovereign or eternal reason is often accompanied by emphasis on the inadequacy of human reason. For example, in his discourse on Socrates, Balzac exclaims, 'Qu'il y a dans le Monde de Foux serieux ; de Foux qui se fondent en raison ; de Foux qui sont déguisez en Sages,' and he urges, 'Fions-nous à la souveraine Raison' (*Socrate chrestien* 41). When Bossuet predicates reason of God he frequently emphasizes the absolute authority of the divine over the human although he considers that God's reason and truth are the fulfilment of man's reasonable nature: 'Il n'y a point de *pourquoi* a ecouter contre Dieu, et tout ce qui met en doute la souveraine raison et la souveraine sagesse devoit dez la nous estre en horreur' (*Traité* 76). Thus he indicates that if human reason is man's pride there is yet a higher reason even more worthy of reverence, a reason which commands an unquestioning obedience and which represents a static absolute. Emphasis on the immutability of eternal reason is often accompanied by descriptions of human reason as manifesting the mobile characteristics of the natural world. Where Pascal uses the metaphor of the wind: 'Plaisante raison qu'un vent manie et à tous sens' (*Pensées* §44), Bossuet describes reason as a sleeping pilot carried unawares on a tempestuous sea: 'Nous allons au gré de nos desirs ; il n'y a plus de pilote, la raison dort et se laisse emporter aux flots et aux vents' (*Traité* 90).

Contrasts between eternal and human reason, although less common and perhaps less dramatic, are also found in Malebranche and Fénelon. Malebranche claims that men must not be too proud in their evaluations and that they must wait upon the judgment of 'la Raison divine' to know their worth (*Recherche* II 51). Remarks to the effect that human reason is weak and wandering by comparison with the eternal are also found in Fénelon. For example, in the *Traité de l'existence et des attributs de Dieu*,[16] Fénelon says: 'Sans doute l'homme qui craint d'être corrigé par cette raison incorruptible, et qui s'égare toujours en ne la suivant pas, n'a pas cette raison parfaite, universelle et immuable qui le corrige malgré lui' (62).

Yet Malebranche, Fénelon, and, to some extent, Bossuet all regard human reason as partaking of the divine. Bossuet considers that man's reason reflects 'la première Raison' and that, like God, man can and should live 'de raison et d'intelligence' (*Discours sur l'histoire universelle* 372). Malebranche and Fénelon expand on Descartes's notion of innate ideas and see eternal reason as constantly available to man's reason. Thus Malebranche says that man is essentially united with 'la vérité éternelle' and 'la souveraine raison' and that it is only through this union that he is able to think (*Recherche* II 126). In Malebranche's and Fénelon's descriptions of reason, the imagery of descending light (used by St Augustine)[17] is more prominent than that of wayward movement. Malebranche compares eternal reason with the rays of the sun: 'elle ne nous manque jamais pour découvrir les choses qui sont naturellement sujettes à la raison. Car le Soleil qui éclaire les esprits, n'est pas comme le Soleil qui éclaire les corps ; il ne s'éclipse jamais, et il pénétre tout sans que sa lumière soit partagée' (ibid 247). Fénelon describes eternal reason as the light which illuminates every soul: 'Où est-elle cette raison commune et supérieure tout ensemble à toutes les raisons bornées et imparfaites du genre humain ? ... Où est-elle cette pure et douce lumière qui non-seulement éclaire les yeux ouverts, mais qui ouvre les yeux fermés... Mon esprit n'est point la raison primitive, la vérité universelle et immuable ; il est seulement l'organe par où passe cette lumière originale, et qui en est éclairé' (*Traité* 63–4). In these passages the predicates *raison*, *vérité*, and *sagesse* are used more or less interchangeably and Malebranche implies that *raison* combines *vérité* and *sagesse*. It may be that the imagery of descending light and of the sun's rays is linked with the phrase *droite raison* which, of course, means 'straight' as well as 'right' reason. Malebranche describes man's will as upright and as following 'une ligne droite' unless it is impeded by corrupt desires (*Recherche* I 45–8). It is in order to distinguish pure reason from man's corrupt reason that these and other authors use adjectives such as 'la droite' and 'la vraie' to qualify *raison. La droite raison*, like eternal reason, appears to embrace *vérité* and *sagesse*: Bossuet uses *droite raison* to refer to the awareness of truth imparted to man by God.

Bossuet, Malebranche, and Fénelon, like Descartes, associate God's reason with order, both moral and physical. Bossuet says that to speak of caprice in the works of God is to blaspheme against his wisdom (*Sermon sur la mort* 277–8), for God is the source of all order whether or not that order is recognized by man: 'C'est ainsi que Dieu règne sur tous les peuples. Ne parlons plus de hasard ni de fortune, ou parlons-en seulement comme d'un nom dont nous couvrons notre ignorance. Ce qui est hasard à l'égard de nos conseils incertains, est un dessein concerté dans un conseil plus haut, c'est-à-dire dans ce conseil éternel qui renferme toutes les causes et tous les effets dans un même ordre' (*Discours* 654). Eternal reason has established immutable rules of behaviour and of morality and this order is evident both in man and in the universe. Bossuet links divine order with 'la droite raison' which he says should be man's guide:

Si nous admirons tous les jours tant d'art, tant de justesse, tant d'économie dans les astres, dans les éléments... à plus forte raison doit-on dire qu'il y a un ordre admirable dans ce qui regarde les hommes. Il y a donc certainement beaucoup d'ordre ; et toutefois il faut reconnaître qu'il n'y a rien qui paraisse moins.... L'experience nous apprend assez que ce qui nous meut, ce qui nous excite, ce n'est pas la droite raison : on se contente de l'admirer et de la faire servir de prétexte, mais l'intérêt, la passion, la vengeance, c'est ce qui agite puissamment les ressorts de l'âme. (*Premier sermon sur la providence* 157–8)

Order, economy, and precision in the universe are presented as the most obvious manifestations of God and sometimes Bossuet refers to God as 'ce divin architecte' and compares the world to 'une grande machine' (*Sermon* 273, 279).

Malebranche and Fénelon also describe God as the origin of moral and physical order. Malebranche characterizes God as the distributor of justice and says that 'la vérité essentielle' informs man of his duties and his faults

(*Recherche* I 14). Fénelon says that God provides man with knowledge of 'la vraie vertu' and that his 'raison supérieure' is the source of unchanging and universal moral values, and acts as a 'centre immobile' to which all men are bound (*Traité* 61). Using the ancient argument from design, Malebranche and Fénelon both take the order of the universe to be indisputable evidence of the existence of God and claim that this order is clearly apparent to man. They use the analogy of the clock (to become so popular in the eighteenth century) which Descartes uses to describe the human body. Thus Malebranche comments admiringly: 'Quand je vois une montre, j'ai raison de conclure, qu'il y a une intelligence, puisqu'il est impossible que le hazard ait pû produire et arranger toutes ces roües. Comment donc seroit-il possible que le hazard, et la rencontre des atomes, fût capable d'arranger dans tous les hommes, et dans tous les animaux tant de ressorts divers, avec la justesse et la proportion que je viens d'expliquer' (*Recherche* I 209). Where Bossuet points to the 'économie' and 'justesse' of the universe, Malebranche admires the 'justesse' and 'proportion.' Fénelon agrees that this order, this 'justesse,' is evidence of the existence of a higher power of reasoning: 'Quand je vois, dans une montre, une justesse sur les heures qui surpasse toutes mes connaissances, je conclus que si la montre ne raisonne pas, il faut qu'elle ait été formée par un ouvrier qui raisonnait en ce genre plus juste que moi' (*Traité* 31). He goes on to equate *raison* with *ordre*, saying that because the universe and its parts do not always function faultlessly, this does not mean that they are 'sans ordre et sans raison' (32) or that they were created at random (3). To maintain that the world is created by chance is, he says, to make chance itself reasonable: 'Je réponds que vous faites le hasard raisonnable jusqu'au point d'être la source de la raison même' (33).

Eternal reason is thus associated by these authors with man's capacity to think and to know truth, with moral order in man and with physical order in the universe. While this order or arrangement is far more explicitly described by Descartes, Bossuet, Malebranche, and Fénelon than by Pascal, and while it is linked with mathematics and with mechanics, it nevertheless remains a conscious design, one which has life and internal equilibrium. Fénelon presents the capacity for conscious order as the very essence of reason and of reasonableness. Busson, in his discussion of Malebranche's conception of eternal reason, suggests that *raison* for Malebranche, as for Descartes, is highly restrictive. He describes it as 'non pas le Logos des platoniciens, mais la raison la plus limitative qui soit: celle des cartésiens.' And he concludes that Malebranche's religion is purely cerebral.[18]

However, the view that order is sterile and limiting is perhaps a post-romantic prejudice and it would seem misleading to approach Descartes's and Malebranche's conceptions of eternal reason with this assumption. For Descartes, eternal reason is the source and origin of man's capacity for an active and conscious striving for order, for an order which will lead man to knowledge both of the external world and of moral truth and which will enable him to grasp and to unify all forms of knowledge.

In Malebranche's view, eternal reason is constantly active in the world and it draws man, his thought and his will, toward the realization of constant and universal truth. If love and obedience are less emphasized than in Pascal or Bossuet, this is because the eternal consciousness in some degree permeates man and gives him a sense of awareness which allows him to perceive and to create order similar to that of the divine. Love is perhaps not the prerequisite for knowledge of truth but this does not mean that the awareness of truth and of true order cannot be retained in an attitude of love. On the contrary, order perfects love as it perfects thought and Malebranche says: 'La charité toute pure est si au dessus de nos forces, que... la raison humaine ne comprend pas facilement que l'on puisse aimer autrement que par rapport à soi, et avoir d'autre derniere fin que sa propre satisfaction (*Recherche* II 46). As Gouhier has commented, by his notion of God as reason, Malebranche emphasizes that God holds everything in its right relationship.[19] This perfect order of God is hardly restrictive or limiting even if, in Malebranche's attempt to comprehend eternal reason, he indulges in lengthy argument.

However, Descartes is indeed in some ways the predecessor of Bayle and of Fontenelle. While for Malebranche and Fénelon human reason is dependent for knowledge on direct contact with God, for Descartes reason does not require a continuous contact with the eternal and consequently it can be seen as a product of nature. Bayle and Fontenelle do not use the phrase *raison éternelle*; they speak rather of a personified *nature* and they treat this *nature* as responsible for the order of the universe. Thus in Bayle and Fontenelle, the association with order, which in other authors is a central feature of *raison éternelle*, becomes an essential aspect of *nature*. Like Bossuet, one of Fontenelle's characters comments that everything in nature is chance 'pourvû qu'on donne ce nom à un ordre que l'on ne connoît point' (*Dialogue des morts* 82). Personifying nature, Fontenelle describes at length the wonderful order of her ways. Nature arranges it so that every planet is provided with moons or, in the case of Saturn, a ring, in proportion to its distance from the sun (*Entretiens sur la pluralité des mondes* 125). If, through habit, the inhabitants of a moon are relieved of the fear of eclipses, some other fear is provided, namely, that of being crushed by its planet (ibid 121–2). In a less light-hearted vein, he points to the balance and precision born from the unity of design in nature: 'Je peindrais volontiers la Nature avec une balance à la main, comme la justice, pour marquer qu'elle s'en sert à peser, et à égaler à peu près tout ce qu'elle distribue aux hommes, le bonheur, les talents, les avantages et les désavantages des différentes conditions, les facilité et les difficulté qui regardent les choses de l'esprit' (*Digression sur les anciens et les modernes* 173). This nature sounds much like providence, but it is a very different providence from that of which Bossuet speaks. It appears to distribute its wares in a quite impersonal way, it does not enlighten man's reason with any specific knowledge of truth, and it does not give to each an equal capacity for reason. Balance is only in the general design.

Like Malebranche and Fénelon, Fontenelle compares the universe to a clock, but he is not concerned to prove thereby the existence of a higher intelligence. He says that, since Descartes, philosophers have become 'des machinistes' and, in the *Entretiens*, his interlocutor, who is in every way his ideal of the lay philosopher, remarks: 'je l'en estime [l'univers] beaucoup plus, depuis que je sais qu'il ressemble à une montre : il est surprenant que l'ordre de la nature, tout admirable qu'il est, ne roule que sur des choses si simples (64). Fontenelle applies the metaphor of a clock also to people – some people are more intelligent than others; some clocks mark the minutes as well as hours and are more finely made (147). Man's intelligence and not just his body now appear as products of nature. Nature can be said to replace *raison éternelle* to the extent that, like eternal reason, it works with supreme order and design and arranges all the parts of creation with balance and simplicity. But the notion of moral order, the backbone of the doctrine of natural law, is entirely absent. Although Fontenelle suggests that man can find true ideals by looking at nature, these are not supplied directly to man's reason. If the Greeks had not given us ideals of the true and the beautiful, he asks rhetorically, whence would we have taken them? And he answers: from the same place as they took theirs, from nature (*Digression* 170–1). By this notion of adopting ideals from nature, Fontenelle does not mean that man has direct knowledge of truth but rather that he is capable of a cumulative knowledge through increasing acquaintance with the external world. Human reason is not provided with innate ideas and has no vertical contact with a superior reason.

Bayle even more explicitly separates nature, as a principle of law and order, from God. He says that it is easy to persuade oneself that the universe is ordered from above but in fact all that happens in the world is a simple effect of nature (*Pensées diverses sur la comète* I 170). The laws of nature are inviolable and are obeyed by God himself (ibid 171). In some ways, Bayle goes further than Fontenelle in separating nature from human ideals for he presents a picture of nature as impervious to man and suggests no connection between providence and justice: 'À la vérité les soins de la Providence descendent jusques à nous, et... nous y entrons pour notre part, mais... leur but est bien autrement considerable que nôtre conservation, et... encore que les mouvemens des cieux nous aportent des grandes utilitez, ce n'est pas à dire pourtant que ces vastes corps se meuvent pour l'amour de la terre' (ibid 217). Consequently, in Bayle and Fontenelle, the pyramid structure in the concept of reason is broken. *Raison* and *nature* cease to refer to two realities: they do not represent a constant moral law and they are not the fulfilment of human potentiality. In some ways *raison* appears to be secondary to *nature*: it is no longer the origin of all order and perfection in the universe and human reason is no longer bound to eternal and immutable truth. Reason is merely another manifestation of nature and it adheres to the same laws as the natural world.

Thus in religious and philosophical authors towards the end of the seventeenth century we find two different structures in the concept of reason. For Bossuet, Malebranche, and Fénelon, as for Pascal, eternal reason provides a constant touchstone for assessment of the functions of human reason and human ideals. In Fontenelle and Bayle, in contrast, no immutable reference point is provided: for them, reason is simply another manifestation of nature.

The use of the phrase *raison éternelle* greatly magnifies certain aspects of the meaning of *raison* and these may provide a clue to the predominant associations of this word in the seventeenth century as a whole. In the predication of reason for God, *raison* becomes virtually synonymous with truth and refers to the source of all order and proportion in the universe. Consequently, the notions of truth and order – both of which are important in the etymology of the word *raison* – may be central to the meaning of *raison* in contemporary usage, and not only for authors who predicate reason of God.

However, truth and order are vague terms which can have very different meanings. The predication of reason for God gives a particular sense to these concepts which is not necessarily present when *raison* is not hypostatized and identified with the Godhead.

First, the use of *raison* to refer to God denies any distinction between structural order and moral truth. The dictionaries define *raison* as *cause* and as *justice*. In the concept of eternal reason, these disparate senses of the word become unified: eternal reason is the source and origin of all causality and also of all justice and moral order. In this sense, the principles underlying the physical structure of the universe are united with the principles underlying true morality.

Second, the predication of reason for God suggests that the order or logic of thought is correct and true only if it coincides with moral truth. The faculty *raison* is defined by the dictionaries as the capacity to distinguish the true from the false, good from evil, and also as the capacity for discursive thought. The first of these meanings is clearly present in the notion of eternal reason which is identified with *sagesse* and *vérité* and described as the origin of man's ability to distinguish between truth and falsehood. The connection between discursive reason and eternal reason is less obvious. Lalande says that *raison discursive* is usually considered peculiar to man. He quotes Aquinas: 'Rationale est differentia animalis et Deo non convenit nec Angelis.'[20] Fénelon uses the verb *raisonner* of God but this use is probably metaphorical since by definition any movement pertains to the mutable world and not to the constant and eternal. However, man's discursive reason may be regarded as emanating from the eternal in so far as it acts as an aid to distinguish the true from the false and to create conscious order.

Thus it would seem that the structure in the concept of reason is fundamental in determining the connotations and meaning of *raison* in many of its different forms. As long as the pyramid structure is present, *raison* refers to two levels of reality: on the one hand, to a purely human reason and, on the other, to a unified and objective truth which may or may not be accessible to human reason. The dictionaries indicate that *droite raison* can be used both of correct discursive thought and of correct judgment. It is now apparent that the notion of what is correct is dependent on belief or lack of belief in a constant and unchanging truth. As long as *raison* can refer to an immutable and unified truth, *droite raison* will be that reason, discursive or judging, which coincides with the universal and which links knowledge to virtue. When the pyramid structure in the concept is broken, reason may be correct or right on different grounds: the test may be logicality or demonstrability. Thus the change from the use of *raison éternelle* to *nature* is reflected in many uses of the word *raison* and is accompanied by a narrowing in the conception of reason as an ideal and as a faculty. In the next chapters these themes are examined in greater detail in these and other authors.

3

Reason as norm

Norme : type concret ou formule abstraite de ce qui doit être, en tout ce qui admet un jugement de valeur : idéal, règle, but, modèle, suivant la cas.

Lalande *Vocabulaire*

In many of its acceptations, the word *raison* implies a value judgment. It most obviously conveys such a judgment when it means right, as in 'il a raison.' But *raison* in the sense of justice, duty, vengeance, explanation, or cause may also carry some imperative or justifying force, and this force, its strength and connotations, will be determined by the conception of the reasonable which lies behind particular instances of use. According to seventeenth-century dictionaries, *raisonnable* can refer either to that which is adequate or to that which is perfect. What is meant by adequate and by perfect will of course depend on an author's frame of reference which will perhaps never be explicitly described. Consequently, the underlying conception of the reasonable must often be surmised indirectly. It may be investigated through an author's doctrinal affiliations, his sociological and cultural background, or the ideas and attitudes conveyed by his work as a whole. It may also be examined in terms of the changing structure in the concept of reason and this approach has some advantages: it allows concentration on the use of the word without introduction of extraneous material and it permits assessment of the relative status of conceptions of the reasonable, whether they represent some form of high ideal or justify baser, personal motives.

Raison as a norm or standard is closely connected with human reason and, where this notion is present, with eternal reason. Eternal reason represents a norm in the sense of an ideal or model. Human reason may carry a variety of values: it may be partly identified with the eternal, it may be opposed to an inferior or animal nature (senses, passions), or it may be regarded as the means of progressing towards an ideal. In all these senses, *raison* implies some kind of value judgment. This means that the norm is highly variable and ranges through a wide spectrum of evaluations. It means also that different standards of the reasonable may conflict. Where eternal reason is in close contact with the human, both may be expected to have a high normative status and the prescriptions of the one will be in harmony with those of the other. Where human reason lacks contact with the eternal or is regarded as unable to fulfil the requirements of higher truth, there is likely to be disharmony or conflict between the norms of reason. Where the presence of eternal reason is minimized or denied, human reason may again have a high normative status but its prescriptions will require no superior sanction. The mobility of the norm can be traced through this structured framework.

Accordingly, this chapter is divided into three sections, examining *raison-vérité*, *raison-prudence-necessité*, and *raison-raisonnement*, respectively. The first is concerned with a norm of reason which, most characteristically, arises from close contact between human and eternal reason. Whether or not God is actually invoked, *raison* is linked with absolute truth and with a constant and unchanging ideal of perfection: it is hypostatized and spoken of as an entity outside man, a point of perfect judgment recognizable and attainable by all men at all times. This *raison* represents a high ideal and appeals to an awareness of a perfect reality above sense-experience, an awareness which is believed to be inherent in man's reason. Owing to the association with absolute truth and to the frequent use of the word *vérité* in connection with *raison*, this norm is here called *raison-vérité*.

The second section considers a norm which, in its most distinctive form, arises out of discord between the prescriptions of human and eternal reason. *Raison* is linked with *prudence* or with *nécessité*. In these connections, it sometimes represents an ideal compatible with *raison-vérité*: it may be predicated of God and, in man, it may be regarded as the expression of 'la droite raison.' However, *raison* linked with *prudence* or *nécessité* can reflect also a regrettable need to compromise with imperfect reality. *Raison* then justifies actions only because higher ideals are considered inaccessible to man or are regarded as incompatible with the harsh demands of government. Finally, the reasons, explanations, and motives arising from necessity may be separated from justification and this avoidance of value judgment is itself significant. *Raison-prudence-nécessité* thus appears in a variety of guises and is a norm of shifting and uncertain status.

The third section examines a norm of reason predominant in authors who minimize the presence of eternal reason. The notion of the reasonable is here closely linked with *raisonnement*, with clarity of thought and demonstrable proof or argument. Reason is connected with truth but with a truth which is verifiable by reasoning. Unlike the first norm, this *raison* is treated as something which changes as human understanding grows. It rests on the assumption that without divine aid human reason can provide and approach the ideals which man sets for himself.

These three standards of reason exist in the seventeenth century side by side and most authors at one time or another appear to use all three in some form or degree. However, gradually the third, that which permits change and demands clarity and evidence without claiming to represent an absolute perfection, comes to take the shape of a distinct and separate standard. In broad outline this shift in emphasis accompanies the change from *raison éternelle* to *nature*. With the disappearance of the notion of an eternal reason and, with it, of a constant human judgment, the norm of reason becomes mutable since it has no sanction other than that derived from reasoning. And yet, to some extent, the third norm incorporates the second and bears important similarities to the first.

The study of reason as norm supports Thuau's thesis that scientific thought towards the end of the century incorporates political tendencies which had conflicted with religion.[1] In the *Pensées*, Pascal contrasts 'la justice éternelle' with 'la légale' (§269), and he treats human justice as right owing to man's ignorance and his incapacity for divine justice. By contrast, the third norm of reason (used by Pascal in his scientific work but prevalent towards the end of the century) does not measure human reason against an unchanging absolute. Consequently, it is able to absorb the imperfections of human reasoning and justice into a conception of progress towards the ideal.[2]

The third norm also bears a significant likeness to the first which suggests a parallel between scientific and religious thought. It is Descartes who forges the link between the first and the third norm: he hypostatizes the ideal and treats it as a universal existing prior to our knowledge about it and yet he seeks to attain it both in ethics and in science by means of clear thought and demonstrable argument. He thus retains the first norm but strips it of mystery. Science was later able to discard the 'Platonic' aspect of Cartesian thought and to set up clarity and demonstrability as a standard relevant to all aspects of life. For Fontenelle, the norm of reason is dependent on man's developing definition of the reasonable and it brings its criteria to bear in morality and aesthetics as well as in science. Like Descartes and unlike political thinkers contemporary with Descartes, Fontenelle propounds only one ideal of reason. The similarity between Descartes's and Fontenelle's use of *raison* as a standard is consequently deceptive in that it overlooks the essential difference of immutability versus mutability, a priori ideas versus a posteriori. But it may be precisely because of this deceptive similarity that the 'crise de la conscience,' described by Hazard, was resolved and that science was able to satisfy the idealism and the desire for a coherent and all-embracing system which accompany the first norm of reason. Lalande has described two types of rationalism, one religious and the other non-religious; he claims that both are characterized by confidence in human reason and by the belief that reason in some way corresponds to the nature of things.[3] He compares Malebranche and Fénelon with Kant but a similar parallel exists between the rationalism of Descartes or Malebranche and that of Fontenelle. Fontenelle sees human ideals not simply as changing but as developing in a direction defined in some sense by nature.

RAISON-VÉRITÉ

This norm has two main characteristics. First of all, *raison* is linked with a constant and immutable truth and, secondly, it is spoken of simultaneously as a hypostatized ideal and as pertaining to man. The latter use is not simply metaphorical: it derives from a belief in a true human nature and in a true reason not usually manifest but nevertheless available to man, even present within him. To strive for the ideal is, in this sense, to strive for the true self, and consequently this norm is opposed to personal whim and caprice and tends to promote a form of individualism. Although the ideal *raison* is not always linked with God, it is identified with an immutable truth, and the norm *raison-vérité* is one which Descartes, Bossuet, Malebranche, and Fénelon share with authors who do not present a theological system.

While La Bruyère sometimes links *raison* and *vérité* with God (*Des esprits forts* §47), he also asserts the identity of reason and truth without mentioning the divine. Thus he says 'La raison tient de la vérité, elle est une' (*De l'homme* §156), and he speaks of 'ceux qui convenant de principes, et connoissant la raison ou la vérité qui est une, s'arrachent la parole l'un à l'autre pour s'accorder sur leurs sentiments' (*De la société* §75). The words 'connoissant la raison ou la vérité' suggest that *raison* and *vérité* are in some degree synonymous and refer to a single ideal which may be known to man but which exists whether or not he is aware of it. Similar uses are found earlier in the century. Naudé says: 'La vérité demeure toujours une et invariable' (*Instruction à la France* 73). Méré, in a passage comparing different forms of 'justesse,' connects 'vérité' with 'le bon sens' and 'la droite raison.' Although he makes no mention of God, he insists that the ideal is unchanging and unified and that it permits of no degrees: 'L'autre Justesse consiste dans le vray rapport que doit avoir une chose avec une autre soit qu'on les assemble ou qu'on les oppose ; et celle-cy vient du bon sens et de la droite raison... et s'exerce sur la vérité simple et nue, qui n'est point sujette au plus ni au moins, et qui demeure toûjours ce qu'elle est' (*Oeuvres* I 96). The ideal represents an absolute, excluding anything mixed or imperfect, and yet the human and the ideal are subtly fused.

Without reference to God, the pyramid structure emerges again. The ideal is a unified and perfect point but in man it can be described in various ways – as self-knowledge, the removal of faults, virtue generally. Méré says that if a man recognizes perfection in one thing he will do so in all for 'toutes les bonnes choses se ressemblent par une conformité de perfection' (ibid II 92). Nicole also insists, 'Toutes les vertus sont nécessairement liées ensemble, et... il n'y a aucune qui puisse subsister seule et sans l'union des autres' (*Essais de morale* I ix 563), and Boileau suggests that perfections can be sought close at hand, one by one, and each in its particular form:

Mais sans t'aller chercher des vertus dans les nües,
Il faudroit peindre en toy des veritez connuës :
Décrire ton esprit ami de la raison.   (*Epistre IX* 155–7)

The words *raison*, *vérité*, and *vertu* offer different ways of referring to a single ideal and, in their plural form, *vertus* and *vérités* merely designate particular instances of that perfection.

The unity of the ideal is often emphasized by the use of the metaphor of a straight path, comparable to that of descending light used by Malebranche and Fénelon to link eternal reason with human reason. At the beginning of the *Discours de la méthode*, Descartes says that in order to become reasonable and to approach truth, it is necessary to follow 'le droit chemin' (2). La Bruyère agrees: 'L'on n'y arrive [à la raison et à la vérité] que par un chemin et l'on s'en écarte par mille' (*De l'homme* §156). The path is easily lost and Boileau describes it as slippery and difficult:

Tout doit tendre au Bon sens : mais pour y parvenir
Le chemin est glissant et penible à tenir.
Pour peu qu'on s'en écarte, aussi-tost on se noye.
La Raison, pour marcher, n'a souvent qu'une voye.   (*L'art poétique* I 45–8)

Several critics, including Brody and Edelman, have remarked on the apparent identity in this passage between Boileau's goal and his means.[4] *Raison* and *bon sens* are first presented as a fixed point which it is hard to reach. Then Boileau turns the tables: *raison* is not a fixed point; on the contrary, it is reason which advances towards the fixed point and which knows the path leading to it. It would seem that the faculty reason can choose from a variety of directions only one of which will lead to truth: having found this direction, reason is already in touch with truth and so, in a sense, has arrived at its goal. Thus reason is both guide and journey's end. For Descartes, the strivings of reason begin only once the true method has been found; for Pascal's Christ, the truth is already possessed by the man who seeks it: 'Tu ne me chercherais pas si tu ne me possédais' (*Pensées* §929). Boileau's view would seem, if anything, more like Pascal's. Edelman says: 'It is something of a miracle road on which journeying and arriving are synchronized into one act.'[5]

Human reason and the ideal for which it strives are thus brought very close – so close that the ideal is a form or quality of human reason itself. This proximity between the ideal and the human is found on occasion throughout the seventeenth century and some passages from Boileau bear an interesting similarity to lines from Corneille's plays. Both Corneille and Boileau refer to reason as prescribing rules of conduct as if it were a voice which addresses man from outside himself. Polyeucte, about to give up his life, calls upon the authority of reason:

> Toujours prêt à la rendre [la vie] au Dieu dont je la tiens :
> La raison me l'ordonne, et la loi des chrétiens.   (*Polyeucte* V ii 1517–18)

Boileau speaks of reason as informing man of certain laws:

> Avant que la Raison, s'expliquant par la voix,
> Eust instruit les Humains, eust enseigné des Loix.
>   (*L'art poétique* IV 133–4)

In other passages, the reason which commands is connected with the individual self. Thus Laodice links *raison* with 'moi' as well as with 'les Dieux':

> Et ce grand nom de reine ailleurs ne m'autorise...
> A vivre indépendante, et n'avoir en tous lieux
> Pour souverains que moi, la raison, et les Dieux.   (*Nicomède* III i 773–4)

And Boileau suggests that his own voice is the vehicle through which a higher reason may communicate:

> Penses-tu qu'aucun d'eux veuille subir mes lois,
> Ni suivre une raison qui parle par ma voix ?   (*Epistre II* 3–4)

These passages from Corneille and Boileau are similar in that they indicate an intimacy between the author or character and the law to which he submits. *Raison*, having imperative force, is often associated with nature and with God; now it appears that this *raison* may also be linked with the individual *moi*. This convergence between higher truth and the self has a quite specific nature (there is only one path and only one truth) and yet it is described in vague terms which render interpretation difficult.

The imperative reason which commands submission and is associated with unified truth is certainly not identical with any whim or opinion that might surface in the personality. Reason linked with truth is contrasted with custom and opinion and also with the senses, imagination, and appetites. In other words, like eternal reason which is opposed to *caprice* and *hasard*, the ideal reason is contrasted with all that pertains to the world of change and mutability. In his essay *De la coutume*, Montaigne distinguishes 'la raison et la vérité' from 'ce violent préjudice de la coutume' and says that the sage should consult only his reason and so shield himself from affectation and falsehood (*Essais* I 23). His words are frequently echoed in the seventeenth century. Naudé remarks: 'Il est très certain que quand nous suivons l'exemple et la coutume, sans sonder la raison, le mérite et la vérité, nous trébuchons' (*Apologie* 128). Descartes regrets that the individual's reason which alone could lead to truth has usually been obscured in childhood by instructions and by appetites (*Discours* 13). Chapelain contrasts 'la raison, qui est immuable' with 'les mœurs des peuples qui sont changeantes' (*Opuscules critiques* 294). Méré opposes 'le bon sens' to the caprice of fashion (*Œuvres* III 100), and he warns: 'On se doit bien garder d'aimer dans son cœur des choses, que la raison ne permet, que parce que le monde s'y est accoûtumé (ibid III 94). *Raison* and *bon sens* point the way to perfection and in obeying reason, he says, 'l'on se prend aux choses comme il faudroit qu'elles fussent, pour estre dans une grande perfection' (ibid II 129). In the same vein, La Bruyère contrasts 'la raison' with 'la prévention du pays' and 'l'orgueil de la nation' (*Des jugements* §22). All these authors hold that the ideal of reason cannot be attained unless the personality is freed from extraneous influences or stimuli whether external or internal: the *moi* with which higher truth and reason are linked is qualitatively different from the self that is swayed by custom, whim, or appetite and, unlike these, it is in some sense stable and constant.

The contrast with custom indicates that although the ideal of reason is immutable and universal it does not necessarily lead to a conformist morality. Lalande has explained that because reason is not an alien law imposed on the individual but is discovered within his own being, belief in the universal may actually promote individualism.[6] However, the degree of individualism to which this notion of the reasonable gives rise is differently conceived by seventeenth-century authors. On the whole, the convergence between the self and the ideal is presented in a considerably more individualistic form in the earlier than in the later part of the century. In Corneille *vertu* is variously interpreted by characters.[7] Descartes's revolutionary overthrow of all former knowledge in his quest for truth through reason is also individualistic. Traces of a similar attitude are found in Méré. Later, in Molière and La Rochefoucauld, the ideal is still presented as deeply personal but it is not on the whole given embodiment in characters or in any single moral stance. In these authors and in Boileau and La Bruyère the individualism of reason is less emphasized and *raison* or *bon sens*, although still separated from custom, are closer to the common consensus. Nevertheless there is a marked similarity in all these authors in that they link the ideal with the human and see some point of possible convergence between constant truth and human reason.

In Corneille, the appeal to reason is often accompanied by what Bénichou calls an 'attitude de défi.'[8] *Raison* is contrasted with *coutume* and with *caprice*. In both instances, it would seem to refer to a conscious will and the contrast is between that which is arbitrary or habitual and that which ensues from choice:

> Oui, Seigneur, dans son mal Rome est trop obstinée,
> Son peuple, qui s'y plaît, en fuit la guérison :
> Sa coutume l'emporte, et non pas la raison.   (*Cinna* II i 526–8)

and

> Ce que peut le caprice, osez-le par raison,
> Et laissez votre sang hors de comparaison.   (*Horace* III iv 909–10)

One of the most contentious examples of Corneille's tendency to identify the reasonable with self-will is Horace's killing of his sister in the name of reason:

> C'est trop, ma patience à la raison fait place ;
> Va dedans les enfers plaindre ton Curiace.   (ibid IV v 1319–20)

Raison, in this passage, may in the first instance mean justice in the sense of reparation or vengeance.[9] However, one meaning does not exclude another. The contrast between *raison* and *patience* is similar to the opposition between *raison* and *coutume* in *Cinna*: both *patience* and *coutume* have a passive content while *raison* suggests conscious purpose and decision. Yet Horace does not view his action as capricious or as simply an expression of his own inclinations: he calls it 'un acte de justice' (*Horace* IV vi 1323). In killing Curiace and his sister, he does violence to his affection for them and he acts in the name of Rome.[10] He thus demonstrates what Corneille in the *Examen du Cid* calls 'la haute vertu' and contrasts with a 'médiocre bonté' (*Oeuvres* III 91–2). This distinction is clearly at least parallel with the mistrust of custom and man's inferior nature seen in Montaigne and it links the self in a highly individualistic way with the ideal. Méré says: 'Ce n'est pas le moyen d'exceller que d'estre toûjours imitateur. Il faut travailler sur l'idée de la perfection' (*Oeuvres* II 71). In his rather peculiar way, this is what Horace does. His action is hardly in accord with 'le bon sens' but it is very much in accord with 'l'idée de la perfection' as he understands it.

While the ideal of reason is given direct expression and is presented in a highly individualistic way in Corneille's characters, it finds only a fleeting *point d'appui* in Molière's plays. The unreason of Molière's principal characters is frequently criticized by characters whom modern critics have dubbed 'les raisonneurs' but the arguments of these characters are also often ridiculous.[11] Reason is nowhere incarnated for long. Characters may be right from one point of view but are shown to be wrong from another and George Dandin cries in exasperation: 'J'enrage... d'avoir tort lorsque j'ai raison' (*George Dandin* I vi). Yet Molière would seem to have had a conception of true reason. A passage from the *Lettre sur la comédie de l'Imposteur*, ostensibly by Donneau de Visé, explains that in order to depict the ridiculous it is necessary to know the reasonable: 'Le ridicule est... la forme extérieure et sensible que la providence de la nature a attachée à tout ce qui est déraisonnable... Pour connoître ce ridicule, il faut connoître la raison dont il signifie le défaut, et voir en quoi elle consiste... nous estimons ridicule ce qui manque extrêmement de raison' (Molière *Oeuvres* IV 560). Moore considers that even if this letter was not dictated by Molière, the views here expressed are 'very probably what he thought, and what he wished to be publicly said.'[12] Whether or not any conclusions concerning Molière's views can be drawn from this letter, Molière does appear to have had a conception of the reasonable. Although in his plays no character is constantly reasonable, the ideal of reason seems to be present in the background, evoked by the very inadequacy and obvious ridiculousness of claims to reasonableness and of pedantic reasonings.

Sometimes the ideal appears to be referred to directly. Cléante's admonition of Orgon in *Tartuffe* certainly gives this impression. *Raison* is linked with 'vérité' and with 'la juste nature':

Éh quoi ? vous ne ferez nulle distinction
Entre l'hypocrisie et la dévotion ?
Vous les voulez traiter d'un semblable langage,
Égaler l'artifice à la sincérité,
Confondre l'apparence avec la vérité,
Estimer le fantôme autant que la personne,
Et la fausse monnaie à l'égal de la bonne ?
Les hommes la plupart sont étrangement faits !
Dans la juste nature on ne les voit jamais ;
La raison a pour eux des bornes trop petites. (I v 331–41)

Reason, as presented in this passage, has a limiting or restraining function
and yet it also offers a form of liberation. If the ideal is realizable, as Cléante
assumes, then through reason a man can be freed from himself, from his
taste for falsehood and hypocrisy. Molière's language thus opens vistas onto
a hidden reality, a way of being which one imagines to be rich in its very
simplicity. The words *raison*, *vérité*, and *nature* all refer in these lines to the
same perfect and unseen truth; the reason to which Cléante addresses himself would seem to be a right reason, one which man can discover and manifest but which is related to a higher truth as well as to the human faculty:
'Dans la droite raison jamais n'entre la vôtre,' Cléante complains (ibid v i
1609). Molière's notion of the reasonable, if indeed it is expressed in this
passage, is similar to that of Corneille in that reason is presented as a superior law that may become a personal quality directly affecting the individual's thought and behaviour. In other respects Molière's conception is very
different: it savours of tranquillity rather than heroism and the association
with 'la juste nature' suggests a stronger resemblance to Boileau than to
Corneille. Lanson has remarked that in Boileau reason, truth, and nature
form one ideal[13] and Thibaudet says that in Boileau's use the word *raison*
always imposes constraints.[14] The notion of conforming to reason, truth, and
nature does indeed impose limits since it involves adherence to a narrow way
which is easily lost. But it is important (and Thibaudet perhaps agrees)[15] to
stress the positive qualities which ensue from following this reason. If in
Molière and Boileau obedience to reason does not lead to grand gestures, it
does guarantee a perfect judgment in all things.

La Rochefoucauld's conception of the reasonable in some ways resembles
that of Molière. Far from destroying moral categories, the questioning of the
content of human virtues in the *Maximes* may force the reader to look
beyond custom and habit to a more genuine understanding. This has been
suggested by Culler and Starobinski[16] and it may be that, as in Molière's

plays, the ideal is present in the background of La Rochefoucauld's writings. Certainly, at times, La Rochefoucauld expresses awareness of an ideal reason. In his presentation of this ideal he emphasizes the immediate and active experience involved in the attainment of the reasonable. Where Méré says of *honnêteté*: 'L'honnesteté n'est pas une simple spéculation, il faut qu'elle agisse et qu'elle gouverne' (*Œuvres* I 55), La Rochefoucauld remarks: 'Celui-là n'est pas raisonnable à qui le hasard fait trouver la raison, mais celui qui la connoît, qui la discerne et qui la goûte' (*Œuvres* I 76). He argues that the reason which is opposed to custom and chance is a truly personal reason and its very individualism is the measure of the universal truth of its judgments. Speaking of the 'honnête homme,' he says that to judge well, 'il y faut une grande proportion et une grande justesse : il faut savoir discerner ce qui est bon en général, et ce qui nous est propre, et suivre alors avec raison la pente naturelle qui nous porte vers les choses qui nous plaisent.' This 'pente naturelle,' which conforms with reason, is discovered through a rare combination of discipline and inner freedom and La Rochefoucauld goes on to say that if men sought to excel only in this way, 'il n'y auroit rien de faux dans leur goût et dans leur conduite ; ils se montreroient tels qu'ils sont ; ils jugeroient des choses par leurs lumières, et s'y attacheroient par leur raison ; il y auroit de la proportion dans leur vues et dans leurs sentiments : leur goût seroit vrai, il viendroit d'eux et non pas des autres, et ils le suivroient par choix, et non pas par coutume ou par hasard' (ibid 313–14). As in Corneille, the opposition between reason and custom implies a contrast between conscious choice and automatic or habitual judgment. As in Molière, the attainment of the ideal is linked with naturalness.

Molière and La Rochefoucauld thus give greater emphasis than Corneille to the identity of reason in all its manifestations and they assume that if the ideal were realized in human thought and action it would give rise to a consensus of opinion and so to a degree of conformity: yet the nature of this conformity would be quite different from a habitual obedience. Their unwillingness to present an embodiment of reason in any single character or moral stance is perhaps due to a greater awareness of the narrow margin which separates adherence to the ideal from servitude to whim and self-will. It is the 'how' rather than the 'what' that distinguishes the true virtue, thought, or gesture from the false and this difference in quality is not easily defined.

The difficulty of recognizing the distinction between an expression of universal truth and conformity to custom besets many discussions[17] and intrudes in the argument between the Ancients and the Moderns. It can confidently be said that this argument turns on the question of whether the reason of the ancients, their judgment and taste, is that of all ages. It is an argument not about whether the authority of the ancients should hold sway but whether a judgment can be different from theirs and still be reason and not merely custom, imagination, and caprice. Boileau and La Bruyère, like Molière and La Rochefoucauld, belong to a generation which does not stress as strongly as Méré and Corneille the individualism involved in obedience to reason. Thus Boileau maintains that what is reason for the ancients must be reason for modern man and he says that most men foolishly fear to repeat the thought another has had before them, foolishly because 'le droit sens' is always 'le droit sens' and must not be sacrificed in a vain attempt at originality:

La pluspart, emportez d'une fougue insensée
Toûjours loin du droit sens vont chercher leur pensée.
Il croiroient s'abaisser, dans leur vers monstrueux,
S'ils pensoient ce qu'un autre a pû penser comme eux.

(*L'art poétique* I 39–42)

But who is to decide and how can one distinguish between personal whim and true conformity to the ideal? La Bruyère, an ardent upholder of the ancients, sees reason as beholden to truth, a truth that comes from above and is not subject to human discretion. Consequently, he admits that what looks like an 'esprit de singularité' may in some instances be precisely that which best conforms to 'la droite raison': 'Le commun des hommes est si enclin au déréglement et à la bagatelle, et le monde est si plein d'exemples ou pernicieux ou ridicules, que je croirois assez que l'esprit de singularité, s'il pouvoit avoir des bornes et ne pas aller trop loin, approcheroit fort de la droite raison et d'une conduite régulière' (*Des jugements* §10). As long as reason is considered to be a constant universal, superior to custom and opinion, there can be no easy solution to the difficulty of distinguishing a true from a false individualism. Consequently, this problem is actually an important corollary of the norm *raison-vérité*: it arises because there are no tangible criteria whereby the expression of the universal can be classified and imposed on anyone who fails of his own accord to recognize truth.

In Descartes, this difficulty is partly overcome by the introduction of another standard of reason. Descartes sets out alone, in what La Bruyère would call an 'esprit de singularité,' to find a truth or reason which he too believes is eternally unchanging: 'Tout mon dessein ne tendoit qu'a m'assurer, et a rejetter la terre mouvante et le sable, pour trouver le roc ou l'argile' (*Discours* 29). But he seeks this truth largely by means of reasoning, thus exposing his conclusions to assessment by quite a different standard of reason – that of *raison-raisonnement*.

RAISON-PRUDENCE-NÉCESSITÉ

The second norm is characterized by compromise with imperfect reality. It is a norm of practical reason answering to realities of government and of individual and social need. The degree of compromise believed to be necessary varies according to the extent of contact posited between the human and the eternal world. Thus the second norm takes various forms. It can 1) represent an ideal in which the politically viable and the eternally just are combined and with which simple expedience is contrasted; but where the human is further divorced from the eternal, it takes the form of 2) expedience justified by man's ignorance and weakness or 3) explanations and motives conveying no specific value judgment. The different forms of the norm are here treated in this order. Although sometimes this arrangement distorts the chronology of authors (Bossuet is considered with Richelieu and Corneille), it highlights the gradual abandonment of a constant and static norm in favour of emphasis on explanation. Lalande has drawn attention to the increasing importance given to explanation as a form of value judgment during the seventeenth century.[18] In non-religious literature, explanation and motive are less and less measured against a constant and eternal norm and while this development is not obvious in Bossuet it is apparent in his contemporaries – Mme de La Fayette and Racine.

The two words *prudence* and *nécessité* span the different forms of this norm of reason. Balzac speaks of God as 'la prudence supérieure' (*Le prince* 251), and Corneille predicates *prudence* of God and equates it with 'la sage équité' (*Cinna* II i 539–40, 545–6). In such uses, *prudence* is the same as divine *sagesse, équité,* or *raison.* Furetière, in his dictionary, defines *prudence* as a cardinal virtue 'qui enseigne à bien conduire sa vie et ses mœurs, ses discours et ses actions, suivant la droite raison' and Bossuet describes it as a virtue 'qui nous apprend ce qui est bon ou mauvais' (*De la connoissance de Dieu et de soi-même* 75). The meaning of *prudence* clearly overlaps considerably with that of *raison,* but *prudence* tends to emphasize the practical aspect of wisdom and justice and is often used in political contexts.[19] One of Corneille's characters exclaims: 'Une vertu parfaite a besoin de prudence,' (*Nicomède* III ii 816), and Furetière gives examples where *prudent* means cautious or circumspect, 'prudent comme le serpent.' Sometimes *prudence* is actually separated from truth; in his translation of *The Imitation of Christ*, Corneille uses it to mean false counsel:

O Dieu de verité, pour qui seul je soupire...
Parle seul à mon âme, et qu'aucune prudence,
D'aucun autre docteur ne m'explique tes lois.   (*Œuvres* VIII 40–1)

Thus the status of *prudence* as of *raison* is highly variable and both words may be used to refer to a high ideal or to argument, explanation, and motive of questionable validity. The word *nécessité* has fewer variations in meaning and usually refers to that which is imposed by circumstance in contrast to that which is just. It thus leans towards the explanation / motive end of the norm.

Corneille and Bossuet often present the ruler as acting in the service of eternal truth. Corneille describes the benevolent king as administering *raison* and *équité*. Thus, in *Agésilas*, the prince appears as the human counterpart of God:

La Grèce a de plus saintes lois,
Elle a des peuples et des rois
Qui gouvernent avec justice :
La raison y préside, et la sage équité ;
Le pouvoir souverain par elles limité,
N'y laisse aucun droit de caprice.   (II i 441–6)

The ruler's power is here described as held in check by a higher principle, that of true reason and justice. The same type of statement is found in *Cinna*, although the order which the ruler imposes is attributed more directly to 'le bien commun de tous' (II i 619):

Avec ordre et raison les honneurs il dispense,
Avec discernement punit et récompense...
Mais quand le peuple est maître, on n'agit qu'en tumulte :
La voix de la raison jamais ne se consulte.   (II i 505–6, 509–10)

In both passages, *raison* is called upon as an informing principle providing the ruler with an awareness of true justice and order. Clarke, referring to Auguste's pardon of Cinna, says: 'The ruler acts in harmony with the highest form of reason, that heroic inspiration of Right Reason.'[20] Certainly, the inspiration for Auguste's action seems closer to a divine love than to a Machiavellian prudence.

Bossuet expresses a vision of the earthly prince acting in the service of truth and justice which is similar to that of Corneille. A ruler can and should be swayed by the reason of religion and should use his power and force to further the reign of truth, virtue and reason. Thus Bossuet asks: A quoi la force doit-elle servir, qu'à défendre la raison ? et pourquoi commandent les hommes, si ce n'est pour faire que Dieu soit obéi ? (*Oraison funèbre de Henriette Marie de France* 520). He praises the king, saying: 'Louis est le rempart de la religion : c'est à la religion qu'il fait servir ses armes redoutées... il ne l'établit partout au dehors, que parce qu'il la fait régner au dedans et au milieu de son cœur' (*Oraison funèbre de Marie-Thérèse d'Autriche* 182). A good ruler does not act on self-interest and does not abuse his power; he bows to a higher principle, that of reason, which represents in Corneille the common good and in Bossuet the authority of religion. The standard here is a divine standard to which it is believed a ruler can and should conform and to which practical considerations appear to be no impediment. The reason of state and the reason of religion are shrouded in the mystery of a higher principle which is necessarily true and good but which is not clearly defined in relation to practicalities.

In Corneille, this reason of state has a different end in view from private conscience and may incorporate political and circumstantial considerations that overrule private conscience. Owing to the particular nature of his responsibilities, the ruler is justified by criteria different from those applicable to the individual:

> Un roi dont la prudence a de meilleurs objets
> Est meilleur ménager du sang de ses sujets :
> Je veille pour les miens, mes soucis les conservent,
> Comme le chef a soin des membres qui le servent.
> Ainsi votre raison n'est pas raison pour moi :
> Vous parlez en soldat ; je dois agir en roi...
> Et quoi qu'on veuille dire, et quoi qu'on ose croire,
> Le Comte à m'obéir ne peut perdre sa gloire.   (*Le Cid* II vi 595–601)

In this passage of *Le Cid*, *prudence* is used to refer to the prince's care, his practical concerns, while *raison* conveys the sense of 'that which justifies.' A question that arises when Horace kills his sister is whether, as a subject, Horace is justified in taking on the norms of state and abandoning private conscience. For the king this is recommended (*Nicomède* IV iii 20–1) but

Horace is not justified in retaining this stance after his immediate duty is done, and he is then absolved from the duties of private conscience only by the king's pardon (*Horace* V iii 1759–63). Thus both personal and public or state virtue have high standing in Corneille's plays, but, where they conflict, the latter prevails.[21]

In both Bossuet and Corneille, the true reason of state or of religion is contrasted with a *prudence* and with *raisons* and *raisonnements* – whether of ruler or subject – which do not look to a higher principle and are entirely personal or whimsical. These assume the status of arguments and explanations having no validity. Bossuet says: 'Quand les malheurs nous ouvrent les yeux... nous ne savons plus par où excuser cette prudence présomptueuse qui se croyait infaillible. Nous voyons que Dieu seul est sage' (*Henriette Marie* 543–4). Man's prudence is nothing beside the wisdom of God. Equally, reasoning must bow to the superior authority of the church and the church borrows the mysterious quality of a higher truth: 'Si notre esprit naturellement incertain, et devenu par ses incertitudes le jouet de ses propres raisonnemens, a besoin... d'être fixé et déterminé par quelque autorité certaine : quelle plus grande autorité que celle de l'Eglise catholique' (*Discours sur l'histoire universelle* 564). In Corneille, the phrases *raisons d'état* and *maximes d'état* in the plural form are given a similar status and are associated with tyranny and self-interest. Laodice exclaims:

> La vertu trouve appui contre la tyrannie.
> Tout son peuple a des yeux pour voir quel attentat
> Font sur le bien public les maximes d'Etat.   (*Nicomède* III ii 848–50)

And Flaminius says:

> Quant aux raisons d'État qui vous font concevoir
> Que nous craignons en vous l'union du pouvoir,
> Si vous en consultiez des têtes bien sensées,
> Elles vous déferoient de ces belles pensées.   (ibid II iii 681–4)

The voice of reason to which Cinna appeals presents a contrast to such *raisons d'état*. The latter take on the status of *raison* meaning motive, explanation or cause, *raison* meaning vengeance or satisfaction, and *raisonnements* referring to arguments of uncertain truth. In all such uses, of which there are many examples in Corneille's plays, no clear justification is conferred on the motives or arguments of his characters.[22]

The marked distinction in Corneille and Bossuet between the true reason of state and individual motive or reasoning accentuates and preserves the difference between that which is eternally just and that which merely conforms with personal needs and expediency. In Richelieu's language, such a distinction is not usually made and individual reasoning is often confused with the reason of state. Richelieu argues that because man is 'souverainement raisonnable' it is his duty to God to see that reason prevails. Thus confusing the faculty with the ideal, he draws two conclusions: the ruler must desire only that which is 'raisonnable et juste' and, secondly, he must see to it that all his orders are obeyed since if they are not obeyed 'la raison ne régneroit pas souverainement.' Finally, he declares: 'Il est impossible que des sujets n'aiment pas un prince, s'ils connaissent que la raison ne soit la guide de toutes actions. L'autorité contraint à l'obéissance, mais la raison y persuade.' (*Testament* 325–6). What is this reason? Is it power? Is it the order of strong discipline? Is it reasoning and foresight? Or is it the capacity to persuade rather than to constrain? All these meanings seem to be present. La Fontaine's fable *Les poissons, et le berger qui joue de la flûte* separates persuasive reason from power:

Ô vous, pasteurs d'humains et non pas de brebis,
Rois, qui croyez gagner par raisons les esprits
D'une multitude étrangère,
Ce n'est jamais par là que l'on en vient à bout.
Il y faut une autre manière :
Servez-vous de vos rets ; la puissance fait tout.[23]   (*Œuvres* III 58)

But Richelieu avoids this distinction and uses the connection of the word *raison* with right and truth to cloak a variety of meanings and to give all of them the sanction of God.

The ambiguity recurs in many passages of the *Testament*. The title of the chapter 'Que la raison doit être la regle et la conduite d'un État' sounds as if Richelieu is calling upon some high principle, but the chapter opens with the statement that for man to honour reason and serve God means that he must use 'raisonnement' and 'prévoyance' and that he must consider the future of the state if necessary at the expense of conscience: 'Quand même la conscience pourroit souffrir qu'on laissât une action signalée sans récompense et un crime notable sans châtiment, la raison d'État ne pourroit le permettre. La punition et les bienfaits regardent le futur plus que le passé' (345). Ultimately, Richelieu says, God helps those who help themselves: 'Dieu concourt à toutes les actions des hommes par une coopération générale, qui suit leurs desseins, et c'est à eux d'user en toutes choses de leur liberté selon la prudence dont la divine sagesse les a rendus capables.' (336). The difference between true justice and expedience is here lost. The Machiavellian notion that 'a prince, in order to hold his position, must acquire the power to be not good, and understand when to use it and when not to use it, in accord with necessity'[24] is concealed by and absorbed into a picture of the ruler as servant of God.

The idea that necessity can in itself be a source of justification has so far been suggested only in La Fontaine's fables and it is not surprising that modern critics have described the atmosphere of the fables as Machiavellian.[25] 'La raison du plus fort est toujours la meilleure' (*Le loup et l'agneau*: *Oeuvres* I 88) plays upon the ambiguities contained in the word *raison*: he who is strongest is right, he is justified and reason is on his side; or *la raison*, the argument of the strongest, always wins whether or not it is justified. The ambiguity is two-fold: it lies in whether *raison* means explanation or justification; and, if the latter, whether justification rests on criteria of the standard *raison-vérité* or on criteria of the standard *raison-nécessité*. Molière uses similar word play when Sganarelle concedes to his master: 'Assurément que vous avez raison, si vous le voulez; on ne peut pas aller là contre. Mais si vous ne le voulez pas, ce seroit peut-être une autre affaire' (*Dom Juan* I ii). However, it is doubtful whether either La Fontaine or Molière really approved a Machiavellian morality: their sympathetic treatment of the victim and of the weaker party suggests otherwise. Ironic recognition of the justifying force of power is obviously not equivalent to a serious commitment to the idea that compromise with circumstance and with nature is desirable and neither La Fontaine nor Molière explicitly creates a norm of reason from expedience. Such a notion appears only among contemporaries and admirers of Richelieu – in the writings of Balzac and more particularly of Chapelain and it is explored in relation to a particular perspective by Pascal.

Balzac, like Corneille, usually uses the phrase *raison d'état* to refer to affairs or interests of state without thereby suggesting that these are in any way worthy or right. He says of Spanish rulers: 'Les raisons d'Estat les tourmentent jour et nuict. Ils ne sont maigres ny malades que de cela, et leur jaunisse perpettuelle est le signe exterieur, et non une impression violente de la convoitise de regner qui les brusle et les consume au dedans' (*Le prince* 317). Sometimes, however, he contrasts human affairs with eternal ideals which he rejects as too demanding for this world. In a letter to de Scudéry (27 August 1637), he says plainly that the ideal reason which he calls 'la souveraine raison' must often be discarded and he indicates that a less demanding standard may be valid: 'N'insistez point sur cette exacte et rigoureuse justice. Ne vous attachez point avec tant de scrupule à la souveraine raison : Qui voudroit la contenter, et suivre ses desseins et sa regularité, seroit obligé de luy bastir un plus beau Monde que cettui-cy ; il faudroit luy faire une nouvelle Nature des choses, et luy aller chercher des Idées au dessus du Ciel' (*Les œuvres* I 543). The actions and laws which Balzac says cannot be justified in terms of an 'exacte et rigoureuse justice' may still be in accord with *raison*: that is, with a different norm of reason. Chapelain makes this possibility explicit. He justifies expedient action in terms of *raisonnement* and *nécessité*. In *De la lecture des vieux romans*, he says of the knights of the Round Table:

Encore que l'expédient pris par ces princes fût violent et déshonnete, il ne laissait pas toutefois d'aller à leurs fins ; et... si du côté de l'équité et de la pudeur, ils n'en étaient pas excusables, ils le pourraient être du côté du raisonnement et de la nécessité, puisque leur peu d'industrie ne leur faisait point voir d'autre moyen de se maintenir et de s'étendre.   (*Opuscules* 232)

Pudeur and *équité* are rejected as unsuitable measures of merit in political matters. As long as actions can be explained in terms of their objective they are defensible: reasoning and explanation are sufficient. The norm of reason as presented in Chapelain's statement is specifically one which is arrived at by reasoning, not one which is constant or which can be recognized and experienced. In Corneille, Bossuet, and Richelieu this norm is not singled out or given a justifying force of its own: it remains hidden and is drawn into the polarities of the true reason and justice of God and false explanations or motives. Sutcliffe remarks (with reference to an unidealistic statement of Naudé resembling that of Chapelain): 'Jamais le Cardinal ni ceux qui le servaient n'aurait usé de pareil langage.'[26]

Pascal, more than any other author, examines and faces up to the difference between true justice and the demands of circumstance and human nature. In his social and political discussion, Pascal presents two distinct norms by which the human order may be assessed. The one is true reason and justice (which everyone thinks he knows but in fact does not know – (*Pensées* §33); the other is necessity. Ideally, true justice would reign, but, since this is not possible, it is necessary and, in this sense, right that force be obeyed (ibid §103). This transformation of the necessary into the just means that, in relation to necessity, demands for true justice are inexcusable, and Pascal says, 'De là vient l'injustice de la Fronde' (§85). Both standards, true justice and necessity, are valid in their right place and if they are understood in the right way. Ideally, Pascal says, man would obey force with a 'pensée de derrière' realizing that it is not true justice and that it is justified only because it is necessary (§91). Thus Pascal separates *raison-nécessité* from *raison-vérité* and, unlike Richelieu, he is at pains to avoid any confusion between these standards.

However, in relation to the human order, Pascal, like Richelieu, to some extent treats explanation as a form of justification. *Raisons* in the phrase 'Raisons des effets' (which in the title of the *laisse* appears in the plural form) probably refers in the first instance to explanations or causes. Speaking of St Augustine and Montaigne, Pascal explains: 'Toutes ces personnes ont vu les effets mais ils n'ont pas vu les causes... Car les effets sont comme sensibles et les causes sont visibles seulement à l'esprit' (*Pensées* §517). In another fragment, he introduces the Latin word *causa*: 'Rem viderunt, causam non viderunt' (§266). In a sense the explanations for the human order also justify that order and in some fragments Pascal takes advantage of this dual sense of *raison* in order to stress the paradox of his argument. Referring to the words 'par une raison qu'ils ne pénètrent pas, on a raison,'[27] Harrington says: 'Le mot *raison* se rencontre deux fois, non pas dans le même sens. La première fois, il signifie l'explication profonde comme dans "raison des effets." La seconde fois, il fait partie de l'idiotisme "avoir raison".'[28] Several other passages involving similar word play might be cited: 'L'usurpation... a été introduite autrefois sans raison, elle est devenue raisonnable' (§60) and 'Les choses du monde les plus déraisonnables deviennent les plus raisonnables à cause du dérèglement des hommes' (§977). The phrase *raisons des effets* is used as the title of fragments bearing diversely on the cause, the necessity, and the justification of the human order and within these fragments *raison* is given all three meanings. By playing on the double sense of *raison*, Pascal, like Richelieu, is able to slide between the meanings of explanation and justification.

For Pascal, as for Balzac and Chapelain, *raison-nécessité* is honourable only because man is incapable of higher standards. Consequently, a degree of uncertainty surrounds the status of this norm. Both Pascal and Bossuet call upon expedience as a justifiable means of bringing man to religion. Reasoning and a sense of expedience make it reasonable, Pascal holds, to wager on the truth of religion: 'Tout joueur hasarde avec certitude pour gagner avec incertitude... sans pécher contre la raison' (*Pensées* §418). Gouhier has suggested that the *raison* of the *Pari* is not intended to prove or disprove the existence of God but to take cognizance of the human situation and to weigh the advantages and disadvantages of living as if God existed.[29] Necessity demands not knowledge, since that may not be possible, but choice. Similarly Bossuet, speaking of the pleasures of this life, says: 'Pourquoi ne pas mépriser par raison ce qu'il faudra un jour mépriser par force ? (*Oraison funèbre de Henriette Anne d'Angleterre* 680). Both appear to consider this type of argument based on *raison-prudence* or *nécessité* a valid means to religious conversion. But to what extent it is honourable is unclear. There has been much debate about the position of the wager in Pascal's *Pensées* and this uncertainty reflects the ambiguous status given to *raison-nécessité* in the *Pensées* as a whole. The expedient reason which can bring man to seek God, like the 'raison des effets,' is an expression of man's misery as well as of his greatness. As Topliss has commented, 'Pascal is able to establish a close connection between his critique of social institutions and his critique of reason.'[30]

In the second half of the seventeenth century, particularly in novelists and playwriters such as Mme de La Fayette and Racine, the uncertain status of the norm *raison-prudence* and *nécessité* surrounds the motives and explanations of their characters with moral ambiguity. Mme de La Fayette, on several occasions, speaks of 'la raison et la prudence': always the reader is left unsure whether the character's action is admirable and justifiable by this standard. Alphonse says of Nugna Bella: 'Elle s'imagina que la raison et la prudence autorisaient son changement et qu'elle devait quitter un homme qui ne serait point son mari pour un autre qui le serait assurément.' Then he adds: 'Il ne faut pas toujours de si grandes raisons pour appuyer la légèreté des femmes' (*Zaïde* 73). In the first statement, Nugna Bella's action would appear to be justified by the standard of necessity; in the second, the standard to which she appeals is debased to mere argument or excuse having no claim to justification. Equally, when Mme de Clèves resists the temptation to go out into the garden to see if M. de Nemours is really there, it is not clear whether she is acting in a praiseworthy or cowardly fasion: 'Mais enfin la raison et la prudence l'emportèrent sur tous ces autres sentiments' (*La princesse de Clèves* 368). Is it virtuous to follow the precepts of *raison* and *prudence*? We are not told.

In Racine's plays, the uncertain status of the norm often creates an impression of the relativity of standards of the reasonable. Arsace tells Antiochus that he can expect success in his wooing of Bérénice:

Ouvrez les yeux, Seigneur, et songeons entre nous
Par combien de raisons Bérénice est à vous.
Puisque aujourd'hui Titus ne prétend plus lui plaire,
Songez que votre hymen lui devient nécessaire.   (*Bérénice* III ii 817–20)

Further on he says:

> Tout parlera pour vous, le dépit, la vengeance,
> L'absence de Titus, le temps, votre présence,
> Trois sceptres que son bras ne peut seul soutenir,
> Vos deux États voisins, qui cherchent à s'unir.
> L'intérêt, la raison, l'amitié, tout vous lie. (823–7)

In the first statement, *raisons* refers to arguments from necessity and self-interest which are of questionable justification. In the second, *raison* probably means logic or good sense and Arsace no doubt intends it to justify Antiochus's ambition and yet it is preceded by considerations of vengeance and self-interest and is ambiguously placed between 'l'intérêt' and 'l'amitié.'

In Corneille's plays, *raison(s)* and *raisonnement(s)* referring to cause, explanation, and satisfaction have clearly a lower status than 'la raison,' the justifying principle. In Racine's plays, such a contrast is not usually provided. The characters themselves often seem more concerned that their *raison(s)* should be persuasive to themselves or to others than that they be justifiable or true. Racine's characters rarely hear the voice of reason. When they do, they usually seem unconvinced, unwilling or unable to obey.[31] As Orgel says of Racine's characters, 'Reason gives no power to refrain, it is almost an accomplice.'[32] Indeed, in many passages of *Phèdre*, *raison* refers not so much to a higher law as to lucidity or sanity, to a human faculty having a normative status only in so far as it is superior to *fureur* and *passion*. Phèdre speaks of her 'raison égarée' and of the 'fol amour qui trouble ma raison' (I iii 282, II v 675); similar uses are found in Mme de La Fayette's novels (*La princesse* 285–6; *Zaïde* 136 and 217).

The tendency of Racine and Mme de La Fayette to avoid value judgment is in itself significant for the development of reason as norm. References to reasonings and reasons are more frequent in Racine's plays than in Corneille's; while Corneille contrasts these with true reason and Pascal contrasts explanations based on necessity with eternal truth, in Racine explanation and motive are provided with no *point d'appui*. The third norm of reason, considered next, in a sense fills this gap and provides a new yardstick by offering a form of justification derived solely from human reasoning.

RAISON-RAISONNEMENT

In its most distinctive form the third norm coincides with the replacement of *raison éternelle* by *nature* and is a mutable, evolving standard deriving its validity from human reasoning. Consequently, like *raison-vérité*, this norm is closely linked with human reason, but this time the norm is determined by the human rather than the human by a hypostatized norm. In other words, instead of human reason remaining constant because the norm of reason is constant, the norm changes because human reason changes. Owing to its foundation in reasoning and to its mutability, the third norm resembles *raison-nécessité*. However, like the first norm, *raison-vérité*, it represents an ideal standard and its status is unquestioned. In Pascal it appears mainly in his scientific work, in Descartes it represents only a means to a higher *raison-vérité*, but in others, such as Fontenelle, Saint-Evremond, and Bayle, it prevails over all other norms and is used as a measure of reasonableness in all areas of experience.

Raison-raisonnement, because it rests on a denial of the reality of higher truth, is to some extent apparent in all authors who reject the possibility of attaining such truth or who admit the need for acceptance of things as they are. Thus, it is glimpsed in Richelieu's insistence on the importance of reasoning and perspicacity, in Balzac's and Chapelain's recognition of the reasonableness of expedience, in Pascal's acknowledgement of the validity of the human order, and in La Fontaine's practical morality. It is also seen, if in a rather negative form, in those uses of Mme de La Fayette and Racine where *raison* refers to sanity or lucidity.

In addition, the third norm may be apparent in embryonic form in Molière and La Rochefoucauld. Fernandez has distinguished two standards of reason in Molière. He calls them 'la raison-idéal' and 'la raison-science' and maintains that since the former is rarely incarnated in Molière's plays, the latter is the norm which ultimately prevails: 'La raison-science s'occupe de connaître le monde comme il est, avec ses opacités et ses incohérences... En vérité la raison qui triomphe chez Molière, c'est la raison-science. "Voilà nous dit-il, comment fonctionne la nature. Adaptez-vous à elle, non pas elle à vous. Sinon l'éclat de rire." La raison molièresque revient à accepter lucidement, quand on le peut, les choses comme elles sont, ce qui suppose assez fatalement une personnalité faible.'[33] To some extent, this statement could be applied to La Rochefoucauld, since in the *Maximes*, as in Molière's plays, the ideal of reason is on the whole secondary to the recognition of human weakness and man's imperfect world.

However, the third norm emerges clearly only in philosophical work of a positive and progressive kind. While traces of this standard are found in Pascal's *Pensées* as in '2 excès : exclure la raison, n'admettre que la raison' (§183), this norm is most evident in his scientific work, where clarity of argument and evidence are the only criteria of the reasonable. He rejects authority and requires instead the adaptation of opinion in accordance with evidence. While some things, such as theology, lie beyond the scope of human reason, others, he says, must be referred to its criteria alone:

Il n'en est pas de même des sujets qui tombent sous le sens ou sous le raisonnement : l'autorité y est inutile ; la raison seule a lieu d'en connaître. Elles ont leurs droits séparés : l'une avait tantôt tout l'avantage ; ici l'autre règne à son tour... C'est ainsi que la géométrie, l'arithmétique, la musique, la physique, la médecine, l'architecture et toutes les sciences qui sont soumises à l'expérience et au raisonnement, doivent etre augmentées pour devenir parfaite. (*Préface sur le Traité du vide* 230–1)

In this passage Pascal identifies *raison* with *raisonnement* and claims that in the perfecting of certain sciences and arts[34] reasoning and experiment alone are helpful. Validity and truth are conferred only on that which meets the requirements of reasoning: no higher standard is called upon.

Reason as a standard of clear thought and argument sets boundaries for itself: it lays down where reasoning and experiment are useful and where they are not. It also tells man just how far his admiration for the ancients should extend: 'Comme la raison le fait naître [ce respect], elle doit aussi le mesurer.' *Raison* is both human reason – a developing faculty – and a standard against which scientific achievement should be measured. Pascal is not concerned with whether our judgment is the same as that of the ancients but with furthering factual knowledge and skill in order to acquire new scientific truths. To expect reason to be static and constant throughout the ages is to equate it with the instinct of animals: 'N'est-ce pas indignement traiter la raison de l'homme et la mettre en parallèle avec l'instinct des animaux, puisqu'on en ôte la principale différence, qui consiste en ce que les effets du raisonnement augmentent sans cesse, au lieu que l'instinct demeure toujours dans un état égal ? (ibid 231). Standards of reason evolve and become more rigorous, and knowledge builds on previous knowledge; consequently, Pascal suggests, the standards of the ancients cannot be those of today.

This norm of reason, which Pascal confines to subjects other than religion and 'la morale,' in many ways resembles Descartes's demand for clarity in reasoning. Descartes's scientific thought is, however, welded to his ethical and moral thought: in his view science and ethics require the same criteria and he considers that his method is adequate for the attainment of greater knowledge in both areas. Also, *raisonnement* remains a part of Descartes's method; it represents a means of developing human reason, already endowed with good judgment, towards an ideal *raison-vérité*. *Raisonnement* is a means to an immutable truth.

Only in the work of Fontenelle, Bayle, and Saint-Evremond is the norm *raison-raisonnement* both mutable and relevant to all areas of experience. Fontenelle adopts Descartes's method and takes the criteria of reasoning as the test of reasonableness in all matters, but he does not believe in a universal reason and he does not cultivate his reason in order to approach an a priori and perfect *raison*. In his *Digression sur les anciens et les modernes*, he speaks very much like Pascal about the supremacy of human reason and its criteria in science: 'La physique, la médecine, les mathématiques, sont composées d'un nombre infini de vues, et dépendent de la justesse du raisonnement, qui se perfectionne avec une extrême lenteur, et se perfectionne toujours.' Unlike Pascal, he does not limit the evolution of reason to subjects outside religion and ethics. On the contrary, he claims that progress in 'la manière de raisonner' 'se répand sur tout' (166). *Raison* is a purely human standard and yet it is relevant to all matters and not just to science.

On these points, Saint-Evremond's thought is similar. In his essay *Sur les anciens*, published a year after Fontenelle's *Digression*, he concedes that there may be some eternal standards based on 'une raison ferme et solide qui subsistera toûjours,' but, he says, 'il en est peu qui portent le caractere de cette raison incorruptible. It is doubtful whether he really believes in any such standards: his list of the areas in which they do not apply includes morality, government, social custom, poetry, art, religion, and law. He stresses that human values are impermanent – 'Elles ont leur age et leur durée.' Yet, he claims, 'rien ne nous contente aujourd'hui que la solidité de la raison' (*Œuvres* III 357–9). Saint-Evremond thus opposes one standard of reason to another: *raison* is the word or concept by which validity and truth are measured. But reason takes two forms, that of an ideal and immutable standard and that of a changing human standard. Like Fontenelle, he attaches considerably more importance to the latter.

Owing to their conception of reason as a mutable norm, Fontenelle and Saint-Evremond enter the discussion of the ancients and moderns from a fundamentally different perspective from that of La Bruyère. Like Pascal, Fontenelle criticizes the followers of the ancients for treating their opinions as truth and for failing to see that human reason acquires new knowledge and better tools for reasoning (*De l'origine des fables* 31–2; cf *Digression* 176). Unlike Pascal, he does not exclude good judgment and taste from this evolution of reason: 'Que les admirateurs des anciens y prennent un peu garde ;

quand ils nous disent que ces gens-là sont les sources du bon goût et de la raison, et les lumières destinées à éclairer tous les autres hommes... en vérité ils nous les font d'une autre espèce que nous, et la physique n'est pas d'accord avec toutes ces belles phrases. La nature a entre les mains une certaine pâte qui est toujours le même' (*Digression* 161–2). La Bruyère would not have disagreed that all men everywhere have reason. But he would have contested the view that the taste and judgment of modern man could be different from that of the ancients and still be reasonable. For Fontenelle reason is a part of nature and capable of growth: there is no inconsistency in calling good judgment *raison* while speaking of *raison* as mutable and changing. To be reasonable does not mean recognizing or knowing a universal judgment but abiding by that which is demonstrated and proven.

The position of Fontenelle and Saint-Evremond is quite explicit. They state clearly that human ideals have no existence outside man and that man's ideas of justice, wisdom, and reason are subject to historical change. Fontenelle says: 'Les hommes commencent à avoir des idées de la sagesse et de la justice ; les dieux y gagnent ; ils commencent à être sages et justes, et le sont toujours de plus en plus à proportion que ces idées se perfectionnent parmi les hommes' (*De l'origine* 19–20); and Saint-Evremond: 'La justice n'est qu'une vertu établie pour maintenir la société humaine ; c'est l'ouvrage des Hommes' and 'Je scay que la raison nous a esté donnée pour regler nos mœurs, mais la raison, autrefois rude et austere, s'est civilisée avec le temps, et ne conserve aujourd'huy presque rien de son ancienne rigidité' (*Œuvres* III 310 and 13–14). *Raison* is the norm which dictates our values and informs us of what we should admire. Yet it is human faculty and as it develops norms of reason change.

Thuau claims that scientific thought at the end of the seventeenth century incorporates political tendencies which had conflicted with religion. A blending of considerations derived from necessity with *raison-raisonnement* is apparent in many passages of Saint-Evremond. While reason in some sense represents an ideal, it is nevertheless adaptable to time, place, and need: 'Je n'entends pas cet honeur formaliste et fassonier, qui nous est à charge par des regles et par des mines ridicules... Je parle d'une droite raison qui s'accorde avec les imperfections de nôtre nature, qui les redresse du mieux qu'elle peut' (ibid II 168). The use of 'la droite raison' in this passage is surprising and unusual. Right reason is not, as in Méré, Molière, and La Bruyère, something fixed and unchanging. On the contrary, Saint-Evremond says that reason is 'droite' because it takes account of human imperfection. He thus adopts the language of authors concerned with immutable truth but distorts that language, giving it quite a different sense. Potts has remarked that Saint-Evremond's *libertinage* had 'its roots in the very tradition to which it was opposed.'[35] The same might be said of his language and indeed the linguistic similarity with the first norm of reason is an important feature of *raison-raisonnement*. The conflict between religious and political thought in the seventeenth century perhaps could only be resolved by a standard which appeared to incorporate both tendencies. While the similarity of *raison-raisonnement* with the first norm may be largely deceptive, it is not entirely so. Reason, for Saint-Evremond and Fontenelle, is linked with custom and circumstance but it is also superior to them.

For both, *raison* on occasion refers to the norms, whatever they may be, by which a given people regulate their behaviour. Thus, to some extent, *raison* itself becomes an expression of custom. In other countries, Saint-Evremond says, people seem to have a different conception of reason: 'Les hommes y paroissent tout autres par la différence des visages, et plus encore si j'ose dire, par une diversité de raison ; une morale, une sagesse singuliere à la Region, y semble regler et conduire d'autres esprits dans un autre monde' (ibid 87–8), and again, 'Les hommes y sont aussi tout-autres ; leur sagesse et leur raison mesme, singuliére à la région, nous y font voir tant de diversité, qu'on pense estre dans un autre monde' (ibid 79). *Raison* in these statements refers to the directing principles or norms of a culture whatever form they may take. Fontenelle makes a similar observation, only he speaks of 'principes de raisonnements': 'Voyez combien la face de la nature est changée d'ici à la Chine ; d'autres figures, d'autres mœurs, et presque d'autres principes de raisonnement' (*Entretiens sur la pluralité des mondes* 89). Although the principles by which a people regulates its behaviour change from place to place, they are still called, if a little hesitantly, 'raison' or 'principes de raisonnements' and not 'coutumes.'

While they thus relate reason to custom, Saint-Evremond and Fontenelle nevertheless view norms of reason as evolving in a direction of increasing separation from necessity. Consequently, like *raison-vérité*, the third norm of reason attains a degree of superiority over and independence from fashion and whim. Saint-Evremond considers that gradually standards become more civilized and that the norms of his time are in some sense better and more reasonable than those of the past. Speaking of ancient Rome, he comments:

Il faut avoüer... que des mœurs si rudes et si grossieres convenoient à la Republique qui se formoit : cette aspreté de naturel qui ne se rendoit jamais aux difficultez, éstablissoit Rome plus fortement que n'auroient fait des humeurs douces avec plus de lumiere et de raison.

Neantmoins à dire vray, cette qualité considerée en elle-mesme, estoit bien sauvage, et ne merite de respect que pour avoir donné commencement a la plus grande puissance de l'Univers.   (*Œuvres* II 234)

The words 'cette qualité considerée en elle-mesme' suggest that it is weighed independently from the necessities of the time. Ultimately then, norms of reason are not all alike and some are more reasonable than others. Fontenelle suggests that they become more civilized. He does not say that reason changes but that 'la raison se perfectionnera.' And when he speaks of men as possessing or lacking reason, he usually refers to their level of civilization: 'Quand on va vers de certaines terres nouvellement découvertes, à peine sont-ce des hommes... ce sont des animaux à figures humaines, encore quelquefois assez imparfaites, mais presque sans aucune raison humaine' (*Entretiens* 89). Fontenelle says that the American Indian may be capable of developing his reason but for the time being he is uncivilized, lacks understanding of what it is to be reasonable, and, as if this meant the same thing, has very little reason.

Thus norms of reason are superior to custom despite their mutability and Fontenelle and Saint-Evremond also give human reason a high normative status. As in Pascal's contrast of *raison* and *instinct*, Saint-Evremond and Fontenelle imply that reason is superior beause, of all human attributes, it alone has the capacity to develop. When Fontenelle says 'La coûtume a sur les hommes une force qui n'a nullement besoin d'estre appuyée par la raison' (*Histoire des oracles* 70), he does not mean to suggest that reason is something static and unchanging or external to man's imperfect world but simply that, whereas custom is irrational and has no foundation in evidence, reason rests on sound argument and proof and is capable of developing on those terms. He speaks from the same position as Bayle who, in the face of superstition, says: 'Nous cherchons si les Comètes sont un signe envoyé de Dieu, ou non. Rien ne nous en assure ; c'est à nous à examiner par la voye du raisonnement ce qu'il en faut penser' (*Pensées diverses sur la comète* II 221). These statements once again sound remarkably like comments of La Bruyère and Descartes. In the following passage Saint-Evremond speaks of human reason as if it had some constant perspective from which to assess things:

Ainsi à la honte de nos jugements, celuy [Corneille], qui a surpassé tous nos Autheurs, et qui s'est peut-estre icy surpassé luy-mesme à rendre à ces grands noms tout ce qui leur estoit deu, n'a pû nous obliger à luy rendre tout ce que nous luy devions, asservis par la coûtume aux choses que nous voyons en usage, et peu disposez par la raison à estimer des qualitez et des sentiments qui ne s'accomodent pas aux nostres.   (*Œuvres* II 90–1)

This remark is so much like passages from Méré, Descartes, and La Bruyère that without a careful investigation of what Saint-Evremond means by *raison*, one might conclude he was in complete agreement with the authors who use raison in the sense of *raison-vérité*. But by 'par la raison' he probably intends no connection between *raison* and higher truth.

The contrast between the views of the first and third norms can be illustrated by comparing a remark from Saint-Evremond with one from Bossuet. Saint-Evremond says: 'Mais quand on en vient à ces termes, ce n'est plus la Raison qui nous conduit, c'est la Passion qui nous entraine ; ce n'est plus le discours qui agit en nous, c'est la vanité' (ibid 137). *Raison* is opposed to *passion*; it is held up as a higher principle. But it is not in contact with a truth external to man, it is 'le discours qui agit en nous.' Boussuet says something which sounds similar, but in his statement *raison* is both human reason and a higher eternal truth which may in fact be contrary to the thought of the individual. Thus he says: 'Et comme nous voulons toujours plier la raison à nos désirs, nous appelons raison ce qui est conforme à notre humeur naturelle, c'est-à-dire à une passion secrète' (*De la connoissance* 70). The following passage from Bayle reads like an answer to Bossuet made from the perspective of the standard *raison-raisonnement*: 'Nous éprouvons tous les jours dans des choses purement spéculatives, que les mêmes raisons paroissent convaincantes à quelques personnes et fort probables à quelques autres, pendant qu'un troisième n'en fait aucun cas... Il seroit donc ridicule de soûtenir, que toutes les fois que nous preferons une raison à une autre, nous le faisons pour favoriser l'envie d'offenser Dieu... [ou par une] inclination au mal' (*Pensées diverses* II 73–4). Human reason in Bayle, Saint-Evremond, and Fontenelle achieves a high normative status without any support from an external or superior reason, simply because it is a faculty capable of reasoning and of assessing evidence. Although human reason is a part of a mixed and imperfect reality and although men have different conceptions of what it is to be reasonable and have attained various degrees of civilization, the norm of reason makes no dishonourable compromise with imperfect reality. Saint-Evremond and Fontenelle are confident that in time human reason will improve and standards of reason will become more perfect. Without being a universal and hypostatized standard, *raison* will again be a unified norm, one by which the purely human and mutable are united to the ideal.

CONCLUSION

Although the three norms described in this chapter are distinct and reflect important differences in outlook, they have a shared underlying theme: each refers to some form of order. *Raison-vérité* represents an order which is universal and known to the individual through an entirely personal insight. *Raison-nécessité*, in its most positive form, refers to an order created out of practical needs and circumstance. *Raison-raisonnement* derives its criteria from the methodical order of thought and argument and of knowledge building on previous knowledge. Thus the several standards of the reasonable found in the seventeenth century all indicate the fundamental association of the word *raison* with order. The differences in the notion of what this order is or should be are reflected at all levels of the concept, and the first and third norms of reason are based on different conceptions of human reason. To a large extent these conceptions of human reason determine the status given to the second norm, *raison-prudence-nécessité*, since they define reason differently in relation to human fallibility and to the ideal.

4

Human reason as
universal reason

I wondered ... what it was that enabled me to make correct judgments about
things ... and I realized that, above my own mind, which was liable to change,
there was the never-changing true eternity of truth.
St Augustine *Confessions* VII xvii 23

The view that reason or good judgment is constant and knows no distinction
of language, nationality, race, or creed is common in the seventeenth century
and is a central feature of the classical conception of reason. Balzac says: 'Il
est certain que la raison est de tout pays' (*Les œuvres* 1 462); Chapelain
agrees: 'La raison... n'est point sujette au changement' (*La pucelle* 266); and
d'Aubignac remarks: 'La raison [est] semblable partout à elle-mesme' (*La
pratique du théâtre* 26). Racine takes the good reception of his plays as evidence that 'la raison' and 'le bon sens' have not changed since the time of
Homer and Euripides (Préface *Iphigénie* 142). In Bouhours's treatise *La
manière de bien penser dans les ouvrages d'esprit*, Philanthe exclaims on the
diversity of human custom and Eudoxe replies that indeed anyone would
think there was no single truth, no unquestionable right and wrong, available
to all reasonable men: 'Comme si la justesse du sens, repartit Eudoxe,
n'estoit pas de toutes les langues, et que ce qui est mauvais de soy-mesme,
deust passer pour bon en aucun païs parmi les personnes raisonnables' (1
54).

In these statements, the word *raison* contains the ambiguity of the norm
raison-vérité: it refers both to higher truth and to human judgment. Consequently, the notion of a universal reason or judgment is fundamentally paradoxical. *Raison* might be expected to mean something like 'common sense,'
that is, 'the general sense, feeling or judgment of mankind, or of a community.'[1] Wright has said: 'Raison ... to the critic like Boileau, far from being a

formidable philosophical expression, merely meant the dictates of common sense.'[2] But universal reason is not the same as conventional wisdom. On the contrary, it is prized precisely because it overrides custom and accepted opinion.[3] Reason is cosmopolitan, shared by Frenchman, Persian, and American Indian, by civilized and savage, and yet, as Philanthe and Eudoxe remark, men live by different customs, often disagree, and are frequently unreasonable.

The assertion that all men possess reason implies that they are all capable of being reasonable and of knowing the same truths. This statement of belief represents a reaction to the increasing scepticism and libertinism of the early seventeenth century. Montaigne was content to observe the diversity of man's ways and he accepted the uncertainty of human opinion. But Descartes, Pascal, and many others seek a firmer ground: there must be a constant universal truth and man must be capable of attaining certainty. Most of the authors – including Descartes, Chapelain, Méré, Boileau, La Bruyère, Malebranche, Fénelon, and even, to some extent, Bossuet – considered in this chapter conclude that the obstacles to reasonableness are, at least initially, external to reason. Reason alone can be trusted. It must not be allowed to succumb to imagination, passion, and self-love, which interfere with its correct functioning, lead to false reasoning, and prevent men from recognizing truth. Because these authors retain a fundamental faith in reason and regard truth as available to all men through reason, they are here called 'universalists.' Pascal, in contrast, offers a different explanation for the diversity of human opinion: he concludes that reason is fallen, that it is not as it should be, and that man must place his trust in other faculties and in religion. For him, the obstacles to reasonableness have infected reason itself. But Pascal's view of reason as corrupt is only meaningful in relation to a conception of a true and reliable reason and since he offers the heart, instinct, and faith as alternatives to reason, his use of *raison*, *cœur*, and *instinct* contributes to an understanding of the universalists' conception.

Despite the different roles they give to *raison*, both Pascal and the universalists are concerned to refute the amorality of the sceptic or *libertin*. The *libertin* does not deny that reason may attain certainty in mathematics but he does deny that reason can know moral truth. His position may be illustrated by a passage from Molière's *Dom Juan*. Dom Juan says: 'Je crois que deux et deux font quatre, Sganarelle, et que quatre et quatre font huit.' In response Sganarelle mocks: 'La belle croyance et les beaux articles de foi que voici ! Votre religion, à ce que je vois, est donc l'arithmétique ? (III i; see *Œuvres* V 140–1n). Dom Juan's remark is not as trite as it may seem: it summarizes the philosophical attitude of sceptics such as Maurice, prince of Orange, who deny that man may know whether God exists and the difference between right and wrong. Pascal and the universalists are concerned to challenge this type of view. They maintain that man has the capacity for a non-ratiocinatory awareness of truth and that the sceptic merely refuses to acknowledge or to use it. Pascal attributes this capacity to the heart, instinct, or *nature*; the universalists attribute it to reason. Pascal says: 'Il n'y a jamais eu de pyrrhonien effectif parfait. La nature soutient la raison impuissante et l'empêche d'extravaguer jusqu'à ce point' (*Pensées* §131). Nicole and Arnauld remark: '[Les] vaines raisons des Pyrrhoniens... ne détruisent pas l'assûrance raisonnable que l'on a des choses certaines, non pas même dans l'esprit de ceux qui les proposent' (*La logique ou l'art de penser* 18–19). These two statements are fundamentally similar: 'natural' or 'reasonable' knowledge is available to all men – even to those who will not admit it. Although Pascal sees this knowledge as inaccessible to reason and in this sense irrational, his conception of the foundations of certainty resembles that of the universalists.

For both Pascal and the universalists, the immediate knowledge which undermines the reasonings of the sceptic is moral as well as mathematical: it is only by including a moral element in man's non-ratiocinatory capacity that the scepticism of the *libertin* can be refuted. Pascal says that through the heart or instinct man knows the first principles of mathematics and geometry (space, time, and number), can attain awareness of the existence of God, and find a moral perspective (*Pensées* §110). Descartes treats knowledge of God and of the mathematical method as the foundations of all other certainty. He considers that the mathematical method must be applied to all disciplines except theology and poetry and that it will lead eventually to a full 'sagesse.' Thus for Descartes both mathematical and moral knowledge lie within the capacities of universal human reason. But it is the moral component in *raison* which distinguishes the reason of the universalists from that of Pascal and of the *libertin*. Consequently, in seeking the distinctive feature of the reason attributed to all men, it is necessary to stress the moral aspect of universal human reason and attempt to understand the way in which a rational faculty may have a moral function.

The reliable reason of the universalists is often referred to as 'la droite raison' and Bush, in his study of 'right reason' in seventeenth-century England, describes this faculty as combining rationality with moral capacities:

The doctrine of right reason predicates certain absolute values of good and evil, reason and unreason ... Right reason is not merely reason in our sense of the word; it is not a dry light, a nonmoral instrument of inquiry. Neither is it simply the religious conscience. It is a kind of rational and philosophic conscience which distinguishes man from the beasts and which links man with man and with God. This faculty was implanted by God in all men, Christian and heathen alike, as a guide to truth and conduct.[4]

The universalists often contrast true reason with false reasonings, and the distinctive quality of this true reason is its moral capacities: true reason is not separated from discursive reasoning so much as from non-moral reason, whether judging or discursive. Reason is a rational and logical faculty and yet its reliability depends on capacities of a non-ratiocinatory kind – on innate knowledge and, it will be argued, on contact with feeling, will, and inclination. In statements to the effect that all men have reason, it is apparent that when *raison* becomes *raisonnable* the definition of *raison* is extended or broadened. *Raison* contains an intuitive, even an instinctive, element resembling the intuitive awareness of Pascal's *coeur*. It represents an immediate sense of rightness having a direct effect on the whole personality. In religious authors it becomes analogous in function to faith. By contrast, when *raison* is separated from the *raisonnable* (as it is in Pascal's and the universalists' notion of corrupt reason), the definition of *raison* is narrowed. Thus corrupt reason, which contributes to diversity and separates man from man and from universal truth, highlights the essential characteristics of the reason attributed to all men.

The idea that reason and good judgment are available to all men may underlie a great many seventeenth-century uses. In the literature and philosophy of the period, *raison* is often used to mean good sense and is contrasted with false reasonings. In some instances, these contrasts form part of an attack on the ability of the rhetorician and sophist to distort truth by clever argument. For example, they are found in Pascal's *Lettres provinciales* (Lettre XVI: *Œuvres* 449) and in Saint-Evremond's *Réponse au plaidoyer de M. Erard* (*Œuvres* IV 340). In authors here called 'universalists,' such contrasts tend to have a particular import: they emphasize the value of a reason which does not depend on learning or cleverness, which may be obscured or hindered by subtle reasoning, and which consequently appears to be the natural heritage of all men. The widespread expression of this view indicates the depth and extent of belief in a more than ratiocinatory reason.

In the *Regulae*, Descartes isolates *raison* from formal structures of reasoning: reason is able to perceive the truth and falsehood of these subtleties if it remains detached and shielded from their influence. 'Les Dialecticiens,' he says, 'pensent gouverner la raison humaine, en lui prescrivant certaines formes de raisonnement,' but truth, he argues, escapes such shackles and shows itself only to him who uses his pure reason: 'C'est pourquoi ici, craignant surtout que notre raison [rationem humanam] ne demeure oisive... Nous rejetons ces formes de raisonnement [formas disserendi] comme contraires à notre but, et nous cherchons plutôt tout ce qui peut aider à retenir l'attention de notre pensée' (96–7). Descartes describes this reliable reason as natural to man, and he says, 'On ne peut rien ajouter à la pure lumière de la raison qui ne l'obscurcisse de quelque manière' (29). He expresses the same idea earlier in the *Discours de la méthode* (13) and, in the *Principes*, he remarks that the logic of the schools tends to corrupt 'le bon sens' rather than to improve it (13).

Descartes's view that *raison* or *bon sens* gives man a natural discernment independent of acquired knowledge and of the capacity for clever argument is echoed in many writers.[5] Balzac, in an essay entitled *Qu'il y a des gens naturellement sçavans*, exclaims: 'La Raison peut faire toute seule de grandes choses, sans l'assistance de l'Art et de la Science' (*Les entretiens* XVI 269). Méré similarly questions the value of learning and erudition: 'Je prens garde, que ce qu'on entend par la profonde science, et la grande erudition, produit un grand nombre de sots, et fort peu de gens raisonnables' (*Œuvres* II 92–3). Elsewhere he writes: 'L'étude peut nuire [au bon sens] du moins il ne faut pas prétendre qu'elle fasse infailliblement des chefs-d'œuvre' (ibid I 67). Boileau complains of 'raisons subtiles,' which destroy man's sense of values (*Epistre XII* 219–22), and, in *L'art poétique*, he contrasts *raisonnements* with *raison*, observing:

On a beau refuter ses vains raisonnemens :
Son esprit se complaist dans ses faux jugemens   (IV 65–6)

and

Il est certains Esprits, dont les sombres pensées
Sont d'un nuage épais toûjours embarrassées.
Le jour de la raison ne le sçauroit percer.   (I 147–9)

Perhaps Boileau's thought is similar to that of Bouhour's Ariste who, speaking of the disputes of philosophers, remarks: 'Aprés tout, ces Philosophes que vous croyez les plus raisonnables, ne sont pas mieux fondez en raison que les autres' (*Les entretiens d'Ariste et d'Eugène* IV 125). The message is clear: truth and reason are not the privileged possessions of the erudite. In Molière's plays many passages are found to this effect. Chrysale says:

Mes gens à la science aspirent pour vous plaire,
Et tous ne font rien moins que ce qu'ils ont à faire ;
Raisonner est l'emploi de toute ma maison,
Et le raisonnement en bannit la raison. *(Les femmes savantes* II vii 595–8)

And Sganarelle opposes his natural good sense to his master's wit and logic: 'Ma foi ! j'ai à dire... je ne sais que dire, car vous tournez les choses d'une manière, qu'il semble que vous avez raison ; et cependant il est vrai que vous ne l'avez pas. J'avois les plus belles pensées du monde, et vos discours m'ont brouillé tout cela. Laissez faire ; une autre fois je mettrai mes raisonnements par écrit, pour disputer avec vous' (*Dom Juan* I ii). Further on, Sganarelle, unable to express his feeling or perception of truth by logical reasoning, substitutes arbitrary word association for logical relationship and Dom Juan mocks: 'O beau raisonnement' (v ii). The capacity to reason well is acquired and of little worth compared to natural good sense.

Time and again, this natural good sense is identified with *raison*, and, although Boileau and Molière do not explicitly speak of the universality of reason, it would seem likely that, together with other authors who use the norm *raison-vérité*, they share the universalist conception of this faculty, its nature, and its functions. Bossuet warns: 'Il y a des erreurs où nous tombons en raisonnant, car l'homme s'embrouille souvent à force de raisonner' (*Discours sur l'histoire universelle* 515; cf 654). Malebranche remarks: 'Lorsque ce n'est point la raison qui régle les études, non seulement les études ne perfectionnent point la raison, mais même... elles l'obscurcissent, la corrompent et la pervertissent entièrement' (*Recherche* I 293). And Fénelon says of philosophers: 'A force de raisonner subtilement, plusieurs d'entre eux ont perdu même une vérité qu'on trouve naturellement en soi' (*Traité de l'existence de Dieu* 98).

Since reason or natural good judgment is contrasted with subtle reasoning, universal human reason might be expected to correspond to the judging aspect of reason as identified by seventeenth-century dictionaries. However such a description of universal reason would be too simplistic. The dictionaries show that both discursive and judging reason can be called 'droite raison.'[6] Also, in the above passages, discursive reason is presented as false not so much because it is discursive as because it rests on erroneous motivations and assumptions. It is false because it is not in accord with *raison-vérité*. Clearly, judgment may be false on the same grounds: it too may contravene the precepts of reason, truth, and nature.

More satisfactory than the distinction between judging and discursive reason for the characterization of universal human reason is the model of two realities. Since the notion of two realities is implicit in the natural law tradition as well as in Christianity, this model may apply, in a modified form, even to non-religious authors. The notion of two realities impinges directly on the conception of the human mind, giving rise to a vision of the mind as capable of submission to two distinct principles, one universal and transcending the individual, the other binding him within his own limitations.

The second principle, the temporal, is sometimes identified with the body, while the mind is connected with a higher reality. This type of opposition is seen in Malebranche's words: 'Il est plus de la nature de l'ame d'être unie à Dieu par la connoissance de la verité, et par l'amour du bien, que d'être unie à un corps... Dieu a fait les esprits pour le connoître et pour l'aimer, plûtost que pour *informer* des corps' (*Recherche* I 11). The two principles are also described at times as operating within the mind itself in the form of mental attitudes or different types of thought. Pascal says that man must choose between love of the universal and love of self (*Pensées* §423), and Nicole emphasizes that evil thoughts belong to man alone: 'Lors donc que nous nous entretenons de choses mauvaises dans notre cœur, c'est notre pensée : mais lorsque c'est des choses bonnes, c'est Dieu qui nous parle' (*Essais de morale* I 508).

The tension between the two orientations of the mind is sometimes presented in the form of an internal dialogue. Fénelon says that without God 'nous nous trompons, nous bégayons, nous ne nous entendons pas nous-mêmes,' and he goes on: 'Nous trouvons comme deux principes au dedans de nous : l'un donne, l'autre reçoit ; l'un manque, l'autre supplée ; l'un se trompe, l'autre corrige ; l'un va de travers par sa pente, l'autre le redresse' (*Traité* 62–3). Both voices in this dialogue can be attributed to reason and Fénelon does actually describe them in this way: 'Voilà donc deux raisons que je trouve en moi : l'une est moi-même ; l'autre est au-dessus de moi. Celle qui est moi est très-imparfaite, fautive, incertaine, prévenue, précipitée, sujette à s'égarer, changeante... L'autre est commune à tous les hommes, et supérieure à eux ; elle est parfaite, éternelle, immuable, toujours prête à se communiquer' (ibid 65–6). In this passage, unreliable reason appears discursive because it is described as in motion and contrasted with a constant reason. Yet Fénelon almost certainly does not intend a distinction between discourse and judgment. Elsewhere, he says that human judgment (and not just reasoning) is false unless it yields to eternal truth (ibid 42). Reason as a whole, judging and discursive, can submit to either of two orientations and the movement ascribed to unreliable reason is due to its affiliation with an inconstant and changing world rather than to a discursive function.

The implication that reason has, as it were, a choice between two orientations is seen in many of the universalists' uses. Balzac says: 'N'est-ce pas convertir les remedes en poisons que d'user de la Raison pour pecher ? (*Le prince* 290). Chapelain remarks (in a letter to Balzac, 6 October 1640): 'Nostre raison ne peut estre soumise qu'à la raison.' And he goes on: 'Des maximes que posent les philosophans, je n'admets que celles qui s'ajustent à ma conception, et qui sont universellement receues par les personnes de bon sens' (*Lettres* I 697–8). Bossuet contrasts true reason with one which is swayed by the senses: 'La raison qui suit les sens n'est pas une véritable raison, mais une raison corrompue, qui au fond n'est non plus raison qu'un homme mort est un homme' (*De la connoissance de Dieu* 77).

Often the word *raison* is used to indicate a true orientation of the mind rather than a specific function. In such uses it may be contrasted with both discourse and judgment in so far as these comply with the world of movement and change. Thus the use of *raison* is highly complex: *raison* may refer to a formal faculty, to a variety of functions associated with this faculty, or to a true orientation and a true knowledge. This complexity can be illustrated by some passages from Nicole.

Nicole says that everyone agrees that reason is given to man to be his guide and that it reflects, if only feebly, higher truth and justice. Hence man could in some measure be guided by truth and justice: 'Il n'y a personne qui ne demeure d'accord que la raison nous est donnée pour nous servir de guide dans la vie, pour nous faire discerner les biens et les maux, et pour nous regler dans nos desirs et dans nos actions. Mais combien y a-t-il peu qui l'emploient à cet usage, et qui vivent, je ne dis pas selon la vérité et la justice, mais selon leur propre raison, toute aveugle et toute corrompue qu'elle est ?' (*Essais de morale* I 22). *Raison* as Nicole here presents it has two main characteristics. First, by virtue of reason, man should be able in some degree to distinguish the true from the false and to judge accordingly, and secondly, through reason, he should be able to give effect to this knowledge and to regulate his desires and behaviour. Reason is an organ of perception and it also has a regulating function.

But, Nicole says, men use their reason badly. In the following passage *raison* is described as unreliable and as inventing maxims to support man's wayward inclinations: 'Il est... necessaire que les hommes voulant s'estimer eux-mêmes, se rangent sous la conduite de leur raison pour éviter ses reproches ; mais parce qu'ils veulent aussi contenter leurs passions, ils font en sorte que leur raison se rendant flexible à leurs inclinations, se forme des maximes de conduite qui y sont conformes, et selon lesquelles elle peut approuver leurs actions' (ibid I 112). Here *raison* still judges but it judges falsely, in accord with shifting and unreliable impulses.

Nicole usually reserves the word *raison* for a reason which is in touch with truth. Consequently, wishing to describe a judgment and reasoning which are false, he sometimes separates these functions from *raison* and ascribes them to passion and self-love:

Lorsqu'on est emporté de part et d'autre en des paroles de chaleur et de passion, chacun s'occupe ensuite à se justifier soi-même, à chercher des raisons pour montrer qu'il a eu raison de parler comme il a fait... c'est que les ressorts qui font agir notre esprit, et qui l'appliquent aux objets, sont l'orgueil et l'amour-propre, et non pas la raison, le vérité et nos intérêts réels... Qui ne considereroit les choses... que par la raison... [ne feroit pas ainsi]. (ibid II 145)

In this passage *raison* is closely linked with the truth, so much so that in the words 'et non pas la raison, la vérité et nos intérêts réels' it appears to refer to the true in man or to his knowledge of truth.

An identification of reason with truth is seen even more clearly in a passage where Nicole distinguishes reason from fantasy:

Il faut tâcher de connoître en soi ce qui est fantaisie et ce qui est raison... J'appelle raison une connoissance véritable des choses telles qu'elles sont, qui fait que nous en jugeons sainement... J'appelle fantaisie, une impression fausse que nous nous formons des choses, en les concevant autres qu'elles ne sont... ce qui nous engage en plusieurs jugemens faux, et produit des passions déraisonnables. (ibid II 29–30)

Raison here means a true knowledge or perception on which thought or behaviour may be based. Reason is not just a formal faculty. It possesses an ingredient of truth and only those operations of the mind that are true and reliable are referred to it. Nicole would seem to conceive of reliable reason as having a natural capacity for truth, perhaps even some form of innate knowledge. Indeed it may be that belief in innate knowledge is essential to the universalists' conception of reason and this notion may underlie many of those uses where *raison* means good sense and where it is described as man's source of truth.

While the model of two realities does not imply a distinction between judging and discursive reason, it does assume a certain receptivity in reason which determines the value of discourse and judgment. Thus *raison* would seem to include something like the *intellectus* associated by Aquinas with rest and possession of truth. Aquinas says: 'Intellect [*intelligere*] is the simple grasp of an intelligible truth, whereas reasoning [*ratiocinari*] is the progression towards an intelligible truth by going from one understood [*intellecto*] point to another. The difference between them is thus like the difference between rest and motion or between possession and acquisition.'[7] Descartes similarly describes an aspect of reason, sometimes called 'lumière naturelle' and sometimes 'intuition,' as having an immediate grasp of truth. Like Aquinas, he says that intuition is different from deduction since in the latter 'on conçoit... un mouvement ou une sorte de succession' (*Regulae* 23). Both intuition and deduction are a part of true reason provided deduction takes intuition as its premise. If it does so, a second reliable intuition may be attained, and Descartes concludes: 'Presque tout le travail de la raison humaine consiste à préparer cette opération ; car, quand elle est claire et simple, il n'est besoin d'aucun secours de la méthode, mais des seules lumières de la nature, pour avoir l'intuition de la vérité qu'elle découvre' (ibid 159). This *intuition* or *lumière naturelle* is closely associated by Descartes with innate knowledge which often appears to consist not so much in actual ideas as in a capacity for direct or intuitive vision.

Gilson has remarked that the doctrine of innate ideas was common in the seventeenth century even in the early years and that Descartes could not have escaped its influence: 'Descartes ne pouvait pas ne pas rencontrer à chaque instant la doctrine des idées innées, tant elle germait en abondance autour de lui, dans le milieu philosophique et théologique où nous le rencontrons aux environs de l'année 1628.'[8] Descartes, Malebranche, and Fénelon all describe a Socratic conception of learning which has innate ideas as its basis. Descartes says that the ideas which others impart 'ne sont point si approchantes de la verité, que les simples raisonnemens que peut faire naturellement un homme de bon sens' (*Discours* 13–14). Malebranche explains: 'Les hommes ne peuvent pas nous instruire en nous donnant les idées des choses, mais seulement en nous faisant penser à celles que nous avons naturellement' (*Recherche* I 147). And Fénelon says: 'Les hommes peuvent nous parler pour nous instruire ; mais nous ne pouvons les croire qu'autant que nous trouvons une certaine conformité entre ce qu'ils nous disent et ce que nous dit le maître intérieur. Après qu'ils ont épuisé tous leurs raisonnements, il faut toujours revenir à lui, et l'écouter, pour la décision' (*Traité* 64).

The doctrine of innate knowledge is often advanced by philosophers as proof of the existence of God[9] and as such it could not be expected to be found in an author such as Méré. Also, as a philosophical theory, it is not usually given direct formulation in drama or poetry. Yet in these literary forms, innate knowledge has its corollary in the form of natural good judgment. Consequently, it may be an essential assumption in the conception of reason as universal.

The theory of innate knowledge is used by the philosophers as a guarantee of the potential reliability of reason. Reason and innate ideas are often described as qualitatively different from the senses, passions, and imagination and are assimilated to a higher reality. As in Nicole's use, *raison* is said to be that which is real or true in man as if it were man's only source of reality and truth. Innate knowledge ensures this link between reason and constant truth. Descartes asserts: 'Tout ce qui est en nous de reel et de vray, vient d'un estre parfait et infini.' For him, this real and true aspect of the self consists in reason and in the true ideas contained in reason. Thus he concludes:

Soit que nous veillions, soit que nous dormions, nous ne nous devons jamais laisser persuader qu'a l'evidence de nostre raison... la raison ne nous dicte point que ce que nous voyons ou imaginons... soit veritable. Mais elle nous dicte bien que toutes nos idées ou notions doivent avoir quelque fondement de verité ; car il ne seroit pas possible que Dieu, qui est tout parfait et tout veritable les eust mises en nous sans cela. (*Discours* 39 40)

Nicole and Arnauld hold the same view and criticize Hobbes for considering that man's ideas may derive from the senses and the temporal world (*La logique* 43–4). By means of innate knowledge, reason is linked with a more solid reality.

Although Bossuet considers man's reason largely corrupt, he too thinks that if any part of man could or should have direct contact with higher truth, that part is reason. According to him reason originally possessed true knowledge and in order to know God 'les hommes n'avoient à consulter que leur raison et leur mémoire.' But reason became weak and, with time, 'les hommes brouilloient les idées qu'ils avoient reçues de leurs ancêtres' (*Discours* 383). Malebranche is more optimistic about the continuity of contact between human reason and universal truth. He goes beyond the notion of innate ideas to the possibility of actual and continued contact with God through reason. Reason, he says, is 'la principale partie de nous mêmes' (*Recherche* I 492). He draws a direct parallel between man's submission to eternal reason and his attention and submission to his own reason and refers his readers to 'les véritables idées des choses, que la Verité éternelle nous représente dans le plus secret de nôtre raison' (ibid I 24). Fénelon speaks similarly. 'En un sens' he says, 'mes idées sont moi-même, car elles sont ma raison,' but he goes on: 'Ce qui paraît le plus à nous, et être le fond de nous-mêmes, je veux dire notre raison, est ce qui nous est le moins propre et qu'on doit croire le plus emprunté' (*Traité* 61, 142).

Innate knowledge or contact with eternal reason ensures the reliability and the correct orientation of reason. It also broadens the definition of *raison*. The meaning of the word *idées* in the above passages is not very precise. As Kenny has remarked, it is difficult to see what is meant by ideas if these constitute a faculty of the mind.[10] Among philosophers who adhere to the doctrine of innate knowledge, innate ideas are not always treated as pertaining to reason. Gilson has shown that Berulle, Gibieuf, Silhon, and Mersenne use the words *âme*, *cœur*, and *lumière naturelle* to refer to the place in man where these ideas, or the capacity to form them, are harboured.[11] The meaning of *raison* may at times be so vague as to be the equivalent of *cœur* or *âme*. Where St Augustine says that God inspires man and turns him toward his principle, Malebranche translates him as saying that God communicates with man through his reason: 'Nullo modo cessat occulta inspiratione vocationis loqui ei creaturæ cui principium est, ut convertatur ad id ex quo est' (*De Gen, ad litt*, ch 50); 'Cette sagesse demeurant toûjours la même, ne cesse jamais de parler à ses créatures dans le plus secret de leur raison' (*Recherche* I 17). *Raison*, in this passage, refers to man's soul or inner self and, if it can in this way be substituted for *âme* or *cœur*, it must have a very broad sense.

Raison may consist in a form of consciousness which penetrates feeling as well as thought. This is suggested by similarities between the *raison* of the universalists and Pascal's cœur. For Pascal *cœur* is clearly a feeling faculty: yet, as Laporte has shown, when it is given a positive value, *cœur* often appears to contain ideas.[12] Cruickshank describes it as the focal point of the personality which 'holds together thought, feeling and will in such a combination that they can provide a knowledge which is direct, concrete and, to that extent, intuitive.'[13] Keefe has remarked that Descartes's reason is intuitive even in the modern sense of that word[14] and Brody points to a close similarity between the *raison* of Boileau and intuition. He also suggests that whenever Boileau urges 'Sentez ce que tous les hommes sentent d'abord,' he may be referring to this *raison-intuition*.[15] This contention cannot easily be substantiated. Boileau does not usually mention *raison* in connection with the 'universal feeling'[16] and even where he does – as in the words 'les Chrestiens doivent estre persuadez d'une verité si claire... qu'un Payen même a sentie par les seules lumières de la raison' (*Traité du sublime* 46) – he may not be referring to feeling so much as to insight, judgment, or opinion. Yet Brody shares the view of the eighteenth-century critic Vauvenargues, who says: 'La raison n'était pas distincte, dans Boileau, du sentiment : c'était son instinct' (*Réflexions critiques sur quelques poètes* 248). And, without relying on the use of the words *sentir* or *sentiment*, which are often vague, there is some evidence to suggest that the reason of the universalists is related to feeling.

Raison is often employed to refer to a non-reflective sense of what is right and fitting. In *Le prince* Balzac praises Louis XIII, saying: 'Il trouve souvent la verité sans prendre la peine de la chercher, et le plus subit mouvement de sa pensée est d'ordinaire si raisonnable et si concluant, que le discours qui vient apres, ne fait qu'approuver ce premier acte, et sans y rien adjouster de nouveau' (252). The perception of what is right and reasonable is here attributed to an immediate insight supported perhaps by reflective thought but having its origin in an awareness which, as it were, controls the strings of the personality. While Balzac does not mention reason directly in this passage, *raison* often refers to a spontaneous insight having instant effect. In some instances it is presented as directing or converting feelings. When Corneille's Sabine chokes the joy she feels at her brother's success, she says:

Soudain, pour l'étouffer [la joie] rappelant ma raison,
J'ai pleuré quand la gloire entroit dans leur maison.   (*Horace* I i 77–8)

A similar power is attributed to reason by Molière's character Done Elvire:

Vous n'avez que les maux que vous voulez avoir,
Et toujours notre cœur est en notre pouvoir :
Il peut bien quelquefois montrer quelque foiblesse ;
Mais enfin sur nos sens la raison, la maîtresse.
                              (*Dom Garcie de Navarre* III ii 961–5)

The view that reason can resist and overcome the influence of custom also suggests that it exerts or calls forth a form of energy.[17] Malebranche speaks of 'la force de la raison': 'Il n'y a que ceux qui font usage de leur esprit, qui puissent par la force de leur raison se mettre au-dessus des méchantes coutûmes' (*Recherche* I 284). Reason gives everything its rightful place or value and it holds the balance between extremes. Nicole and Arnauld say: 'La vraie raison place toutes choses dans le rang qui leur convient' (*La logique* 18). And Molière's Philinte remarks: 'La parfaite raison fuit toute extrémité' (*Le misanthrope* I ii 151). In a passage quoted above (51) La Rochefoucauld explains that if men used their reason there would be 'de la proportion dans leurs vues et dans leurs sentiments' (*Œuvres* I 313–14).

The sense of proportion and balance available to reason thus affects feeling as well as thought and it can be retained within strong emotion. La Rochefoucauld's remark is reminiscent of Richelieu's words 'Mes colères ne sont fondées qu'en raison'[18] and of La Fontaine's surprise that to be a prophet it might be necessary to lose the power of reason:

> Ne peut-on être prophète,
> Si l'on ne perd la raison ?
>
> (*Daphné* IV ii 647–8)

Certainly, reason is considered by the universalists to be suited to all aspects of life and not just to abstract thought. The ubiquity of reason among men is paralleled by the possible universality of its application. Descartes says: 'La raison est un instrument universel, qui peut servir en toutes sortes de rencontres' (*Méditations* 57). Nicole and Arnauld agree: 'Toutes les autres qualités d'esprit ont des usages bornés ; mais l'exactitude de la raison est generalement utile dans toutes les parties et dans tous les emplois de la vie' (*La logique* 15). Malebranche remarks: 'On se peut donc servir de sa raison en toutes choses' (*Recherche* I 491). La Bruyère says: 'Je ne haïrois pas d'être livré par la confiance à une personne raisonnable, et d'en être gouverné en toutes choses, et absolument, et toujours... je jouirois de la tranquillité de celui qui est gouverné par la raison' (*Du cœur* §71).

This passage is particularly interesting: 'une personne raisonnable' is identified with 'celui qui est gouverné par la raison.' If a man is governed by reason he becomes a reasonable person and his life and attitudes are affected accordingly. The moral and directive effect of *raison* would seem to depend on this absorption of the *raisonnable* into *raison* which is accompanied by a *rapprochement* between reason and feeling, desire, or will. If human reason submits to true reason, to that awareness of the right, proportioned and fitting (ensured, for the philosophers, by innate knowledge), it becomes itself reasonable and is the source of reasonableness in the whole personality.

It is this capacity to render reason reasonable which is attributed to all men. All men of course have a faculty called reason but this endows them with different degrees of intelligence and cleverness. What they all possess in equal share is the capacity to become reasonable by using the light of reason in such a way that it affects both thought and feeling and has an immediate impact on behaviour, rendering them moral in some objective sense. Clearly, the attainment of universal reason is then only a potential – innate and inalienable perhaps – but nevertheless no more than a potential. Bossuet complains: 'Comment prouverons-nous un tel paradoxe, que l'ordre le plus excellent se doive trouver dans une confusion si visible ? ' (*Premier sermon sur la providence* 158). His sentiment is shared in some degree by most of the universalists and the view that all men have reason in fact refers to a latent capacity, not an actual manifestation.

Statements on the universality of reason invoke a particular form of reason, one which is distinct from intelligence and which contains moral and non-ratiocinatory elements which render it potentially reasonable. At the beginning of the *Discours de la méthode*, Descartes asserts that all men are equally endowed with *raison* or *bon sens* and he uses the two terms interchangeably: 'La puissance de bien juger, et distinguer le vrai d'avec le faux, qui est proprement ce qu'on nomme le bon sens ou la raison, est naturellement esgale en tous les hommes ; et ainsi... la diversité de nos opinions ne vient pas de ce que les uns sont plus raisonnables que les autres, mais seulement de ce que nous conduisons nos pensées par diverses voies, et ne considerons pas les mesmes choses.' He goes on: 'Car pour la raison, ou le sens, d'autant qu'elle est la seule chose qui nous rend hommes, et nous distingue des bestes, je veux croyre qu'elle est toute entiere en un chacun' (2). In this passage, Descartes describes *raison-bon sens* as a common denominator which distinguishes man from animal and consequently pertains to all men. He clearly does not mean that all men are equally intelligent or equally capable of abstract thought. Elsewhere he distinguishes men by the degree to which they possess what he calls 'esprit' (*Principes* 12, 22). And in the *Discours*, he explains: '[Je veux] suivre en cecy l'opinion commune des Philosophes, qui disent qu'il n'y a du plus et du moins qu'entre les *accidens* et non point entre les *formes*, ou nature, des *individus* d'une mesme espece' (2–3). In some fundamental sense all men have reason; Descartes must then be referring to some basic and essential form of reason.

The reason which he attributes to all men would seem to be the embryonic equivalent of true wisdom, the quality which renders man capable of attaining or of recognizing a full 'sagesse.' Gilson has commented: 'Le bon sens est l'instrument qui, si nous en usons bien, nous permet d'atteindre la *bona mens*, ou Sagesse ; et, inversement, la Sagesse n'est que le bon sens parvenu au point de perfection le plus haut dont il soit susceptible, grâce à la méthode qui n'en est elle-même que l'usage régulier.'[19] The slight hesitation shown in the above passages, as in the words 'je veux croyre,' may be indicative not so much of irony as of Descartes's awareness that the reason of which he speaks is not usually manifest and consequently that its existence is not susceptible to conclusive proof. In a letter to Mersenne, 16 October 1639, Descartes says that men differ in their opinions because reason is frequently ill used and 'il n'y a presque personne qui se serve bien de cete lumiere' (*Oeuvres* II 598). Nevertheless, men are nearly all capable of recognizing truth when it is shown to them: 'Encore que plusieurs ne soient pas capables de trouver d'eux mesmes le droit chemin, il y en a peu toute fois qui ne le puissent assez reconnoistre, lorsqu'il leur est clairement monstré par quelque autre' (lettre à Elizabeth, 18 août 1645, *Œuvres* IV 272). Despite differences in custom, there are 'd'aussy bien sensez, parmi les Perses et les Chinois, que parmi nous' (*Discours* 23), and without education or cultural influence, men are able to reach the same eternal conclusions (*Recherche de la vérité* 506).

While Descartes does not consider that a full moral knowledge is immediately accessible to reason, he attributes considerable moral powers to that faculty. The understanding has an immediate influence on the will: 'Je ne pouvois pas m'empescher de juger qu'une chose que je concevois si clairement estoit vraye, non que je ne m'y trouvasse forcé par aucune cause exterieure, mais seulement, parce que d'une grande clarté qui estoit en mon entendement a suivy une grande inclination en ma volonté' (*Méditations* 47). And it has moral insight enabling men to become virtuous, each according to his capacity: 'Nostre volonté ne se portant a suivre ny a fuir aucune chose, que selon que nostre entendement la luy represente bonne ou mauvaise, il suffit de bien juger, pour bien faire, et de juger le mieux qu'on puisse, pour faire aussy tout son mieux, c'est à dire pour acquerir toutes les vertus' (*Discours* 28). Thus intellectual perception gives rise to order in the personality and this order is spontaneous in the sense that it follows immediately upon perception. Rodis-Lewis has drawn attention to a passage in which Descartes compares man's natural light with a form of instinct[20]: 'Pour moy, je distingue deux sortes d'instincts : l'un est en nous en tant qu'hommes et est purement intellectuel ; c'est la lumiere naturelle ou *intuitus mentis*, auquel seul je tiens qu'on se doit fier, l'autre est en nous en tant qu'animaux, et est une certaine impulsion de la nature a la conservation de nostre cors, a la jouissance des voluptez corporelles etc., lequel ne doit pas toujours estre suivi' (lettre à Mersenne, 16 octobre 1639, *Œuvres* II 599). Descartes is concerned to separate the mind from the body. Yet he does not separate reason or man's natural light from the sources of energy and direction in the personality. The power of reason over the will and the comparison of reason with a form of instinct suggest that reason possesses a directive capacity having an immediate effect on the personality as a whole. Perhaps it is significant that, at the beginning of the *Discours de la méthode*, the universality of reason is deduced from the assumption that man is a reasonable being.

In authors with less philosophical concerns, the link drawn between *raison* and the *raisonnable* shows clearly the moral effectiveness of *raison*. In the preface of *La pucelle*, Chapelain speaks first of an immutable hypostatized reason separate from custom and then of a constant community of judgment among reasonable men of all time. In preparing his work, he says, he was at pains to accommodate 'la pratique des derniers temps aux maximes anciennes, autant que la raison, qui est immuable, et les mœurs des peuples, qui sont changeantes, l'ont ou permis, ou desiré' (*Opuscules* 274). He goes on to say that he wants reasonable, just, and equitable men in all places to judge his poem and seems confident that they will reach the true judgment and be in agreement:

Lorsque je dis toute la terre, lorsque je dis tous les temps, je veux dire ce qu'il y aura de sensé et d'équitable dans tout le monde, ce qu'il y aura de juste et de raisonnable dans toute la suite des âges ; et pour prendre de solides conclusions sur des matières poétiques, je n'exclus pas moins les barbares et les stupides que les malins et les jaloux. Je ne compte pour rien cette populace grossière qui n'a ni raison ni savoir.   (ibid 294)

Being reasonable is here equated with having reason. Chapelain excludes 'cette populace grossière' from the community of reasonable men: he may be giving way to prejudice or he may, like Descartes, consider that most men do not realize their potential. In an unpublished letter to Guez de Balzac, 18 November 1640, he writes: 'Comme il est vray que la droitte raison est le seul juge naturel de toutes choses, il est aussi véritable qu'elle n'est guère connue et qu'il n'y a point d'homme qui se puisse asseurer de l'avoir... Mais en l'homme la raison la mieux constituée s'abuse et tombe en erreur ; elle ne voit rien de bien clair et toute son opération ne consiste à bien parler qu'en soupçons et en conjectures' (see G. Collas *Jean Chapelain* [1912] 61–2).

Méré offers a wealth of comment on the universality of reason. Like Chapelain, he considers that the individual can adhere either to the changing customs of his society or to a true and universal reason and judgment. He attributes the following remark to La Rochefoucauld: 'Nous devons quelque chose aux coûtumes des lieux où nous vivons pour ne pas choquer la reverence publique, quoi que ces coûtumes soient mauvaises. Mais nous ne leur devons que de l'apparence : il faut les en payer, et se bien garder de les approuver dans son cœur de peur de choquer la raison universelle qui les condamne' (*Lettres* I 88). The idea of giving lip-service to present custom and morality is reminiscent of Descartes's 'morale provisoire.' But Méré considers that true morality is immediately available provided man uses a sincere and natural reason:

C'est un grand point, que de pouvoir découvrir ce qui semble le meilleur selon la raison sincere et naturelle, et de s'en servir le plus qu'on peut, quand les Coûtumes le souffrent... Cependant comme les institutions de ceux qui nous ont précedez, nous reglent malgré nous, il faut observer ce qu'on approuve dans les Cours et dans les Païs, où nous avons à passer nôtre vie, et ne pas offenser la reverence publique ; mais pour ne pas être d'un méchant goût, on se doit bien garder d'aimer dans son cœur des choses, que la raison ne permet, que parce que le monde s'y est accoûtumé.   (*Œuvres* III 94)

The words *sincere* and *naturelle* recall uses in Boileau, Molière, and La Rochefoucauld: they suggest that true reason has a distinctive quality and is accompanied by certain right attitudes.

Méré also draws into his conception of universal reason both *bienséance* and *honnêteté*. He says that Alexander the Great cannot be forgiven for his conduct on the grounds that *mores* were different in his day. 'La bienséance' and 'les grâces' are the same in all periods. At all times, some men are acquainted with them and express them in their behaviour while others do not (ibid III 83). In the following passage, he distinguishes a true and a false *honnêteté* and identifies that which is 'juste' and 'raisonnable' with the 'réel' in much the same way as *raison* is described as 'réel' by the philosophers:

Pour démêler la vraie honnêteté de la fausse, on se doit assurer, qu'elle n'a rien que de bien réel ; rien qui ne soit juste et raisonnable en tous les endroits du monde : car elle est universelle, et ses manieres sont de toutes les Cours depuis un bout de la Terre à l'autre, encore ne sont-elles pas plus des Cours que des Deserts. Le changement des lieux, la revolution du temps, ni la difference des coûtumes ne leur ôtent presque rien : C'est du bon or, qui vaut toûjours son prix.   (ibid III 93)

The moral content of *raison* is stressed by this association with *honnêteté* which refers specifically to attitude, manners, and behaviour. Méré's distinction between a true and a false *honnêteté* and his insistence that only a sincere and natural reason may attain truth suggest a distinction between a constant moral reality and the temporal world. Thus, although not concerned with God, he uses language which is shared by the theologian and implies awareness of higher reality.

Another passage from Méré illuminates the connection between the moral content of reason and the absorption into reason of contact with feeling. Linking reason with the reasonable, Méré describes it as a power of the soul common to thought and feeling:

Il ne faut pas confondre l'esprit et la raison, comme si c'estoit une mesme chose, et je trouve qu'on peut bien estre fort raisonnable et n'avoir que fort peu d'esprit. Pour entendre ce que je veux dire, on peut considerer la raison comme une puissance de l'ame commune à l'esprit et au sentiment : de sorte que ce que nous appellons raisonner, n'est autre chose que l'action de l'esprit, ou du sentiment, qui vont d'un objet à un autre, et qui reviennent sur leurs pas. L'esprit fait plus de reflexions que le sentiment, et d'une maniere plus pure et plus distincte. Mais comme j'ay dit qu'on pourroit estre fort raisonnable, et n'avoir qu'un esprit mediocre, il me semble qu'on peut avoir l'esprit au dessus du commun, et n'estre que fort peu raisonnable... Et pour revenir à ceux qui sont fort raisonnables sans avoir beaucoup d'esprit, c'est que si peu qu'ils en ont... ils ont le sentiment de plusieurs choses que n'ont pas ceux qui ont plus d'esprit.   (ibid II 69–70)

In this passage *raison* is distinguished from cleverness and intelligence and refers to an awareness of what is right and true which may originate in thought or in feeling. The relationship drawn between *raison* and *esprit* is similar to that seen in Descartes, and Méré's interpretation of the nature of *raison* may have some general application.

His conception proves helpful in explaining Boileau's notion (discussed briefly in the last chapter) of reason as guide and journey's end. Boileau hopes that his reason will be salvaged by the submission of his whole being to a reason which ensures virtue and order:

Ainsi donc Philosophe à la Raison soûmis,
Mes defauts desormais, sont mes seuls ennemis.
C'est l'erreur que je fuis ; c'est la vertu que j'aime...
Je songe à me pourvoir d'esquif et d'avirons,
A regler mes desirs, à prévenir l'orage,
Et sauver, s'il se peut, ma raison du naufrage.   (*Epistre V* 23–40)

The first *raison* mentioned in this passage contains the *raisonnable*: it has a moral content and induces certain attitudes and aims which Boileau considers laudable and desirable. Thus it resembles the reasonable reason described by Méré. In its second use, *raison* refers to a personal faculty the fate of which is still undetermined. This faculty may be corrected and saved by obedience to true reason. Thus Boileau expects that his thought, feeling, and desire will be affected by submission to reasonable reason which represents both the source and the fulfilment of harmonious order in the personality. There is a clear similarity here with Descartes's *raison-bon sens* which represents the embryonic seed of a true wisdom. There is also a resemblance to Chapelain's view that 'reason must submit only to reason,' to La Bruyère's idea of becoming reasonable by obedience to reason, and to Bossuet's belief that the individual's reason must be corrected by submission to the reason of God and religion.

Like Méré, La Bruyère speaks as if both thought and behaviour were influenced by the reason which he attributes to all men. He says that reason is possessed equally by the barbarian and the civilized and claims that education is no guarantee of reasonableness:

Si les ambassadeurs des princes étrangers étoient des singes instruits à marcher sur leurs pieds de derrière, et à se faire entendre par interprète, nous ne pourrions pas marquer un plus grand étonnement que celui que nous donne la justesse de leurs réponses, et le bon sens qui paroît quelquefois dans leurs discours. La prévention du pays, jointe à l'orgueil de la nation, nous fait oublier que la raison est de tous les climats, et que l'on pense juste partout où il y a des hommes. Nous n'aimerions pas à être traités ainsi de ceux que nous appelons barbares ; et s'il y a en nous quelque barbarie, elle consiste à être épouvantés de voir d'autres peuples raisonner comme nous.

Tous les étrangers ne sont pas barbares, et tous nos compatriotes ne sont pas civilisés : de même toute campagne n'est pas agreste, et toute ville n'est pas polie. (*Des jugements* §22)

In this passage, La Bruyère makes a direct transition from the statement that 'la raison est de tous les climats' to 'l'on pense juste partout où il y a des hommes.' That men have reason means that they may be 'raisonnable' and 'juste' and that they may express these characteristics both in thought and action or manner. It enables them to be polite regardless of the customs of their society and whether or not they have been educated. Yet the possession of reason does not guarantee such reasonableness: only some men, educated or uneducated, realize their potential.

Bossuet attributes reason to all men by implication. Like Descartes, he says that reason is that which distinguishes man from animal and in this sense it necessarily belongs to all human beings. He sees true reason as akin to conscience – 'la raison, en tant qu'elle nous détourne du vrai mal de l'homme, qui est le péché, s'appelle le *conscience* (*De la connoissance* 49) – and he emphasizes that, through the possession of reason, man is likened to God and could be morally upright:

Dieu a fait l'homme droit... et cette droiture consistoit en ce que l'esprit estant parfaitement soumis à Dieu, le corps aussi estoit dans l'ordre et c'est cet ordre que nous appellons la justice et la droiture originelle... Tout le desordre vient de la chair et de l'empire des sens, que toujours prevaloient sur la raison... La creature raisonnable... est libre... en se soumettant volontairement à la raison souveraine de Dieu, dont la sienne est emanée... O homme... tu estois fait pour estre avec Dieu un mesme esprit et participer par ce moyen à son immutabilité. (*Traité de la concupiscence* 19, 21, 45, 91)

Being a reasonable creature means that man is capable of true order and justice. The potentiality of human reason is due to its origin, to the fact that it emanates from God, and it allows man in some measure to participate in the constancy and immutability of God. Where Méré associates *raison* and *honnêteté* with *droiture* and *justesse*, Bossuet connects *raison* above all with *droiture* by which he means the capacity to give inner order and true direction to the personality as a whole. Thus reason becomes 'droite' and 'raisonnable' when it has contact both with higher objective truth and with man's lower nature, his inclinations and emotions.

In Malebranche and Fénelon the notion that all men have reason is related to a confluence between human and eternal reason. Unlike Bossuet, they regard divine inspiration as actual rather than as pertaining to man's original and lost nature. God speaks through reason, informing men everywhere of right and wrong and providing them, should they care to listen, with the capacity for true and identical judgment.

Concerned like Méré with the morality of Alexander the Great, Malebranche explains that God, the light of truth and the voice of nature 'qui ne parle ni Grec, ni Scythe, ni Barbare [mais] un langage trè-clair et très-intelligible,' speaks to every man 'dans le plus secret de sa raison.' No man is therefore excused for ignorance of the true and the good, for 'l'ame reçoit de la Verité éternelle qui préside à son esprit, la connoissance de son devoir et de ses déréglemens' (*Recherche* I 13–15). Human reason is presented as a divine principle within man and its function is primarily moral. Intelligence is not mentioned; it appears almost irrelevant. What concerns Malebranche is to stress that even the most criminal – 'les assassins et les voleurs' – have reason. Together with this moral sense, Malebranche attributes to all men a basic mathematical knowledge. He makes no distinction between these for he says that both are possessed by men everywhere and at all times: 'Nous voyons en Dieu certaines idées et certaines loix immuables, selon lesquelles nous sçavons avec certitude, que Dieu agit également dans tous les esprits. Je sçais que deux fois deux font quatre, qu'il vaut mieux être juste que d'être riche, et je ne me trompe point de croire que les autres connoissent ces véritez aussi bien que moi' (ibid 454). The contact between human and eternal reason provides a foundation which is secure and reliable for both thought and behaviour.

Fénelon also includes both elements, the mathematical and the moral, in reason. Men, he says, are reasonable by virtue of the infinite reason of God:

Les hommes de tous les pays et de tous les temps, quelque education qu'ils aient reçue, se sentent invinciblement assujettis à penser et à parler de même... Tous les hommes sont raisonnables de la même raison, qui se communique a eux selon divers degrés... C'est elle qui fait qu'on juge au Japon comme en France, que deux et deux font quatre. C'est elle qui fait que les hommes, tout dépravés qu'ils sont, n'ont point encore osé donner ouvertement le nom de la vertu au vice.

Man cannot escape awareness of what is right, for, Fénelon says, 'Le maître intérieur, qu'on nomme raison, le reproche intérieurement avec un empire absolu... Les hommes les plus vicieux ne peuvent venir à bout d'effacer en eux l'idée de la vraie vertu' (*Traité* 60–3).

In all the statements on the universality of reason, *raison* endows man with a sense of order, with a capacity for seeing things in their right proportion, for giving them a true value and weight, and for achieving an inner rectitude and harmonious direction. Indeed, in some uses, it informs man of his duty and of the rules and laws of justice. Thus the moral aspect would seem to be the most essential component of universal human reason. Although mathematical knowledge also depends on a sense of order and so is closely linked with the moral, it is the moral element which differentiates the reason of the universalists from that of the *libertin*. Malebranche and Fénelon's statements on the universality of reason read like an answer to Dom Juan who claims to know only the elementary truths of mathematics. Unlike the *libertin*, they assert that men share knowledge of right and wrong, virtue and vice, as well as the first principles of mathematics.

Contact with the feeling side of the personality is implied by moral knowledge and the connection between reason and feeling is extended and magnified by Malebranche and, particularly, Fénelon. *Raison* comes to be analogous in function to faith and its action is so swift and deeply felt that it resembles the directives of instinct. Malebranche links *raison* with desire and inclination: he regards both as deriving from God and as turned towards their origin unless diverted by the temporal (*Recherche* I 45). Thus he ties human will and motivation as well as reason to higher universal reason. Like Bossuet he relates true reason to conscience, referring to 'les reproches de nôtre raison, et les remords de nôtre conscience' (ibid I 57). He also treats faith simply as a short cut to greater knowledge of God. Faith does not contradict reason but can achieve more immediate results and therefore it is advisable, he says, 'd'écouter plutôt nôtre foi que nôtre raison' (ibid II 454).

This attitude to faith is an extension of the view of Descartes, Nicole, and Arnauld. Maritain and Laporte point out that for Descartes faith expands the light of reason and that both reason and faith are treated as forms of 'évidence.' The knowledge of God's existence through reason is a foretaste of the actual vision of God.[21] Nicole and Arnauld say explicitly that faith does not contradict reason; reason itself informs man of God's perfection and the truth of his word. For them, true reason teaches the first articles of faith and, if reason does not yet know God, they hope that it will lead to such knowledge: 'Il est certain que la foi suppose toujours quelque raison... La vraie raison nous apprend que Dieu étant la vérité même, il ne nous peut tromper en ce qu'il nous revele de sa nature ou de ses mysteres' (*La logique* 337).

In Fénelon, the link between reason, feeling, and faith is further strengthened as the vertical bond with the eternal becomes more direct and continuous. Extending the empire of reason within the personality, Fénelon relates reason to instinct and, speaking of the instinct of animals, he concludes. 'Mais ce nom d'instinct n'est qu'un beau nom vide de sens : car que peut-on entendre par un instinct plus précis et plus sûr que la raison même, sinon une raison plus parfaite ? ... Elles [les bêtes] n'ont étudié ni dialectique, ni géométrie, ni mécanique ; elles n'ont aucune méthode, aucune science, ni aucune culture : ce qu'elles font, elles le font sans l'avoir étudié ni préparé ; elles le font tout d'un coup, et sans tenir conseil' (*Traité* 31). The capacity to know 'tout d'un coup' and without argument or reflection is reminiscent of Balzac's immediate insight and of Méré's *raison-sentiment*. An association of reason with a form of instinct is suggested by Descartes. La Fontaine, in contrast, attributes to animals a kind of reason. He says they possess:

Non point une raison selon notre manière,
Mais beaucoup plus aussi qu'un aveugle ressort.

(Discours à Madame de la Sablière 476)

Thus, these authors regard reason as a source of conscious order which resembles to a greater or lesser extent the instinct of animals in that it functions in an immediate way, compelling the submission of the whole personality.[22] Fénelon, in an ecstatic passage, says that God imparts to man 'une règle droite et simple... une raison qui n'est point une raison, une raison qui renverse la raison même' (*Traité* 109). Paradoxically, his quietism may actually be an extension of the universalists' conception of reason. Reason dominates the personality not by imposing a purely cerebral knowledge on non-cognitive faculties but by permeating will and feeling with the light of consciousness.

Further evidence for the importance of contact with the feeling side of the personality in securing the moral reliability of reason is contained in the relationship drawn by these authors between corrupt reason and the inner self. Here Pascal's conception parallels that of the universalists. For both, reason is unable to make contact with universal truth unless it can establish an order and coherent direction within man. The universalists' faith in reason is based on their conviction that reason can act as guide and regulator of man's passions and imagination, although it is not always used to this end. Pascal's mistrust of reason arises from his belief that reason unaided cannot control or direct wayward impulses. To this extent, the notion of a corrupt reason in the universalists matches the description of corrupt reason in Pascal. Together they reveal the necessity of direct and effective contact between reason and the inner personality if reason is to be the source of reliable judgment.

For the universalists, one important hindrance to the realization and manifestation of right reason is discord in the personality. Like subtle reasoning, various forms of internal disorientation obscure and corrupt reason. This corruption is attributed to the *déréglement* of the will, passions, and senses. Since true reason is closely associated with, even dependent upon, a correctly functioning will and desire, the opposition of reason to passion and imagination often signifies a contrast between the two possible orientations of man and between the mutable and immutable within him rather than a contrast between specific faculties. The universalists' critique of the will and passion represents an attack on the misuse of these and does not indicate a mistrust of feeling *per se*.

The will, undirected or misdirected, is frequently held responsible for error. Descartes explains that it often moves ahead of the understanding, causing men to reach mistaken conclusions (*Méditations* 46). Nicole and Arnauld also blame the will for false judgments: 'Le déreglement de la volonté... trouble et déregle le jugement' (*La logique* 261). Malebranche says: 'Nôtre volonté... nous trompe par ses jugemens précipitez' (*Recherches* I 77); he concludes: 'Les hommes... doivent un peu reprimer et arrêter l'inconstance et la legereté de leur volonté, s'ils veulent penetrer le fond des choses : car leurs esprits seront toûjours foibles, superficiels et discursifs, si leurs volontez demeurent toûjours legeres inconstantes et volages' (ibid II 30).

Diversity and error in human opinion are attributed also to self-love, self-interest, and the passions. Nicole and Arnauld remark that the desire to speak of oneself 'corrompt étrangement la raison' and that self-interest is the main cause of differences in opinion: 'À ne juger des choses que par les regles de la raison... il est visible que cette diversité de jugement ne peut venir d'autre cause, sinon qu'il plaît aux uns de tenir pour vrai ce qui leur est avantageux, et que les autres n'y ayant point d'interêt, en jugent d'une autre sorte' (*La logique* 262 and 269).

La Bruyère agrees. He describes the various impediments to the proper function of reason during the individual's lifetime:

Il y a un second temps où la raison se développe, où elle est formée, et où elle pourroit agir, si elle n'étoit pas obscurcie et comme éteinte par les vices de la complexion, et par un enchaînement de passions qui se succèdent les unes aux autres, et conduisent jusques au troisième et dernier âge. La raison, alors dans sa force, devroit produire ; mais elle est refroidie et ralentie par les années, par la maladie et la douleur, déconcertée ensuite par le désordre de la machine, qui est dans son déclin : et ces temps néanmoins sont la vie de l'homme. (*De l'homme* §49)

Elsewhere he says, 'avec la raison... croissent les passions et les vices, qui seuls rendent les hommes si dissemblables entre eux, et si contraires a eux-mêmes' (ibid §52).

Reasoning can contribute to this process whereby the light of reason is dimmed and distorted. Bossuet says: 'Il faut... remarquer... que le raisonne-ment peut servir à faire naître les passions... Un homme s'échauffe lui-même par de faux raisonnemens, qui rendent plus violent le désir qu'il a de se venger' (*De la connoissance* 76–7). As a result of such inner turmoil the mind becomes 'le jouet de ses propres raisonnements' (*Discours* 564). Male-branche speaks similarly: 'Toutes les passions se justifient... Les faux juge-mens et les passions contribuent sans cesse à leur mutuelle conservation' (*Recherche* II 225).

Reason itself need never err; it reaches mistaken conclusions and judg-ments only if the temporal interferes. The understanding, Bossuet explains, 'n'est jamais forcé à errer.' If it errs, it does so because it is not supported by 'une droite volonté' or because it is undermined by the passions and senses (*De la connoissance* 72–3). Malebranche claims that if men used their reason and did not allow the influence of the body, 'qui... ne dit jamais la vérité,' there would be no diversity of opinion and 'l'approbation universelle seroit une raison.' But, he says, 'c'est tout le contraire.' He concludes with this warning: 'Que l'on soit donc averti une fois pour toutes qu'il n'y a que la Raison qui doive presider au jugement de toutes les opinions humaines, qui n'ont point rapport à la foi... Que l'on rentre dans soi-même, et que l'on s'approche de la lumiere qui y luit incessamment, afin que nôtre raison soit plus éclairée' (*Recherche* I 25). Clearly inner order is essential for reason to function and to be made manifest. If reason fails to establish an alliance with non-cognitive elements in the personality good judgment is not possible and neither are right reasoning and deduction for these also depend on the right orientation of reason.

The *raison* of Pascal's *Pensées* is to a large extent defined within the same framework as that of the universalists. One should not expect a rigorous consistency in thoughts jotted down at different times, yet in many ways Pascal's view of reason is at least as consistent as that of the universalists.[23] The clue to understanding his conception of the human faculty lies in approaching it from two different perspectives: that of the norm *raison-vérité* shared by the universalists and that of the standard *raison-raisonnement*. From the first perspective, reason as a whole is condemned because it fails to give man access to objective moral truth; from the second perspective, it is lauded because as a fallible logical faculty it can perform certain highly constructive functions. Where Pascal's conception falls within the model of two realities and two possible orientations of the mind, his use of *raison* highlights the moral and feeling elements involved in the universalists' conception of right reason.

Occasionally Pascal refers in the *Pensées* to a right reason. Thus he says: 'L'homme n'agit point par la raison qui fait son être' (§491) and 'C'est le consentement de vous à vous-même et la voix constante de votre raison et non des autres qui vous doit faire croire' (§505). In these fragments *raison* is the centre of man and the source of moral truth as it is for the universalists. More usually, Pascal points out that while this ought to be the function of reason, reason has been debased and no longer can occupy its rightful place. It is corrupted and has become a purely formal faculty having no necessary access to truth.[24] This *raison* resembles the pliable faculty, uncommitted to its true orientation, seen in the universalists.

In the *Pensées*, Pascal often considers this formal faculty from the perspective of the universalists. Lacking any sense of truth, reason cannot resist the passions and imagination and it follows their shifting and inconstant impulses (§§44, 45, 530). He stresses repeatedly that in doing so, reason is not as it should be: 'La raison a été obligée de céder' (§44). Reason and the senses lie and mislead one another: 'Ces deux principes de vérité, la raison et les sens, outre qu'ils manquent chacun de sincérité, s'abusent réciproquement l'un l'autre' (§45). Consequently, like passion and imagination, reason contributes the great diversity of opinion and Pascal says: 'La corruption de la raison paraît par tant de différentes et extravangantes mœurs' (§600). Like the corrupt reason of the universalists, Pascal's *raison* follows the senses and the passions, justifies and invents false maxims, and, far from providing man with a stable point of reference, promotes disorder and misunderstanding (§60).

In line with the perspective and conception of the universalists, Pascal gives to corrupt reason a tangential relationship both with the *raisonnable* and with the sources of motivation in man. Where for the universalists false or corrupt reason brings out the supreme value of reliable reason in touch with moral truth and the inner personality, for Pascal the weakness of reason shows the need to turn to faith and to the heart. The *raisonnable*, in his use, occupies the same place as for the universalists, but reason is separated from the reasonable and at the same time from feeling and from faith. Thus Pascal assesses reason against the reasonable and finds it wanting 'si la raison était raisonnable' (§76). Through reason alone, a man cannot know of the existence of good and he also cannot know himself (§§131, 418). Reason can lead a man to truth and can help in his quest for morality only when it comes to see its limitations and is prepared to stand down. 'Elle l'est bien assez [raisonnable] pour avouer qu'elle n'a pu encore trouver rien de ferme... [et] qu'il y a une infinité de choses qui la surpassent' (§§76, 188). He who thinks reason can find higher truth is unreasonable (§§131, 428); the Christian who surrenders reason is reasonable: 'Nul n'est heureux comme un vrai chrétien, ni raisonnable, ni vertueux, ni aimable' (§357). Truth can be known by the humble-hearted irrespective of intelligence or by the clever man who dares to see the limitations of reason (§394). Ultimately only the heart, instinct, and faith can provide reliability: 'C'est sur ces connaissances du cœur et de l'instinct qu'il faut que la raison s'appuie et qu'elle y fonde tout son discours' (§110; cf §§199, 424, and 588). The non-cerebral and feeling aspects of the personality can thus have a direct relationship with truth from which reason, as a purely formal faculty, is excluded. *Sentiment*, in contrast, is approved on the same grounds as *raison* is valued by the universalists. It is able to see things in their true perspective: 'le jugement est celui à qui appartient le sentiment' (§513); it acts instantly: 'Il agit en un instant et toujours est prêt à agir' (§821); and it is able to give effect to this insight in that it can provide a rightful orientation for man's desires. So far, Pascal's *raison* fits perfectly into the model of two realities of the universalists and his use supports the contention that for *raison* to be reliable and to have moral and regulative capacities it must have contact with and permeate non-cerebral aspects of the self.

Pascal departs from the model of two realities by giving a certain limited but valuable constructive role to reason as a purely formal faculty. He says that reason becomes reasonable by seeing its own limitations and that it does not live up to its full strength and possibilities unless it does so (§§76, 188). A full use of logical thought can lead to awareness of the limitations of that function and, once this awareness is attained, that same logic can be used to give each faculty its rightful application. In these circumstances, reasoning contributes in an indirect but important way to the attainment of moral knowledge and it also acts rightly by the standards of logic. Pascal says: 'Il faut savoir douter où il faut, assurer où il faut, en se soumettant où il faut. Qui ne fait ainsi n'entend pas la force de la raison' (§170). The formal faculty of reason is here given a constructive and valuable function, that of determining where each faculty should be used. In this sense, corrupt reason is also corrupt or misguided by the standard *raison-raisonnement*: passions, imagination, pride, and pretentiousness interfere with the correct function-ing of reasoning and so contravene the standards of logic as well as those of immutable truth. This positive reason of the *Pensées* is the same as that used in Pascal's scientific work: it is, as it were, an outgrowth of the corrupt reason despised both by himself and by the universalists. The order which it creates is not moral so much as logical, is founded on correct reasoning, depends on intelligence, and has no direct contact with objective moral truth or with feeling. When reason is treated in this way, as a purely formal faculty, the contrast between *raison* and *sentiment, imagination*, or *passion* becomes clear-cut: that is, this contrast represents an opposition between actual faculties of the mind and is not confused by a contrast between that which is morally right and that which is self-orientated. The logic of thought can be evaluated on its own merits without implying any moral evaluation and the order imposed or discovered by reason does not necessarily repair the disorder of man's ways.

But the universalists are unwilling to separate logic from moral rectitude. Even Descartes, who attaches immense importance to the correct method of thought, and Nicole and Arnauld, who present to the literary and philo-sophical world a guide to logic, insist that right thinking is linked with a right attitude of mind, that reason creates that attitude and is in turn freed by it. True reason is not only the reason of logic: it is the capacity for a right perspective in all things. The universalists see reason as a bright light illuminating the whole mind, directing and guiding thought, feeling, and action. In the face of scepticism, they affirm that the impediments to reason, like dark but flimsy clouds, can be blown away, dissolved by a constant and unchanging awareness. Reason does not require the support of authority or, for the most part, of the senses, experience, or experiment. It must be 'freed from the Pedantic dust of the Schools'[25] and from the oppression of opinion, prejudice, and the self-orientated desires of man. Pascal, in the shadow of Descartes and as if forgetting that reason is corrupted, remarks that man must not be guided by authority but only by 'la voix constante de la raison.' Chapelain says, 'Il n'y a rien qui la cabre [la raison] davantage que l'autorité' (lettre à Balzac, 6 octobre 1640, *Lettres* I 697); d'Aubignac proclaims, 'la Raison doît toujours prévaloir sur l'Autorité' (*La pratique du théâtre* 26). This true and assertive reason derives its reliability both from its independence from accepted opinion and from its dependence on higher truth, whether in the form of God or of universal and unwritten law. As Laporte has said, speaking of Cartesian reason: 'Notre condition est indépendance relativement aux êtres finis, mais dépendance totale relativement à l'infini.'[26] True reason is not confined to the clever or educated man but to him who allows the sense, almost the instinct, distinguishing man from animal and linking man with the 'real' order of things to find expression within himself. Thus, despite the manifest unreasonableness of men, the notion that all men are equally reasonable has a logic of its own.

5

Human reason as
empirical reason

Ils laissent là les choses, et s'amusement à traiter les causes. Plaisants causeurs.
Montaigne *Essais* III ix

There appears to be no seventeenth-century French equivalent and no adequate translation of the phrase *empirical reason*.[1] According to the Academy and Furetière *empirique* had a very narrow usage and referred mainly to unorthodox medical practice.[2] *Expérience*, in contrast, could mean both experiment and experience and, in this sense, was closer to the meaning of empirical. The Academy defines *expérience* as 'espreuve qu'on fait de quelque chose, soit à dessein, soit par hasard' and as 'connoissance des choses acquise par un long usage.' Furetière also gives the two meanings: 'Espreuve réitérée de quelque effet qui sert à notre raisonnement pour venir à la connoissance de sa cause... On appelle un homme d'*experience* celuy qui a vescu et raisonné longtemps, qui a veu et leu beaucoup de choses et d'affaires, qui connoist le monde par sa propre *experience*.' Yet the words *raison* and *expérience* are often antithetical. Thevet's *La cosmologie universelle* of 1575 provides an early example of this antithesis. Although he is concerned to stress the importance of sense-experience and observation, he nevertheless contrasts these with *raison*: 'La Cosmographie : les principaux points de laquelle ne se prouvent point par raison, mais par demonstrations et expérience, et par veritez (qu'on allegue) tellement qu'un homme combien qu'il soit raisonnable, et bien instruit aux lettres Grecques et Latines, ne les peut entendre, si premierement ne luy ont esté démonstrées à l'œil' (iv). Montaigne emphasizes this opposition in the medical sphere: 'L'experience est proprement sur son fumier au sujet de la medecine, où la raison lui quitte toute la place' (Essais III 13). This contrast is still found in modern French: Robert gives as possible antonyms of *expé-*

rience 'théorie, raison, ignorance, inexpérience.'[3] Thus the word *raison* would appear to be more readily linked to a theoretical than to an empirical approach and this tendency is expressed in much seventeenth-century thought.

However, the relationship of reason to experience is necessarily affected by the definition of *raison*. If *raison* is narrowly defined and treated simply as a faculty for reasoning and for logical thought, it becomes more clearly differentiated from experience but it also becomes more dependent on experience. As Moore has shown, *raison* in Montaigne's use is associated with a 'professional or bookish-knowledge.'[4] It is largely an instrument of explanation and is dependent on the truth of actual experience as against a theoretical knowledge: 'L'humaine raison est un instrument libre et vague. Je vois ordinairement que les hommes aux faits qu'on leurs propose, s'amusent plus volontiers à en chercher la raison qu'à en chercher la vérité' (ibid 9). While this contrast of *raison* and *expérience* in Montaigne resembles the contrast of *raison* and spurious *raisonnements* in the universalists, Montaigne's narrow definition of *raison* provides an important impetus to the development of empiricism because it emphasizes the dependence of reason on premises external to itself. Deprived of contact with a higher universal, reason participates in the movement and inconstancy of the world and in order to regain reliability it must turn to the external world and to documented fact for its premises. Giving an example of the use of *expérience*, Furetière says: 'La Physique moderne est preferable à celle des Anciens, en ce que celle-cy commençoit à raisonner sur les causes, et celle-là ne raisonne que sur les *expériences*' (*Dictionnaire universel*). Thus an increased separation of reason from direct experience tends to render it an inductive and empirical instrument: reason assesses speculative reasoning with the aid of factual experience rather than by means of a natural good sense.

This conception of human reason is most prominent in the work of Fontenelle and Bayle. While they perhaps owe their confidence in reason to Descartes, their view of reason more closely resembles that of *libertin* writers, of Pascal and generally of those who, like Montaigne, sever the ties of man's reason with eternal truth. But points of agreement can be reached from very different lines of approach and there are many parallels between uses of Bayle and Fontenelle and those of other authors, including the universalists.

Usually the universalists contrast the evidence of reason with that of the senses: reason has contact with a higher reality unknown to the senses. But this does not mean that the senses can in no way contribute to knowledge. Descartes says that he hopes experiment will confirm the conclusions of deductive reasoning (*Principes* 17), and Nicole and Arnauld, on occasion, describe the evidence of the senses as an important part of man's resources. They claim that a first means to knowledge is 'la connoissance que nous en avons [d'une chose] par nous-mêmes, pour en avoir reconnu et recherché la verité, soit par nos sens, soit par notre raison ; ce qui se peut appeler generalement *raison*, parceque les sens mêmes dépendent du jugement de la raison' (*La logique* 335). In this passage, reason and the senses are portrayed as mutually supporting and as forming man's natural instrument for the acquisition of knowledge. Although the judgment of reason is said to be of greater importance than the senses, each contributes to the other in such an intimate way that they can together be called *raison*.

In some instances, there is only a slight distinction between the notion that reason, relying on a priori judgment, must rectify the errors of the senses and the view that reason is dependent on the senses to gain further knowledge and to promote understanding. Montaigne, in his *Apologie de Raymond Sebond*, speaks of a mutual exchange between reason and the evidence of the senses and Nicole and Arnauld echo his argument in the *Logique* (85). La Fontaine discusses the same issue poetically in *Un animal dans la lune*; the senses, he concludes, need not mislead:

> Mon âme, en toute occasion,
> Développe le vrai caché sous l'apparence...
> Quand l'eau courbe un bâton, ma raison le redresse :
> La raison décide en maîtresse.
> Mes yeux, moyennant ce secours,
> Ne me trompent jamais, en me mentant toujours.   (*Œuvres* II 199–201)

Reason consults the senses and yet remains the ultimate arbiter; it perceives the truth hidden beneath appearances and so can use the senses to advantage.[5]

This view of reason as collaborating with the senses and yet maintaining a certain superiority is also found in Bayle and Fontenelle. The latter comments: 'On ne persuade pas facilement aux hommes de mettre la raison en la place de leurs yeux' (*Entretiens sur la pluralité des mondes* 146). He points out that while reasoning is sometimes derived entirely from experience, at other times experience contributes very little: 'Ici, le raisonnement se forme entièrement par l'expérience ; ailleurs, l'expérience y ajoute fort peu de chose' (ibid 107). Bayle on occasion also speaks as if reason informed man independently of the senses, as in the words 'non seulement la raison... mais l'expérience aussi' (*Pensées diverses sur la comète* I 129). Reason remains the final judge and yet these two authors specifically deny that reason has a priori knowledge – a point not raised in La Fontaine's poetical discussion.

The distinction between the position of Bayle and Fontenelle and that of other authors who use the norm *raison-vérité* is also sometimes blurred. For example, Molière and Boileau, who contrast false reasonings with a natural good judgment, sometimes mock speculative argument which pays no attention to factual evidence. Echoing Montaigne, one of Molière's characters remarks ironically that disease must adjust itself to eloquence and that a beautiful argument must not be abused by recalcitrant facts: 'Vous avez si bien discouru sur tous les signes, les symptômes et les causes de la maladie de Monsieur ; le raisonnement que vous en avez fait est si docte et si beau, qu'il est impossible qu'il ne soit pas fou, et mélancolique hypocondriaque ; et quand il ne le seroit pas, il faudroit qu'il le devînt, pour la beauté des choses que vous avez dites, et la justesse du raisonnement que vous avez fait' (*Monsieur de Pourceaugnac* I viii). Boileau's satirical *Arrest burlesque* of 1675 represents the professors of the university as making a declaration in favour of Aristotle and as rejecting reason and the factual evidence on which it draws:

Enjoint au Cœur de continuer d'estre le principe des Nerfs, et à toutes personnes de quelque condition et profession qu'elles soient de la croire tel, nonobstant toute experience à ce contraire... Deffend à la Raison et à ses adherans de plus s'ingerer à l'avenir de guerir les fiévres... Et en cas de guérison... permet aux Medecins de ladite Faculté de rendre, suivant leur methode ordinaire, la fiévre aux Malades... et de remettre lesdits Malades en tel et semblable état qu'ils estoient auparavant ; pour estre ensuite traités selon les regles.

The indictment concludes that the university 'a banni à perpetuité la Raison' (33).

Such criticism of a form of reasoning which attaches little significance to factual evidence is frequent in the writings of Bayle and Fontenelle. Bayle exclaims: 'Une vérité de fait ne renverse-t-elle pas cent volumes de raisonnements spéculatifs' (*Dictionnaire historique, Épicure*, remarque D). He quotes Montaigne's criticism of those who pay no attention to fact and comments: 'c'etoit le défaut d'Avicenne, grand Medecin en raisonnement, mais sans experience' (*Pensées diverses* I 140). In Fontenelle and Bayle, however, this point of view is developed into a systematic philosophy and the notion of reason as dependent on sense-experience and documented fact becomes the central theme in their conceptions of reason.

While there are thus many similarities between statements of Fontenelle and Bayle, on the one hand, and the language of Descartes and the universalists, on the other hand, the differences in their conceptions of reason have been insufficiently stressed.[6] Bayle and Fontenelle make important reservations about their debt to Cartesianism. For the most part, they reject Descartes's philosophy but praise his insistence on the need for precision. Bayle writes to his brother: 'Je le regarde [le cartésianisme] comme une hypothèse ingénieuse... Je ne risquerois pas la moindre chose pour soutenir que la nature se règle et se gouverne selon ces principes là.'[7] Fontenelle admires Descartes's method of reasoning far more than his philosophy, the greater part of which, he says, has been proved false (*Digression sur les anciens et les modernes* 166–9). In their dismissal of Cartesian philosophy, they both reject not only the conclusions Descartes reached by means of deduction but also, in large part, the deductive method itself: their attitude, in other words, is inseparable from their conception of human reason.

Prat, in a footnote to his edition of Bayle's *Pensées diverses sur la comète*, identifies the evidence required by Bayle with that required by the *raison* of Descartes and of Malebranche: 'Toute la doctrine de Bayle et son argumentation contre l'autorité de la tradition est fondée sur le principe Cartésien de l'évidence rationnelle qui a été si fortement énoncé par Malebranche.'[8] Prat goes on to quote Malebranche's statement that one must never accept anything until forced to do so by 'des reproches intérieurs de notre raison.' But Malebranche means by this *raison* something akin to conscience. By using the words 'évidence rationnelle' Prat incorrectly suggests that in these authors there is only one reason and only one type of evidence.

Bayle and Fontenelle define *raison* as a purely human faculty, one which is closely dependent on the senses. A phrase such as Bayle's 'la raison toute pure' might suggest a thought similar to Descartes's 'nous ne nous devons jamais laisser persuader qu'a l'evidence de nostre raison' (*Discours de la méthode* 39). But whereas Descartes distinguishes this evidence from that of the senses and says it is reliable because it derives from God, Bayle identifies 'la raison toute pure' with 'la voye du raisonnement.' Addressing the recipient of his *Pensées diverses*, he says: 'Vous êtes trop habile pour être la dupe de quelque Philosophe que ce soit, pourvue qu'il ne vous attaque que par la voye du raisonnement, et il faut vous rendre cette justice que dans les choses que vous croyez être du ressort de la raison, vous ne suivez que la raison toute pure' (1 39). 'La raison toute pure' is man's capacity to reason, not his capacity for direct knowledge or for sound judgment based on innate ideas. Bayle goes on to point out: 'le temoignage d'un homme ne doit avoir de force qu'à proportion du degré de certitude qu'il s'est acquis en s'instruisant pleinement du fait' (ibid 134). Pure reason, for Bayle, does not mean a reason independent of the senses or having direct access to truth. *Raison* is a power of judgment as well as of discourse and the distinction seen in Aquinas and seventeenth-century dictionaries between discursive and judging reason thus still pertains. However, taken out of the context of two realities, the distinction loses much of its significance. Reason does not make contact simultaneously with higher truth and with the inner self. Judgment is not related to conscience or to a sense or feeling of the true: it is mainly dependent on the capacity to reason and so to examine and assess the factual evidence on which opinion is based.

Illustrative of this relationship is Fontenelle's use of *raison* in relation to *esprit*. He uses the word *esprit* in two ways. It can refer to the mind as a whole, as in 'La raison nous propose un trop petit nombre de maximes certaines, et... notre esprit est fait pour en croire davantage' (*Dialogue des morts* 169). Or it can be a synonym for *raison*: 'Tout le reste des hommes a de la raison ; autrement ce ne seroit rien que de perdre l'esprit' (ibid 91) and 'Ce n'est pas un plaisir comme celui que vous auriez à la comédie de Molière ; c'en est un qui est je ne sais où dans la raison, et qui ne fait rire que l'esprit' (*Entretiens* 62). When they are placed in contrast *esprit* becomes agility and volatility of mind while *raison* refers to methodical thinking. The Greeks, he says, 'étoient fort legers, curieux, inquiets, incapables de se moderer sur rien ; et... ils avoient tant d'esprit, que leur raison en soufroit un peu.' The Romans, in contrast, were a solid and serious people 'qui sçavoient suivre un principe, et prevoir de loin une consequence' (*Histoire des oracles* 67). *Raison* implies mental discipline while *esprit* can refer to a type of mind which is too rapid and too imaginative. Thus *raison* may refer to a capacity for judgment but one which derives from methodical thought rather than an immediate or intuitive awareness.

This view of reason bears a stronger resemblance to Pascal's conception than to Descartes's; the influence of Cartesianism on the work of Bayle and Fontenelle must consequently be carefully qualified. As Delbos has pointed out, 'En triomphant, il [le cartesianisme] ne triomphait pas tout entier.'[9] Similarly, Bayle's and Fontenelle's appeal to reason as an authority above custom and prejudice does not signify an appeal to a constant and unchanging standard and the point of view expressed in the above passages from Molière and Boileau becomes for Bayle and Fontenelle a systematic philosophy relevant in other contexts than those of medicine and the natural sciences. Boileau's use of *raison* in the *Arrest burlesque* as an empirical faculty serves, however, as a reminder of the danger of too rigidly categorizing authors and word use. The dependence of good judgment on discursive reasoning is suggested on occasion by La Rochefoucauld (*Réflexions ou sentences* 73) and by La Bruyère (*De l'homme* §14); and Bossuet remarks in *De la connoissance de Dieu*: 'Le bon jugement est l'effet du bon raisonnement'

(70). These authors belong to a generation for whom the notion of reason as a moral faculty co-exists in many instances with the narrower definition of reason as fallible and discursive and as relying for judgment on reasoning.

The main impetus to the use of the senses and of experiment in conjunction with reason comes from those who lack confidence in reason. The connection between the view that reason must rely on sense-evidence and the rejection of the notion that reason in some way resembles or has access to the eternal can be illustrated from a brief consideration of early *libertin* writers and of Pascal. In *Le libertinage érudit*, Pintard points to La Mothe Le Vayer, Gassendi, and Naudé as the predecessors of Fontenelle and Bayle. He sees their 'libertinage souffrant, hésitant, combattu, embarrassé de scrupules et de craintes' as prefiguring the 'libertinage triomphant' of Bayle and Fontenelle.[10] The important role given to the senses and to experience or experiment by La Mothe Le Vayer, Gassendi, and Naudé derives from their rejection of innate knowledge and of the theory that all men have access to the same eternal truths.

Gassendi claims that 'des nations entières n'ont eu de Dieu ni connaissance ni même soupçon' and denies that human reason lacks any certainty of its own.[11] Describing reason as a purely natural instrument, he compares it with the intelligence of animals: 'J'attribue la vie aux semences ; je restitue la raison aux bêtes ; je n'établis aucune distinction entre l'entendement et la phantaisie.'[12] At the same time, he gives an important role to the senses. Pintard comments:

Il leur ouvre [aux sens] un champ presque illimité, en s'abstenant de séparer les opérations des sens de celles de la 'phantaisie,' qui en rapproche, ordonne, compare, réduit, ou étend les résultats jusqu'à en tirer des idées, – et en doublant ainsi la sensation d'une sorte de raison élémentaire, corporelle comme elle mais comme elle capable de vérité, pour peu que ses créations soient suffisamment répétées, confrontées, éprouvées.[13]

Reason is a corporeal faculty not unlike fantasy and its reliability depends on repeated experience and proof.

A similar point of view is found in La Mothe Le Vayer, who mocks the notion of a constant human reason and, pointing like Montaigne and Pascal to the diversity of man's ways, surmises that a 'droite raison' would not allow for such variation: 'Examinés les façons de faire d'autant qu'il a de peuples au Monde, vous les trouverés presque toutes diverses, ce qui ne devroit pas être, si elles étoient fondées sur une droite et juste raison,

dont nous sommes obligés de présupposer que les maximes sont invari-
ables' (*Œuvres* v ii 66–7). He concludes that man's reason does not know
immutable rules and, complaining of the uncertainty of human reason, compares it unfavourably with the instinct of animals. It is not surprising, he
says, that the Egyptians deified animals since their instinct is in many ways
sound whereas 'tous nos discours raisonnés n'engendrent la plûpart du
tems que de fausses doctrines, qui bien loin de nous servir, ne causent dans
nôtre ame que des perplexités' (ibid v ii 54).

La Mothe Le Vayer's conception of reason as a purely human faculty
leads him, like Gassendi, to place it on a par with the senses and to describe
it as dependent upon them. In the *Soliloques sceptiques*, described by Tisser-
and as 'une petite revanche sur l'immortel *Discours de la méthode*,'[14] La
Mothe Le Vayer says: 'À l'égard de la Morale mesme, il valoit beaucoup
mieux tenir ses préceptes de la Foi, que de nostre raison humaine, qui varie
sans cesse, et qui n'est constante que dans son inconstance. Elle ne peut faire
ses opérations, qu'elle ne s'appuie sur ce que nos sens lui suggèrent ; et
nous sommes enfin contraints d'avouer que ces mesmes sens, et nostre raison, s'entre-abusent à qui mieux mieux' (10). Reason is dependent on the
senses, but reason and the senses constantly abuse one another. Thus La
Mothe Le Vayer and Gassendi give no more reliability to the senses than to
reason; both receive their share of the shafts of irony directed against human
weakness. However, the connection drawn between the senses and reason
and the dependence of one on the other anticipate the confidence placed in
empirical reason by Bayle and Fontenelle.

In the *Pensées*, Pascal, like Gassendi and La Mothe Le Vayer, deplores
the mutual weakness of reason, imagination, and the senses, saying '[Ils]
s'abusent réciproquement l'un l'autre... Ils mentent et se trompent à
l'envi' (§45). The place Pascal gives to experiment in his scientific work is
thus related to his attack on reason in the *Pensées*. The two attitudes complement each other. Since man does not have direct access to truth through his
reason he must take seriously the evidence of the senses in science, just as he
takes seriously the insight of the heart or instinct in morals and in mathematics. Unlike theology and history, physics and the natural sciences are not
subject to authority: 'Il n'en est pas de même des sujets qui tombent sous le
sens ou sous le raisonnement : l'autorité y est inutile ; la raison seule a lieu
d'en connaître' (*Œuvres* 230).[15] In the *Préface sur le traité du vide* reason is
spoken of as functioning with the aid of experiment and factual evidence:
reasoning must be based on these. In his letters to le père Noël, Pascal
rejects the a priori reasoning of Descartes and of Noël. Appealing to the
evidence of reason, the latter accepts the Cartesian definition of matter as

precluding the possibility of a vacuum: 'L'entrée subtile [à travers les pores du verre] de ces petits corps d'air et de feu qui sont partout, paraissant moins aux sens qu'à la raison, fait conjecturer un vide qui soit une privation de tout corps' (*Œuvres* 200). In his answer, Pascal opposes this a priori approach: 'Mais, mon Père, je crois que vous donnez cela pour une pensée, et non pas pour une démonstration... qui *présupposera* le contraire, tirera une conséquence contraire aussi nécessairement... Toutes les choses de cette nature, dont l'existence ne se manifeste à aucun des sens, sont aussi difficiles à croire, qu'elles sont faciles à inventer' (ibid 202). Again Noël protests: 'Le sens est trompé, mais il est corrigé par la raison' (ibid 207), and Pascal comments to M. le Pailleur: 'Monsieur, je vous laisse à juger, lorsqu'on ne voit rien, et que les sens n'aperçoivent rien dans un lieu, lequel est mieux fondé, ou de celui qui affirme qu'il y a quelque chose, quoiqu'il n'aperçoive rien, ou de celui qui pense qu'il n'y a rien, parce qu'il ne voit aucune chose' (ibid 212). Thus in Pascal as well the rejection of innate knowledge and the narrow definition of reason are accompanied by an insistence on the need for collaboration between reason and the senses.

La Mothe Le Vayer compares reason with animal instinct. Later, in an essay entitled *De la véritable définition de l'homme et de la raison*,[16] Boulainviller maintains that reason is essentially an inductive instrument and that it conducts all its operations 'mécaniquement.' He goes on to ask: 'Si l'on avoue que l'induction et la conclusion sont les offices principaux de la raison, qui peut nier que les bêtes raisonnent ? ' It would seem that the comparison of human reason with animal intelligence can serve very different ends. Where Fénelon compares reason with the instinct of animals in order to stress their mutual dependence on eternal reason and consequently their ultimate reliability and non-material nature, La Mothe Le Vayer and Boulainviller make this comparison in order to draw attention to the corporeal, unreliable and, for Boulainviller, the mechanical nature of reason.

Obliquely, Cartesian philosophy may have contributed to the notion of reason as mechanical. Descartes claims that while the 'reasonable' soul is spiritual, man's body and his bodily passions are purely mechanical (*Les passions de l'ame* 364–6). Spink remarks that, in so doing, Descartes allowed the natural philosopher to consider human passions as a part of the natural world.[17] He shows that after Descartes the word *mechanical* was used with increasing frequency to describe human operations[18] and, of course, Descartes's notion of the animal machine was gradually extended until in La Mettrie man himself is described as a machine.[19] The consequences of Boulainviller's view of reason as mechanical, however, are foreign to Cartesianism. His conception of reason as an inductive and reasoning instrument dependent on experience leads him to conclude that the soul 'n'est point essentiellement raisonnable,' a view which resembles the position of La Mothe Le Vayer and Pascal.

In Bayle and Fontenelle, Cartesian confidence in reason is coupled with the idea that reason is weak and fallible. Like La Mothe Le Vayer and Boulainviller, Fontenelle maintains that animals are capable of thought (*Sur l'instinct* 420) and that man's reason is superior only in that it is able to relate one thought to another (ibid 407–8). Whereas the universalists describe reason as the centre of man, Fontenelle claims that man's nature is fundamentally irrational. Like Saint-Evremond, who speaks of 'les passions estant du fond de la nature, et les vertus n'estant purement établies en nous que par les lumieres d'une raison instruite et enseignée' (*Sur les anciens* 353), Fontenelle considers that the passions form the centre of man's being. In *De l'origine des fables*, he says that history reveals man's fundamental folly and he concludes: 'Ne cherchons donc autre chose dans les fables que l'histoire des erreurs de l'esprit humain' (35–9).

Bayle and Fontenelle, like Pascal, question the capacity of reason to know God and do not take the existence of God as the guarantee of human ideas and thought. Proofs of God's existence are by no means self-evident and fail to convince. The knowledge of reason does not convert man's inner being; it is not a deep understanding or an inner light of conscience; it remains cerebral. This incapacity to accept fully the proofs of the existence of God, Bayle says, is not always due to unwillingness or to the presence of some unruly passion (*Pensées diverses* II 149). True philosophy teaches the immortality of the soul, but he asks 'Combien y a-t-il de gens qui ne comprennent pas la force de toutes ces démonstrations ? ' He cites Cicero's experience upon reading Plato's proofs of immortality: 'Il acquiesce à ses raisons ; mais... aussi-tôt qu'il laisse le livre, et qu'il médite là dessus, sa persuasion s'évanoüit... C'est donc à tort que l'on s'imagine, que quand nous ne voyons pas une verité importante dans la Religion, nous avons quelque passion secrete, qui a intérêt que nous demeurions dans l'ignorance' (ibid 150–1). This statement is strikingly similar to Pascal's comment that proofs of God's existence are of little use and are readily forgotten (*Pensées* §190). Whereas Pascal concludes from this weakness of the human mind that some other way to experience God must be sought, Bayle is content to abandon the question of the immortality of the soul since there is no factual evidence with which to examine it.[20]

Nevertheless Bayle's and Fontenelle's conceptions of the relationship of reason to man's heart and will are very similar to Pascal's. Most authors, including the universalists, consider that the power of reasoning, in so far as it is not based on immediate vision and does not draw on the seeds of knowledge of true reason, will not convince or direct the whole of man. When reason is defined as discursive it necessarily lacks this immediate effect on the inner personality, the will and feelings. Saint-Evremond, when he speaks of reason in this sense as a reasoning faculty, also asserts that it lacks the power of converting man; like Pascal, he mocks Descartes's attempts to know the nature of man through reason:

Vouloir se persuader l'Immortalité de l'Ame par la Raison, c'est entrer en défiance de la parole que Dieu nous en a donnée, et renoncer, en quelque façon, à la seule chose par qui nous pouvons en être assûrés.

Qu'a fait Descartes, par sa démonstration pretenduë d'une substance purement spirituelle, d'une substance qui doit penser éternellement ? Il a fait croire que la Religion ne le persuadoit pas, sans pouvoir persuader ni lui ni les autres par ses raisons.   (*Œuvres* II 137)

The intellect is too weak to be man's guide: 'L'activité de nostre esprit nous donne assez de mouvement, mais ses lumieres sont trop foibles pour nous conduire' (ibid 130). The same view of the relationship of reason to the inner self is found in La Rochefoucauld and Racine. Where Pascal says 'Tout notre raisonnement se réduit à ceder au sentiment,' La Rochefoucauld claims 'L'homme croit souvent se conduire lorsqu'il est conduit, et pendant que par son esprit, il tend à un but, son cœur l'entraîne insensiblement à un autre' (*Réflexions* 48) and 'L'esprit est toujours la dupe du cœur' (ibid 75). He uses the word *esprit*, but Mme de Schömberg, commenting on these aphorisms, identifies this *esprit* with *raison*: 'C'est toujours le cœur qui fait agir l'esprit ; l'on suit tous ses mouvements, malgré que l'on en ait, et l'on les suit même sans croire les suivre':

La raison sans cesse raisonne
Et jamais n'a guéri personne.   (*Œuvres* I 377: appendice)

Racine's characters, although they may be lucid and see clearly the horror or folly of their situations, are on the whole unable to regulate their behaviour by means of reason. Confused by the folly of his behaviour, Oreste exclaims: 'Quoi? J'étouffe en mon cœur la raison qui m'éclaire' (*Andromaque* V iv 1569). Often, since reason cannot alter the desires of the heart, the inner direction of passion can only be changed by cutting it off with death. Contemplating suicide, Oreste says:

> Non, tes conseils ne sont plus de saison,
> Pylade, je suis las d'écouter la raison.
> C'est traîner trop longtemps ma vie et mon supplice :
> Il faut que je l'enlève, ou bien que je périsse.   (ibid III i 712–15)

and Antiochus exclaims:

> Je viens de rappeler ma raison toute entière :
> Jamais je ne me suis senti plus amoureux.
> Il faut d'autres efforts pour rompre tant de nœuds :
> Ce n'est qu'en expirant que je puis les détruire.   (*Bérénice* V vii 1456–9)

Bossuet's remarks on corrupt human reason sometimes resemble the protestations of Racine's characters. While Bossuet speaks of the hopelessness of trying to guide one's life by means of a 'raison égarée' (*Discours sur l'histoire universelle* 547), Phèdre, realizing that her thought is following the impulses of fervour, cries: 'Que fais-je? Où ma raison se va-t-elle égarer ? ' (IV vi 1264). While these passages have little to do with empiricism as such, the narrow definition of reason, by which reason lacks immediate control over the inner self, is an important and perhaps a necessary accompaniment of the empirical approach. Consequently it may be no accident that the weakness and fallibility of reason are emphasized in plays, aphorisms, and sermons at a time when empiricism emerges with increasing confidence.

The idea that reason is unable to control the inner self is found also in Fontenelle and Bayle. In Fontenelle's *Dialogues*, Sénèque complains that Scarron's so-called 'sagesse' is not an effect of his reason so much as of his temperament. In words reminiscent of Montaigne, Scarron replies that this is the only form of wisdom worth having since 'la nature garde toujours ses droits ; elle a ses premiers mouvemens qu'on ne lui peut jamais ôter' (I 144). Bayle claims: 'L'inclination à la pitié, à la sobriété, à la débonnaireté, etc. ne vient pas de ce qu'on connoit qu'il y a un Dieu... mais d'une certaine disposition du tempérament, fortifiée par l'éducation, par l'intérêt personnel, par le désir d'être loüé, par l'instinct de la raison, ou par semblables motifs, qui se rencontrent dans un Athée, aussi bien que dans les autres hommes' (*Pensées diverses* II 36–7). The phrase *l'instinct de la raison* suggests that reason is a part of man's physical make-up. Just as he is driven by self-interest, so man has a natural drive to use his reason; this drive is not qualitatively different from his self-interest and does not depend on contact with higher truth. Man's weakness and his faults, as much as his reason, may lead him to virtue. Thus Bayle and Fontenelle give a positive interpretation of the view that reason does not control the personality or have direct access to truth.

The idea that virtue can be moulded from man's weaknesses and self-interest dates from long before the *Maximes* of La Rochefoucauld. Speaking of Senault, Hippeau notes: 'La psychologie religieuse avait déjà accoutumé les esprits à admettre qu'on peut créer la vertu à l'aide de sentiments et de tendances qui ne sont pas, par eux-mêmes, vertueux.'[21] Both Pascal and Bossuet consider that persuasion can justifiably seek to render man virtuous by appealing to his self-interest. Such a conversion of man's weaknesses into strength in many ways characterizes Bayle's and Fontenelle's conception of reason: it is a fallible faculty, but in its weakness nature's laws are expressed and, from it, progress in methods of reasoning and in knowledge is possible. Descartes's notion that the 'semences' in man resemble the 'semences' in nature, because both are implanted by God, becomes in Fontenelle and Bayle the view that human reason, although weak, is a part of nature's order and will develop in accordance with her laws.

For Bayle and Fontenelle the dependence of reason on sense-evidence makes up for the frailty of reason and represents a substitute for Descartes's divine guarantee. In the *Fragmens d'un traité de la raison humaine*, published posthumously and of uncertain date,[22] Fontenelle suggests that sense-experience is a form of guarantee for human ideas:

Si vous prétendez que sur les idées des choses sensibles, il ne faille rien assurer des objets, il ne faut seulement pas assurer leur existence ; ainsi il ne faut pas dire : *il y a quelque chose dans l'objet qui fait que je pense blanc* ; mais il faut dire : *J'ai une idée de blanc.* Or, qui m'assurera qu'il y ait quelque chose au monde de blanc ? c'est que Dieu, disent les Cartésiens, ne permettroit pas qu'on fût dans une illusion perpétuelle, etc. Mais qui m'assurera d'un Dieu ? ôtez-moi toutes les idées des sens, jamais vous ne me prouverez un Dieu.   (392)

For Bayle, facts are the only safeguard against vain argumentation. As Labrouse has pointed out: 'Les raisonnements philosophiques *a priori* sont un peu comme une passerelle ; mais la chair est faible et des discussions de fait sont le rassurant garde-fou qui nous préserve du vertige des hauteurs.'[23] This does not mean that the senses and factual evidence provide a complete certainty but rather that they are the only form of guarantee or guide available to reason.

In *De la connaissance de l'esprit humain*, Fontenelle asserts: 'Toutes les idées sont prises dans l'expérience' (396). He goes on to say that, as Aristotle knew, universal ideas are not grasped directly or by innate knowledge: reason has the capacity to discover the universal from a number of particular or individual ideas furnished by experience (397). Even the first principles of geometry are known by experience and the notion that the whole is always greater than any of its parts differs from, for example, the notion that man is mortal only in that it does not require repeated experience to establish its certainty (398). Thus when Fontenelle contrasts reason with the senses, he does not imply, as does Descartes, that reason is independent of the senses. He says: 'Toutes les idées viennent donc de l'expérience : mais il y en a que l'expérience peut abandonner, pour ainsi dire, dès qu'elle les a fait naître, et qui se soutiennent sans elle ; d'autres qui ont longtems besoin de son secours' (400). Here Fontenelle also goes beyond Pascal. While for Pascal the first principles of geometry and mathematics do not require proof, because they are immediately evident to the heart and instinct (*De l'esprit géométrique* 352), Fontenelle sees no source of knowledge internal to man other than reason and, because reason is incapable of direct vision, it must draw all first principles from the external world.

Reason is superior to the senses mainly in that it can make suppositions and hypotheses. Ideas like that of infinity and perfection are suppositions only; they are not direct perceptions of higher truth: 'Je suppose une chose sans bornes, sans savoir si elle est possible ou non, et sans la concevoir en aucune manière' (*De la connaissance* 409). Carré comments on this attitude: 'Selon Fontenelle... les idées de l'infini et du parfait sont hors de nos prises, et de pseudo-idées.'[24] It would seem more accurate to say that, for Fontenelle, the idea of infinity presupposes no contact with an actual infinity and, like the norms of reason, is true so long as it is conceptually useful and not disproved (ibid 397–8). Bayle similarly suggests that reason can provide hypotheses and that these may be regarded as valid as long as they are not contradicted by experience, but as soon as a hypothesis is so contradicted it is relegated to the status of 'raisonnemens métaphysiques':

Disputer contre ce que je soûtiens, n'est autre chose qu'opposer des raisonnemens métaphysiques à une vérité de fait, comme ce Philosophe qui vouloit prouver qu'il n'y a point de mouvement. On me permettra... de me servir de la méthode de Diogene, qui sans répondre pied à pied aux subtilitez de Zénon, se contenta de marcher en sa présence : car rien n'est plus propre à convaincre un honnête homme, qu'il raisonne sur de fausses hypotheses, que de lui montrer qu'il combat contre l'expérience. (*Pensées diverses* II 35)

Hypotheses and suppositions, in which lie the chief superiority of reason over the senses, are therefore also made to serve fact and experience.

Because reason cannot provide the first principles of knowledge and must rely on experience, Bayle and Fontenelle refuse to adhere to any one system of explanation. The doubt and scepticism they bring to any proposition is formed around the question 'Is there sufficient factual evidence?' Bayle, in the letter (29 May 1681) to his brother in which he refuses the title of Cartesian, asserts that the systems of philosophers must be treated as conjectures: 'Je suis un philosophe sans entêtement et qui regarde Aristote, Épicure, Descartes comme des inventeurs de conjectures' (see É. Labrousse *Pierre Bayle* II [1964] 39). He agrees with the view expressed by the experimenter and dissector Claude Perrault in the preface to his *Essay de physique* of 1680: 'Je ne sçaurois estre de l'opinion de la plus grande partie des Philosophes qui veulent que dans la Physique on s'attache à un seul système.' Given that Fontenelle praised Perrault in his *Éloge de M. Perrault* of 1688, the latter's views may have had some influence on him and on Bayle. Like Galileo and in opposition to Descartes, Bayle and Perrault attach less importance to systematization of thought than to individual facts. Fontenelle exclaims: 'Assurons-nous bien du fait, avant que de nous inquieter de la cause... Je ne suis pas si convaincu de nostre ignorance par les choses qui sont, et dont la raison nous est inconnuë, que par celles qui ne sont point, et dont nous trouvons la raison. Cela veut dire que non seulement nous n'avons pas les Principes qui menent au vray, mais que nous en avons d'autres qui s'accommodent tres-bien avec le faux' (*Histoire des oracles* 30–3). Rejecting a priori ideas and deductive systems, Bayle and Fontenelle seek evidence which stands outside reason and yet satisfies the demands of reason for clarity and precision, for 'raisons suffisantes' (ibid 9) and for 'propositions prouvées demonstrativement' (*Pensées diverses* I 27). Although such evidence, thus pruned by reason, may not always provide certainty and may not be a sufficient basis for generalization, it is in their view preferable to a priori judgment.

Nevertheless, in relation to tradition, custom, and popular opinion, reason performs a function for Bayle and Fontenelle very similar to Cartesian reason. As an instrument of scepticism and critical analysis it achieves a degree of detachment from the inconstancy of the natural and human world. Fontenelle, for example, speaks very much like Descartes: 'Pour quitter une opinion commune, ou pour en recevoir une nouvelle, il faut faire quelque usage de sa raison, bon ou mauvais, mais il n'est point besoin d'en faire aucun pour rejetter une opinion nouvelle, ou pour en prendre une qui est commune. Il faut des forces pour resister au torrent, mais il n'en faut point pour le suivre' (*Histoire* 79). And he deplores the power of 'un faux merveilleux' over the human mind (*Entretiens* 64). Moreover, reason delimits the areas in which credulity is legitimate. Bayle criticizes the recipient of his *Pensées* for his readiness to submit to mystery: 'Vous étiez accoutumez par vôtre caractere de Theologien à ne plus raisonner, dès que vous croyez qu'il y a du mystere, ce qui est une docilité fort loüable, mais qui ne laisse pas quelquefois par le trop d'étenduë qu'on luy donne, d'empiëter sur les droits de la raison, comme l'a fort bien remarqué Monsieur Pascal' (*Pensées diverses* 140).

Thus Bayle and Fontenelle also oppose reason to custom and prejudice, but they do so because reason is capable of examining the factual evidence and not because it can make contact with constant and universal truths above empirical reality. They do not deplore the limitations of reason but, revising the conception of its functions and potential, set aims for man's reason which are within its capacities however limited these may be.

It is through error, they believe, that reason has made and will make progress. Being fallible, reason requires the false in order to discover where and how to seek the truth. Fontenelle pays his famous tribute to the ancients that they exhausted most of the mistakes which could and had to be made and so saved him and his contemporaries a great deal of trouble. The seventeenth century will no doubt do the same for its progeny (*Digression sur les anciens et les modernes* 165–7). Pascal, to some extent, shares this view of reason progressing. In the *Préface sur le traité du vide*, he points out that mankind like a child grows in knowledge, 'car il tire avantage non seulement de sa propre expérience, mais encore de celle de ses prédécesseurs' (*Œuvres* 231). Speaking of advances in knowledge, Fontenelle adds: 'Il faut même souvent qu'elles soient aidées par des expériences que le hasard seul fait naître, et qu'il n'amène pas à point nommé. Il est évident que tout cela n'a point de fin' (*Digression* 166). However, unlike Pascal, he extends the development of reason to all fields of knowledge except revelation. He agrees that man is usually wrongly situated to judge well – too near to himself and too far from others (*Entretiens* 80–1). But he considers that the process of presenting opposing views is essentially creative even in the study of man.

The follies of man are a necessary part of the natural order. For Fontenelle and for Bayle history becomes a science of human error. It can achieve this status because the false in human nature – the *caprices* and *raisons* which direct affairs – may itself be part of a larger order, a natural order as yet unknown to man. Like Pascal, they regard history as the product of whims and inconsequential events. They insist that no great or high reason determines the flow of human events, just as Pascal says that the whole of history would have been different had Cleopatra's nose been shorter. Propounding a view of history which sharply contrasts with that of Bossuet, Fontenelle says: 'J'aime à donner de petites origines aux grandes choses, cela me paroist naturel, et digne du jeu de la fortune' (*Histoire* 88; cf Bayle *Pensées diverses* II 244–7). Unlike Pascal (or Montaigne), however, he maintains that a science can be made of the study of man's past follies and errors: 'Ne cherchons donc autre chose dans les fables que l'histoire des erreurs de l'esprit humain... Ce n'est pas une science que de s'être rempli la tête de toutes les extravagances des Phéniciens et des Grecs ; mais c'en est une de savoir ce qui a conduit les Phéniciens et les Grecs à ces extravagances' (*De l'origine* 40).[25] The historian is himself material for study and cannot be assumed to be correct: 'Les discussions historiques sont encore plus susceptibles de cette sorte d'erreur. On raisonne sur ce qu'ont dit les Historiens, mais ces Historiens n'ont-ils esté ny passionez, ny credules, ny mal instruits, ny negligens ? Il en faudroit trouver un qui eust esté spectateur de toutes choses, indifferent, et appliqué' (*Histoire* 34). Whereas, for Pascal, 'les lois naturelles' are not given expression in human affairs, Fontenelle can treat history as a science because he believes the errors of the human mind are a part of the natural order of things or, as Bayle says, of 'le cours de la Nature' (*Pensées diverses* II 235).

Pascal nowhere suggests (and in the *Pensées* emphatically denies) that the development of reason, which he describes in the *Préface*, will affect man's *mœurs*. Fontenelle, in contrast, is confident that while reason may not direct the inner personality of man it will raise his general standard of civilization even if for the majority this remains only a veneer. Marsak maintains: '[Fontenelle's] recognition of the fact that the *mœurs* of a society are determined by the ideas that are overlaid on the passions allowed him to give reality to the idea of social change.'[26] Despite the apparently haphazard nature of the process, the way in which reason will develop follows a pattern which is, in a sense, preordained. Just as nature must abide by certain laws, so there is a law of human thought. Under the heading 'Analogie de la matiere et de l'esprit,' Fontenelle says: 'Dieu a donné des loix au mouvement. Il a donné des loix à la pensée' (*De la connaissance* 401). There is an order which regulates the progress of thought, for each idea develops only after a certain number of preceding ideas and when its time to flourish has come. Such is his thought in 1727 (*Préface des éléments de la géométrie de l'infini* 42).

The truth of the external world with which the reason of Pascal, Bayle, and Fontenelle can make contact is a constant truth, but unlike the truths of the universalists it cannot be equally accessible to all men at all times. 'Quoique toujours égale en elle-même,' Pascal says, 'elle [la nature] n'est pas toujours également connue' (*Œuvres* 231). Nature, Fontenelle remarks, does not always show itself in its entirety. Consequently, while experimental or experiential truth is liable to be only partial, it nevertheless corresponds with nature: 'Quoique dans les idées des sens la nature des choses ne se montre pas toute, c'est pourtant parce que la nature des choses est telle, qu'elles se montrent d'une certaine manière, en tant qu'elles se montrent. Ainsi ce qu'on en voit a sa vérité' (*Fragmens* 387). Reason is fallible and the truths to which it has access are often incomplete. Nevertheless, it develops in such a way as to represent progress towards ever greater precision, knowledge, and order. Thus Fontenelle integrates Descartes's confidence in reason and his belief that man's ideas derive from the same source as the laws of nature with the view of Montaigne, Pascal, and the *libertins* that reason has no direct access to truth and cannot control or alter man's fundamentally irrational nature. The scepticism concerning man's reason expressed by Fontenelle's contemporaries Racine and Bossuet is absorbed into a philosophy of progress. Although narrowly defined as a human faculty without innate knowledge and without immediate contact with eternal truth, the reason of Bayle and Fontenelle, through its very dependence on empirical reality, achieves an effectiveness similar to the *raison* of the universalists. Its direction, however, is horizontal and lies in the accumulation of factual knowledge rather than in the immediate grasp of eternal truths.

6

Reason and beauty

Aimez donc la Raison. Que toûjours vos écrits,
Empruntent d'elle seule et leur lustre et leur prix.
Boileau *L'art poétique* I 37

Throughout the seventeenth century *raison* is associated with *beauté*. Both the universalists and more empirical writers make this connection. But identical vocabulary does not necessarily reflect identical conceptions: in some uses *raison* links man with higher truth and is the source of inner order; in others it is a cerebral faculty dissociated from feeling and dependent on cumulative knowledge. Awareness of this difference has an immediate impact on the interpretation of aesthetic rationalism. If the use of *raison* to refer to a cerebral faculty is assumed to be the basis of classical doctrine, this doctrine appears to be undermined by contradictory tendencies such as the appeals to nature, to sentiment, and to the pleasure-giving quality of art. Soreil, for example, remarks that these appeals 'sont de nature à ruiner le rationalisme esthétique.'[1] However, this narrow use of *raison*, while found in Montaigne, Pascal, and *libertin* writers and included in the universalists' conception, is not predominant until the latter part of the century and then only in certain authors.

Accordingly, it is only when the ideal of reason comes to be seen as relative and changing and when human reason is separated from feeling that the aesthetics based on reason conflict with those which seek to inspire and to please. On the whole, classical writers regard *raison* itself as ineffable and they seek a beauty which in the first instance corresponds to man's reasonable nature as distinct from the ratiocinations of logic. An understanding of these differences helps to resolve many apparent inconsistencies in individual authors and in classical doctrine as a whole.

For authors who conceive of two realities, or who use words as if they held such a conception, *raison* is ultimately connected with all perfections. Thus, for the universalists, reason is related to beauty as much as to justice and to truth. Reason and beauty have similar attributes: both are seen as constant and can be predicated of God. Chapelain, who calls upon 'la raison qui n'est point sujette au changement' (*La pucelle* 266), speaks also of 'cette beauté universelle, qui doit plaire à tout le monde' (*Les sentimens de l'Académie françoise* 356). While Fénelon refers to God as 'la raison souveraine,' André Félibien calls him 'cette Beauté souveraine' (*Entretiens sur les vies et les ouvrages des peintres* I 42). Since beauty, like reason, can refer to the eternal, Ramsey's conclusion can be applied here[2]: in so far as beauty refers to the eternal, it represents the sum of, and more than the sum of, all perfections. In the light of these similarities, further parallels may be expected. Like reason, beauty is associated with truth and with a true nature which is at once superior to sense reality and yet contained in some degree within that reality. Also, just as there is a right and a corrupt reason, there is a true and a false beauty.

Central to the classical notion of art is the view that there is only one true beauty. This view is held by the universalists and also by Pascal. In a letter to Chantelou (20 March 1642), Poussin compares the beauty of buildings to that of young women: 'Les belles filles que vous aurez vues à Nîmes ne vous auront, je m'assure, pas moins délecté l'esprit par la vue que les belles colonnes de la Maison Carrée, vu que celles-ci ne sont que de vieilles copies de celles-là' (*Lettres et propos* 53). An acquaintance of Méré exclaims: 'Mon Dieu... que je voudrois ressembler à cette lettre, et qu'on me trouveroit jolie ! ' (*Œuvres* II 60). Félibien remarks:

Nous voyons que les Architectes, les Sculpteurs et les Peintres, tiennent tous des chemins différens quoiqu'ils tâchent d'arriver à un même but ; et que les plus éclairez connoissent qu'il y a une raison de beauté positive. Cependant ils n'ont pu encore découvrir cette raison si cachée, et pourtant si vraye, par le moyen de laquelle ils pourroient établir des regles assurées et démonstratives, pour faire des ouvrages qui pussent aussi-bien satisfaire les yeux, comme avec le temps on a trouvé moyen de satisfaire l'ouïe par des proportions harmoniques. (*Entretiens* III 360)

In a famous passage (§585) of the *Pensées*, Pascal explains that the unique model of beauty can be found in a great variety of forms – in a woman, a bird, a song, a poem – and adds that in each this model necessarily pleases and corresponds in some way to man's nature:

Il y a un certain modèle d'agrément et de beauté qui consiste en un certain rapport entre notre nature faible ou forte telle qu'elle est et la chose qui nous plaît.

Tout ce qui est formé sur ce modèle nous agrée, soit maison, chanson, discours, vers, prose, femme, oiseaux, rivières, arbres, chambres, habits, etc.

Tout ce qui n'est point fait sur ce modèle déplaît à ceux qui ont le goût bon.

Et comme il y a un rapport parfait entre une chanson et une maison qui sont faites sur ce bon modèle, parce qu'elles ressemblent à ce modèle unique, quoique chacune selon son genre, il y a de même un rapport parfait entre les choses faites sur les mauvais modèles. Ce n'est pas que le mauvais modèle soit unique, car il y en a une infinité ; mais chaque mauvais sonnet par exemple, sur quelque faux modèle qu'il soit fait, ressemble parfaitement à une femme vêtue sur ce modèle.

Like Félibien, Pascal maintains: 'On ne sait ce que c'est que ce modèle naturel qu'il faut imiter' (§586).

The description of the ideal beauty is sometimes framed in language which suggests a Platonic attitude.[3] The artist and his public are said to have the capacity to perceive a universal beauty and to use this perception as the measure of quality. In this sense, it is implied that a work of art reflects a higher ideal. Thus Nicole says that beauty is the same in all ages and that, while men may be attracted by false beauties, their awareness of true beauty is never entirely destroyed; they can always be drawn back to this constant vision by means of reason:

La vraie Beauté... n'est ni variable, ni passagere ; mais... constante, certaine, et au goût de tous les tems. Car quoi qu'il y ait des esprits assez dereglez pour la mépriser, ils sont en petit nombre, et la force de la raison peut enfin les ramener à la verité. Et si la fausse beauté a ses Partisans, elle ne sçauroit les garder long-temps contre la nature qui leur inspire du dégoût pour ce qui ne vient pas d'elle, et comme dit Ciceron : *Le temps détruit les chimeres de l'opinion, et confirme les jugemens de la nature...* [La lumière de la raison] nous conduira d'abord à la nature ; elle nous apprendra pour regle génerale qu'une chose est belle, lorsqu'elle a de la convenance avec sa propre nature, et avec la nôtre... Affin qu'une chose soit belle, il ne suffit pas qu'elle convienne à sa nature, il faut qu'elle ait rapport à la nôtre. (*Traité de la vraie et de la fausse beauté* 171–3)

Méré insists that, despite appearances to the contrary, there is indubitably one true taste, a taste which is reliable and in no way derived from fantasy:

La pluspart sont persuadez, qu'il ne faut pas disputer du goust, et j'approuve assez qu'on ne dispute de rien ; mais si l'on entend par-là, qu'il n'y a point de raison pour montrer qu'on a le goust bon, ou qu'on l'a mauvais, et que cela ne dépend que de la fantaisie, c'est une erreur. Car le bon goust se fonde toûjours sur des raisons tres-solides ; mais le plus souvent sans raisonner. Il consiste à sentir, à quel point de bonté sont les choses qui doivent plaire, et à preferer les excellentes aux mediocres. (*Œuvres* II 128–9)

La Bruyère thinks that there is a point of perfection in art as in nature: 'Il y a dans l'art un point de perfection, comme de bonté ou de maturité dans la nature. Celui qui le sent et qui l'aime a le goût parfait ; celui qui ne le sent pas, et qui aime en deçà ou au-delà, a le goût défectueux. Il y a donc un bon et un mauvais goût, et l'on dispute des goûts avec fondement' (*Des ouvrages de l'esprit* 10). And La Rochefoucauld says: 'La vérité est le fondement et la raison de le perfection et de la beauté. Une chose, de quelque nature qu'elle soit, ne sauroit être belle et parfaite, si elle n'est véritablement tout ce qu'elle doît être, et si elle n'a tout ce qu'elle doît avoir' (*Maximes supprimées* 263). Elsewhere he observes: 'Il y en a qui sont sensibles à ce qui est bon, et choqués de ce qui ne l'est pas ; leurs vues sont nettes et justes, et ils trouvent raison de leur goût dans leur esprit et dans leur discernement... Mais, à parler généralement, il y en a peu de gens qui aient le goût fixe et indépendant de celui des autres : ils suivent l'exemple et la coutume et en empruntent presque tout ce qu'ils ont de goût' (*Réflexions diverses* 305–6). The Platonic element in this view of beauty is perhaps most evident in a passage of Bossuet's *Logique* to which Brody has drawn attention.[4] Bossuet remarks that the architect takes as his model an inner idea of which temporal buildings are only reflections. He says that this idea remains intact irrespective of the ruins which may surround the artist: 'Dans la pensée de l'architecte est l'idée primitive d'une maison qu'il aperçoit en lui-même : cette maison intellectuelle ne se détruit par aucune ruine des maisons bâties sur ce modèle intérieur ; et si l'archi-tecte étoit éternel, l'idée et la raison de maison le seroient aussi' (*Œuvres complètes* XXIII 291).

In these passages only Nicole uses the word *raison* to refer to the faculty which perceives beauty. He says that reason is capable of ensuring a con-stancy in human response and of recalling man to his 'true nature.' Aware-ness of beauty appears to be dependent, in his view, on man's contact with this true nature. While Méré, La Bruyère, and La Rochefoucauld do not speak of *raison* as a faculty, their conception of good taste is strikingly similar to their notion of a true judgment based on reason.[5] The truth which is in accord with reason, La Bruyère says, 'vient du Ciel toute faite.' Constant beauty and universal good taste would thus seem to be corollaries of the norm *raison-vérité*. In other words, he who recognizes higher truth and reason also recognizes the unique model of beauty and he who uses his reason and exercises good judgment also possesses good taste.

Indeed beauty is often connected with *vérité*, and the constant element in man which perceives beauty is often referred to as *raison*. Numerous examples could be given. Poussin remarks (in a letter to Chantelou, 24 November 1647): 'Nos appétits ne doivent pas juger seulement, mais la raison' (*Lettres et propos* 123). Nicole and Arnauld hold that an awareness that only the true is beautiful is fundamental to the study of rhetoric (*La logique* 30). Nicole says: 'Tout ce qui n'est pas conforme a la raison nous blesse' (*Traité* 183) and 'La source de la beauté est dans la verité, et la fausseté au contraire ne fournit rien que de mauvais' (191). La Rochefoucauld agrees: 'La vérité est le fondement et la raison de la perfection et de la beauté' (*Maximes* 262). These remarks throw light on the theoretical background of Boileau's well-known words: 'Rien n'est beau que le Vrai. Le Vrai seul est aimable' (*Epistre IX* 43) and 'Aimez donc la Raison' (*L'art poétique* I 37).

Commenting on Chapelain's view that 'l'ordinaire des hommes... jugent par leurs sens' (*Les sentimens* 158), Bray has suggested that according to classical doctrine only the well-born and the educated have access to good taste.[6] However, the universalists repeatedly assert that all men have reason. The apparently élitist character of some of the above statements would thus seem to be due to the assumption that most men fail to free themselves from the influence of their appetites and prejudices and so never make contact with a universal truth which is available to them. Chapelain explains: 'Je négligeay de plaire à un si mauvais juge [que le commun]... pensant à me conformer à la raison qui est éternelle au lieu de suyvre le goust variable des siècles qui change à tous coups comme enfant du caprice et qui n'a de règle que le desreglement' (lettre à Ferrari, 15 juin 1667, *Lettres* II 655). Saint-Evremond states this conception of good taste very clearly: 'Si l'idée que tous les hommes ont naturellement de la vraie beauté des ouvrages d'esprit n'étoit effacée par un grand nombre de faux jugemens, il n'y auroit pas de si differentes opinions sur leur mérite ; car cette idée seroit une régle certaine que l'on seroit obligé de suivre' (*De la vraie et de la fausse beauté* 106).

In appealing to truth and to reason these authors stress that there is an element in human nature which is at least potentially constant and through which contact with universal beauty is possible. Although Pascal does not speak of reason as the faculty which perceives beauty, it seems likely that he links the ideal model of beauty with higher truth, justice, and reason, all of which are, in his view, accessible only to man's *cœur* or *instinct*. Because Pascal's model consists in a relationship between 'notre nature' and 'la chose qui nous plaît' it does not follow, as Louis Marin assumes,[7] that this model is purely subjective. Pascal thinks that *l'agrément* should be derived from *le vrai*: 'Eloquence. Il faut de l'agréable et du réel, mais il faut que cet agréable soit lui-même pris du vrai' (*Pensées* §667). Like the universalists, Pascal may therefore connect the unique model of beauty with a constant human nature, although he does not refer to this nature as *raison*. In the fragment in which he attributes beauty to imagination – 'l'imagination dispose de la beauté, la justice, et le bonheur qui est le tout de l'homme' (§44) – he clearly means that imagination usually decides, not that it always does so. Topliss observes that Pascal tends to say always or all when he means usually or most.[8] Like Chapelain and Méré, Pascal considers that man is on the whole swayed by the inconstant in his nature and invents false beauties but is nevertheless capable of a more exact response and of recognizing true beauty. Thus it is arguable that Pascal's view of the relationship between beauty and human nature is similar to that of the universalists.

This conclusion does not take into account what Pascal means when he says that beauty corresponds to man's nature, 'faible ou forte telle qu'elle est.' It is not immediately apparent how this remark can be reconciled with the view that beauty conforms to a constant human nature. But, except in broadest outline, it is still unclear what is meant by this constant nature. Tourneur has suggested a parallel between Pascal's view of beauty and of Christianity[9]: each represents a synthesis which stands above and between the contradictory characteristics of human nature. Pascal's conception of man's reasonable nature – whereby reason or the reasoning faculty submits to the heart and whereby the inconstant movement of the imagination and passions is held in abeyance – resembles that of the universalists except that they tend to identify this reasonable nature with *raison*. It may be that in suggesting a correspondence between the ideal of beauty and human nature both Pascal and the universalists consider that beauty is perceived and experienced by man's reasonable nature. If this is so, imitation of the ideal model of beauty will not necessarily preclude the artist's imitation of man's weaknesses or his appeal to the weaknesses of the public. Provided these can be used to draw man into his reasonable nature, the source of all virtue and truth, they need not contravene the demand for an absolute beauty and reason. While Pascal appeals to a constant model of beauty and at the same time claims that this model corresponds to the ambivalence of human nature, Boileau and other classical writers assert that there is nothing in nature, however deformed and ugly, which cannot be rendered beautiful by art.

Thus the manner in which Pascal perceives beauty as related to the imperfections of human nature may parallel the way in which the universalists
relate beauty to the defects of nature.

Critics have remarked upon naturalistic and custom-orientated tendencies
in classical theory and these have been regarded as inconsistent with the
search for the unique and universal model of beauty. Lanson suggests that
there is a conflict between the desire for the constant and universal and the
acceptance of the imperfections and peculiarities of nature. He says that
Boileau follows the doctrine of Aristotle and considers that poetry, without
copying reality, should seek the truth common to all reality.[10] At the same
time, he sees naturalistic tendencies in Boileau's theory of art. He quotes the
lines 'Un Esprit né chagrin plaist par son chagrin mesme' (*Epistre IX* 88)
and 'Il n'est point de Serpent ni de Monstre odieux, / Qui par l'art imité ne
puisse plaire aux yeux' (*L'art poétique* III 1–2) and concludes: 'Cette
théorie de la poésie classique... est une théorie essentiellement et franche-
ment naturaliste.'[11]

Haley has pointed to a conflict between the desire for the universal and the
concern to please the public. In her discussion of Racine's plays, she says
that the search for the universal is countered by reverence for the 'vraisemblable' and the 'bienséant.' She treats these two principles as referring to
that which is acceptable to the current beliefs and customs of the French
public and concludes: 'We see, then, that the opinions and beliefs of the
public play an absolutely preponderant role in Racine's poetics.'[12]

While such conflicts between the demand for the absolute and acceptance
of imperfection may be present in classical thought, it is not clear that they
are to be found where Lanson and Haley claim to discover them. The words
vérité, *vraisemblance*, and *nature* are not used consistently to represent either
the absolute or the temporal. Thus it must be asked whether Boileau, when
he says 'la Nature est vraye' (*Epistre IX* 86) and then 'le Vrai peut quelquefois n'estre pas vraisemblable' (*L'art poétique* III 48), is suggesting that the
ideal *vérité* associated with *raison* must at some point give way to that which
is in accord with public opinion and whether he really sees the imitation of
imperfect nature as incompatible with the imitation of an ideal truth and
nature.

Both *vérité* and *vraisemblance* are used at times to refer to 'les choses
comme elles doivent être.' La Rochefoucauld, after insisting that 'la
vérité est le fondement et la raison de la perfection et de la beauté,' goes
on to say that nothing is beautiful unless it is all that it should be. Many
authors, in contrast, use *vérité* to refer to things as they are and *vraisemblance*
to signify things as they should be. Thus the latter is used not just to mean a

'semblance of truth,'[13] but also to invoke an ideal truth. Rapin, for example, in *Les réflexions sur la poétique* (41), uses *vérité* to refer to ordinary mixed reality and *vraisemblance* to represent the appearance of perfection bestowed on reality by the artist:

Outre que la vray-semblance sert à donner de la créance à ce que la poésie a de plus fabuleux : elle sert aussi à donner aux choses que dit le poète un plus grand air de perfection que ne pourroit faire la vérité mesme, quoique la vray-semblance n'en soit que la copie. Car la vérité ne fait les choses que comme elles sont ; et la vray-semblance les fait comme elles doivent estre. La vérité est presque toujours défectueuse, par le mélange des conditions singulières, qui la composent. Il ne naist rien du monde qui ne s'éloigne de la perfection de son idée et y naissant. Il faut chercher des originaux et des modèles, dans la vray-semblance et dans les principes universels des choses : où il n'entre rien de matériel et de singulier qui les corrompe.

This passage reveals a concern with Aristotle's distinction between historical and poetic truth but it also shows a distinctly Platonic attitude. Butcher's commentary on Aristotle's *Poetics* is here instructive. He says that nature in Aristotle is not 'the outward world of created things' since (he quotes Aristotle) 'the artist may "imitate things as they ought to be," he may place before him an unrealized ideal.'[14] Thus, in this matter, the Aristotelian influence merges easily with a Platonic attitude. Like La Rochefoucauld, Rapin requires that the artist should seek the universal and pure idea behind the object rather than the particular and unsatisfactory shape of the object itself. This idea, however, he calls *vraisemblance* and contrasts it to *vérité*, which he uses to refer to defective reality.

In his discussion of tragedy, Chapelain often uses these words *vérité* and *vraisemblance* in the same sense as Rapin. He says that in a historical play 'le poète ne considère point la vérité mais seulement la vraisemblance, sans se rendre esclave des circonstances qui accompagnent la vérité des événements' (*Les sentimens* 170). Commenting on Ferdinand's recommendation that Rodrigue should marry despite his crime, Chapelain identifies *vraisemblance* with that which is in accord with reason. *Raison*, he suggests, seeks the *vraisemblable*, if necessary at the expense of historical truth:

Or c'est principalement en ces occasions que le poète doit préférer la vraisemblance à la vérité, qu'il doit plutôt travailler sur une chose toute feinte pourvu qu'elle soit conforme à la raison... il la doit plutôt changer tout entière [l'histoire] que de lui laisser une seule tache incompatible avec les règles de son art ; lequel cherche l'universel des choses et les épure des défauts et des irrégularités particulières que l'histoire, par la sévérité de ses lois, est contrainte d'y souffrir. (ibid 164–5)

Corneille himself uses *vérité* and *vraisemblance* in this sense in the *Examen* of *Pompée*: 'Cette unité [de lieu] n'a rien que de vraisemblable, pourvu qu'on se détache de la vérité historique' (*Œuvres* IV 20). Whether called *vérité* or *vraisemblance*, the aim in these passages is the same: a truth, a reality, beyond that known to the senses, beyond that provided by history, a truth which is 'conforme à la raison.' Praising Leonardo, Félibien says: 'Il parut comme une Aigle généreuse s'élever au dessus de toutes choses visibles, pour contempler les idées plus parfaites dont il formoit ses Ouvrages... La Nature est représentée dans une beauté et une perfection, qu'elle semble n'avoir jamais fait voir qu'à ces grands hommes' (*Entretiens* I 223). Like Bossuet, who explores the hidden direction behind the events of history, and unlike Bayle and Fontenelle who are concerned only with the factual reality of events, La Rochefoucauld, Rapin, Chapelain, and Félibien consider that the artist's task is to seek the perfection and purity which, they believe, lies behind his subject.

Since *vérité* refers sometimes to ordinary reality and sometimes to an ideal reality, it is almost certain that Boileau when he says that the artist must seek only the true means *vérité* in La Rochefoucauld's sense (an ideal truth), while when he remarks that the true is sometimes not *vraisemblable* he means 'le vrai' in Rapin's sense (ordinary mixed reality). This is not to say that the meaning of *vraisemblable* is thus exhausted. But it is clear that *vraisemblance* is not confined, as Haley suggests, simply to that which is currently acceptable to the taste and beliefs of the public. *Vraisemblance* does not represent only a principle of adaptation to custom and public opinion conflicting with *raison-vérité* which stands for the constant, universal, and unchanging. Like *vérité*, it can refer to the universal and, consequently, although Boileau appeals to both principles, he may be consistently requiring that the artist seek only the universal.

Nature, in the aesthetic context as in the moral is also used to refer both to the universal and to the temporal. Pascal calls the invisible model which the artist must imitate 'ce modèle naturel' (*Pensées* §586). As Saint-Girons has noted, *naturel* is used here in the same sense as in the phrase 'les lois naturelles,'[15] that is, to signify a truth which is man's by right but which has been lost through human corruption. Blondel, in contrast, says: 'L'Art ne s'est éloigné du cours severe de la Nature, que pour luy donner plus de grace et de beauté' (*Cours* 143). *Nature* here refers to the temporal, to the same level of reality as the historical truth contrary to reason which, according to Chapelain, the dramatist must surmount. At the same time, Blondel comments that *nature* teaches the artist certain precepts, for example 'L'ordre de la Nature... veut que le fort porte le foible' (ibid 88). Poussin draws on the same precept and says that it is taught by nature and by reason. Speaking of bad artists he remarks (in an undated letter to Sublet de Noyers): 'Ils ne savent pas que c'est contre l'ordre et les exemples que la nature même nous fournit, de poser les choses plus grandes et plus massives aux endroits les plus élevés.' He goes on to explain that buildings must have a natural appearance 'comme la nature et la raison enseignent' (*Lettres et propos* 63–4). In this use of *raison* and *nature*, Poussin is appealing to an awareness of a reality which is above or outside sense-experience. It is to such an awareness that La Bruyère appeals when he says there is a point of perfection in art as in nature and this point is known only to him who has good taste. It could be that Boileau also refers to such a reality when he says 'Mais la Nature est vraye.'

If the function of the artist's reason is to imitate in some sense the perfect idea which he sees within an object of nature, it is no contradiction to suggest, as Boileau does, that by art the ugliest thing can be made beautiful and in accord with reason. In a passage which anticipates the aesthetics of Du Bos and, indeed, of romanticism, Félibien speaks similarly about the painter and dramatist: 'Quoi que les tragédies représentent des actions funestes et fâcheuses, elles ne laissent pas de divertir les spectateurs ; et... j'ai souvent vû des Tableaux où il n'y avoit rien que d'affreux et de difforme, qui arrêtoient agréablement les yeux, parce que ces sortes de choses étoient représentées avec beaucoup d'art' (*Entretiens* I 189). The artist supplies a perfection to nature which is present within it but which is not immediately obvious because of the corruption which, as Rapin stresses, adulterates everything born into the world. Thus it would seem that acceptance of imperfect nature as a suitable subject for the artist does not imply (as Lanson has suggested) naturalistic tendencies contrary to the doctrine of reason.

What then is the beauty and reason which the artist takes as his model? Blondel's thoughts on architecture and painting (in the *Cours*) provide some insight. Like Boileau and Félibien, he remarks that by means of art '[la beauté] éclate... et se fait sentir dans l'ordure, pour ainsi dire, et dans la confusion' (774). He explains that the artist can effect this transformation of the monstrous into the beautiful because he gives order, proportion, and symmetry to his work: 'On trouvera que c'est la seule symmetrie et la disposition bien reglée, c'est à dire le rapport du tout à ses parties d'entr'elles, qui y produisent cette union harmonieuse que l'on appelle la Beauté, et qui nous les font regarder avec plaisir' (755–6). He says that in all the arts it is always order and proportion to which man responds (785–6) and he maintains that this response is natural to man and does not derive from custom: '[La] beauté se rend maistresse de nos esprits et de nos sens, plutost par quelque cause née avec nous et insinuée dans nostre ame par la nature que par l'opinion' (763–4). Hence it would seem that for the classicist the ideal model of beauty consists in an order which the artist perceives and attempts to convey through his materials: it refers to a harmony between the idea and its expression and to a just proportion within the work itself which most closely portrays the perfection of the artist's vision. Clearly, such order can be presented in subjects which in themselves seem ugly, disproportionate, and confused.

The artist consequently may be described as the imitator of God who creates order out of chaos and whom Bossuet speaks of as the supreme architect. Félibien draws this parallel in his *Entretiens*. Speaking of painting, he says:

Cet Art... fournit de grands sujets de méditer sur l'excellence de cette premiere Lumiere, d'où l'esprit de l'homme tire toutes ces belles idées, et ces nobles inventions qu'il exprime ensuite dans ses Ouvrages... Si en considérant les beautez et l'art d'un Tableau, nous admirons l'invention et l'esprit de celui dans la pensée duquel il a sans doute été conceû encore plus parfaitement que son pinceau ne l'a pû executer ; combien admirerons-nous davantage la beauté de cette source où il a puisé ses nobles idées ? Et ainsi toutes les diverses beautez de la Peinture, servant comme de divers degrez pour nous élever jusqu'à cette Beauté souveraine, ce que nous verrons d'admirable dans la proportion des parties, nous fera considerer combien plus admirable encore est cette proportion, et cette harmonie qui se trouve dans toutes les Créatures. L'ordonnance d'un beau Tableau nous fera penser à ce bel Ordre de l'Univers. (142)

Raison, predicated of God, is opposed to *caprice* and to *hasard*; as an aesthetic principle it has the same association with order. Blondel and Perrault often use the word *raison* to mean simply *ratio* in the English sense of proportion, as in 'en la raison de 4 à 3' (*Cours* 754). Also Félibien defines *raison*, in the dictionary appended to *Des principes de l'architecture*, as the place in which things are rightfully situated: '*RAISON*, quand on dispose les pieces de bois qui doivent servir à un bastiment, et qu'estant mises en chantier, on met chaque morceau en sa place ; on appelle cela mettre les pieces en leur raison.' It would seem that the use of *raison* as an aesthetic principle is related to these more technical senses. Beauty is indeed inseparable from reason since both ideals have as their foundation the idea of a perfect order and symmetry.

In a letter to Chantelou (24 November 1647), Poussin uses the word *raison* to refer to measure and proportion in the work itself and he implies thereby that the artist's reason performs a corresponding function, that it is by means of his reason that the artist gives balance and measure to his work:

Cette parole 'mode' signifie proprement la raison ou la measure et forme de laquelle nous nous servons à faire quelque chose, laquelle nous astreint à ne passer pas outre, nous faisant opérer en toutes les choses avec une certaine médiocrité et modération, et, partant, telle médiocrité et modération n'est autre qu'une certaine manière ou ordre déterminé et ferme, dedans le procédé par lequel la chose se conserve en son être. (*Lettres et propos* 123–4)

André Fontaine has commented that Poussin is here suggesting a notion of art whereby the proportions (*raisons*) within the work result from the order (*raison*) of the artist's vision and creates a corresponding unity of impression in his public. Consequently, he says, the external shape of things interests Poussin only to the extent that it reveals the inner and hidden form.[16]

The association of beauty with order is prominent in literary discussion. Many authors emphasize this need for harmony between the idea and its expression. While Pascal believes that the order suited to poetry cannot be clearly defined since 'on ne sait pas en quoi consiste l'agrément qui est l'objet de la poésie,' he nevertheless considers that this 'agrément' does consist in some form of order whereby the expression or form closely suits the idea or content. He claims that we are able to recognize verses which are not in accord with the true model of beauty because they resemble a girl dressed with a lavish ostentation which fails to show off her natural beauty and tends rather to detract from it. Those who have developed a sense of good taste, he suggests, reject a work in which the language is not suited to the content and in which the parts are not harmonious (*Pensées* §586).

Emphasis on a simple and natural order within a work of art rather than on ornament and superficial splendour is the heart of La Bruyère's criticism of the gothic style. He emphasizes that literary style should follow the example of classical architecture in giving primary importance to simplicity, concluding: 'Combien de siècles se sont écoulés avant que les hommes, dans les sciences et dans les arts, aient pu revenir au goût des anciens et reprendre enfin le simple et le naturel' (*Des ouvrages de l'esprit* §15). That 'la parfaite raison fuit toute extrémité' (*Le misanthrope* I i 151) is frequently the theme of aesthetic commentary. Bouhours criticizes the Spanish language on the grounds that it exaggerates and cannot present things in their true size – like the apparentice who being unable to express the features and charm of Helen covered her with gold (*Les entretiens d'Ariste et d'Eugène* II 34). Chapelain speaks similarly of the poet: the number of verses and the richness of rhyme are only 'l'habillement du corps poétique' (*La pucelle* 288). Nicole and Arnauld comment that imagery and purity of language are like colours in a painting: they are 'la partie la plus basse et la plus materielle.' The most important prerequisite for good art is strength and clarity of conception (*La logique* 276). The disposition and form of a poem or of a work of literature or persuasive eloquence must spring from the idea or feeling of the author and are essential to its impact. Classical literature thus gives immense stress to unity and harmony between form and content, between expression and idea.

However, order within the work is insufficient and fails in its purpose unless it is also visible to the artist's public. Here the conflict remarked by Lanson and Haley between the universal and the temporal is of paramount importance. Because the order of a work must be apparent to the reader or audience, the notion of the fitting and of the rightful place, or as Poussin says of *mesure* and *raison*, is more complex than it appears at first sight. As we have seen, *bienséance* is used in moral and social contexts and, like *raison*, the *bienséant* is sometimes described as universal.[17] But *bienséance* can also be used of that which is acceptable to current *mores*. Like *vraisemblance* it can represent the temporal or customary as well as the universal. Boileau and La Bruyère shift easily from one to the other. For example, Boileau connects the reasonableness of Malherbe's poetry with the poet's ability to give the right emphasis to each word:

> Enfin Malherbe vint, et le premier en France,
> Fit sentir dans les vers une juste cadence :
> D'un mot mis en sa place enseigna le pouvoir.   (*L'art poétique* I 131–3)

La Bruyère remarks that les *bienséances* are responsible for perfection and that *raison* dictates them: 'Les belles choses le sont moins hors de leur place ; les bienséances mettent la perfection, et la raison met les bienséances' (*De quelques usages* §18). In these passages, the notion of *bienséance* appears to refer to a universal principle. The idea would seem to be similar to that of Méré who contrasts *bienséance* with custom and relates it to an ideal perfection:

La vraye bienséance ne dépend point de la fortune elle vient du cœur et de l'esprit ; tout le reste est peu considérable... J'entens cette bienseance, que le bon sens qui n'est pas prevenue sçait bien gouster. Que si l'on commet des fautes contre la coustume, elles sont bien reparées ; puisque l'on se prend aux choses comme il faudroit qu'elles fussent, pour estre dans une grande perfection.   (*Œuvres* II 128)

However, Boileau and La Bruyère also link *bienséance* with notions of propriety which, to the modern reader at least, appear to derive from custom. Boileau distinguishes the *bienséance* of different art forms:

Dans un Roman frivole aisément tout s'excuse.
C'est assez qu'en courant la fiction amuse.
Trop de rigueur alors seroit hors de saison :
Mais la Scene demande une exacte raison.
L'étroite bienséance y veut estre gardée.   (*L'art poétique* III 120–3)

La Bruyère claims that while certain things are fitting to a chapel, others are inappropriate (*De quelques usages* §18). Since the authors do not seem aware of any inconsistency it must be asked how the apparent conflict between the universal and the temporal can be resolved. Rather than representing two distinct currents in classical thought, the different emphasis in these remarks may allude to a problem which lies at the very centre of classical doctrine. Although it is believed that all men are capable of recognizing the universal it is also well accepted that the majority of men are too much bound by their appetites, by custom, and by prejudice to do so unaided. Consequently, in order to contact that which is constant in his readers or audience, an author may have to make allowance for their customs and prejudices. Appearance is in this sense of utmost importance, for if the appearance shocks it will block and impede the desired effect. An author, although he takes account of custom, may still make his aim the universal just as the architect, in Félibien's view, cannot be satisfied with correct proportions unless they are apparent to the observer from his particular standpoint: 'Ce n'est... pas encore assez de détérminer les mesures des colonnes et de tous les autres membres de l'Architecture selon la grandeur de l'édifice. Il faut qu'il y ait une proportion de ces mêmes mesures avec l'œil de celui qui les voit, c'est à dire que de l'endroit où ce même œil sera placé, il puisse découvrir toutes les beautez et les graces qui doivent paroître dans un bâtiment' (*Entretiens* I 17). While retaining its resemblance to the eternal model, the order of a work of art must be apparent from the position of the onlooker.

If custom intervenes between man and his response to universal beauty, the senses and appetites represent an even more immediate impediment and this reintroduces the problem, raised by Pascal's fragment, of the relationship of beauty to the variable in human nature. As Malebranche remarks, the beauty of an idea such as justice can be perceived solely through reason: 'Je reconnois par la raison que la Justice est aimable : je sçais aussi par le goût, qu'un tel fruit est bon. La beauté de la Justice ne se sent pas : la bonté d'un fruit ne se connoît pas' (*Recherche* I 72). But the beauty of a work of art is necessarily experienced by means of the senses and so it appeals in the first instance to man's changeable nature. Yet the universalists insist that reason and a constant nature must judge of beauty. Most classical writers resolve this difficulty by distinguishing between two types of pleasure. False beauty affords a pleasure which affects only man's inconstant nature, his senses and his appetites, and so tends to promote a disorder or *déréglement*. True beauty, however, has the virtue of elevating man into his constant or reasonable nature and affords what might be called a reasonable pleasure. Since man's reasonable nature is the source of all virtue and perfection, this pleasure is in some sense morally instructive. Méré's comment on justice – 'la justice même n'est une veritable vertu, que parce qu'elle nous conduit dans nôtre nature raisonnable' (*Oeuvres* III 99) – can thus be applied to beauty: beauty is true only if it renders man reasonable and upright and so leads him away from corruption. In other words, the beauty of a work of art can be measured by the extent to which it enables man himself to become reasonable and beautiful for, as Bossuet says, using Christian language, 'Apres Dieu, il n'y a rien de plus beau ni de plus semblable a Dieu que la creature raisonnable sanctifiée par sa grace, soumise a sa grace, pleine de ses dons, vivant selon la raison et selon Dieu' (*Traité de la concupiscence* 69). Although this second impression, of beauty which stimulates a reasonable pleasure, is, like the first, received through the senses, it penetrates beyond them and has a moral effect.

The notion of two kinds of pleasure can be illustrated first from Descartes whose views on the relationship between beauty and human nature afford an interesting comparison with Pascal. In the *Compendium musicae*, Descartes asserts that the beauty of music depends on a certain harmony between sound and sense-perception (91). But he does not appear to attribute much reliability to beauty in so far as it corresponds only with the senses. In *Les passions de l'âme* he points out that unlike the pure perceptions of reason those of beauty and ugliness 'ont ordinairement moins de verité' (392) because they depend on the intermediary of the senses. Allonnes remarks that Descartes sometimes separates beauty entirely from reason[18] and Tatarkiewicz sees in Cartesian aesthetics a subjectivism which contrasts sharply with the classical ideal.[19] However, Descartes also on occasion suggests that sense-impressions can affect reason and can give rise to what he calls an intellectual joy. Where Boileau, Félibien, and Blondel consider that the naturally ugly or imperfect can be made beautiful through art, Descartes holds that the passions of sadness and fear which are normally unpleasant can be rendered pleasing because they can be transformed by art into an intellectual pleasure:

Lors que nous lisons des avantures estranges dans un livre, ou que nous les voyons representer sur un theatre, cela excite quelquefois en nous la Tristesse, quelquefois la Joye, ou l'Amour, ou la Haine, et generalement toutes les Passions, selon la diversité des objets qui s'offrent à nostre imagination ; mais avec cela nous avons du plaisir, de le sentir exciter en nous, et ce plaisir est une Joye intellectuelle, qui peut aussi bien naistre de la Tristesse, que de toutes les autres Passions. (ibid 441)

When Pascal says of beauty '[Elle] consiste en un certain rapport entre notre nature faible ou forte telle qu'elle est et la chose qui nous plaît,' he may have in mind the same kind of correspondence between beauty and human nature as is here described by Descartes. Beauty solicits diverse emotions in man; it plays on his weakness and his strength but, in both instances, it in some sense elevates him, contributing perhaps to that state of rest between the extremes which alone, in Pascal's view, makes man reasonable and capable of faith. If beauty has this function for Pascal, it would explain why he may have intended to include considerations on aesthetics in his apology for the Christian religion.

Descartes attributes to reason the 'intellectual' pleasure afforded by art and he identifies raison with 'l'âme raisonnable.' In Les passions de l'âme, he stresses that there are no divisions within the soul; unless the impressions of the senses and the physical passions aroused by them are repugnant to reason they become appetites or volitions of reason itself (364-5). Thus, in some passages at least, Descartes appears to allow for two kinds of pleasure. Both are received through the senses, but whereas one is repugnant to reason and creates an inner conflict, the other is acceptable to reason and no conflict ensues.

Other authors also distinguish a purely sensuous pleasure from one which is reasonable. Chapelain argues that most men judge only with their senses and that they go to the theatre to be amused. Others, he says, regard pleasure as irrelevant and seek only to be instructed. He endorses a third position whereby pleasure is the sole end of art, but this pleasure must be of a particular kind. Speaking of this view, he says:

Lequel, sans s'attacher à celle qui fait de la poésie une morale déguisée, estime que le plaisir en est la seule fin, mais fait distinction de plaisir et ne lui attribue que celui qui est raisonnable. Et suivant cette doctrine on pourrait dire encore qu'il ne suffirait pas que les pièces de théâtre plussent pour être bonnes, si le plaisir qu'elles produiraient n'était fondé en raison et si elles ne le produisaient par les voies qui le rendent régulier, lesquels à peu près sont les mêmes qui sont requises pour le rendre profitable. (*Les sentimens* 159)

The pleasure provided by art must be 'fondé en raison' and this pleasure is produced by the same order and proportion which renders the work 'regulier.' Chapelain's idea is very similar to Félibien's conception of the inseparability of the beautiful and the useful in architecture. Félibien says:

Ils [les anciens] ont veû que les choses ne sont excellentes que quand elles sont utiles : qu'elles ne peuvent être utiles que par le rapport qu'elles ont entre-elles. C'est ce qui leur a fait connoître qu'il y en a qui ne sont capables de servir utilement, qu'autant qu'elles sont plus ou moins solides. Ainsi... ils ont donné plus de force aux uns et moins aux autres. Mais ils ont connu en même-temps que ce qui sert à la solidité sert aussi à la beauté. (*Entretiens* I 12)

Solidity in a work of literature lies in its moral instruction and this instructiveness ensues from elements which also engender pleasure.

Nicole, in his *Traité de la vraie et de la fausse beauté* and in the *Traité de la comédie*, argues that beauty which excites only the passions and the senses is a false beauty. Bossuet also rejects 'cette impression de beauté sensible' and, using words very similar to those of Nicole, says that the theatre's presentation of the passions constitutes 'une fragile et fausse beauté' which is 'la honte de la nature raisonnable.' He goes on to explain: 'Ils [les poètes comiques, tragiques, épiques] étalent également les bonnes et les mauvaises maximes, et... sans se soucier de la vérité, qui est simple et une, ils ne travaillent qu'à flatter le goût et la passion, dont la nature est compliquée et variable' (*L'église et le théâtre* 189, 220). Fénelon maintains that if the orator or author is not governed by that which is constant in his own nature he will excite a false and morally undesirable pleasure in his audience or reader, and he concludes: 'Quand on tâche de plaire, on a un autre but plus éloigné [que le plaisir], qui est néanmoins le principal. L'homme de bien ne cherche à plaire que pour inspirer la justice et les autres vertus, en les rendant aimables' (*Dialogues sur l'éloquence* 15–6). Boileau agrees that virtue in the artist is a necessary precondition for beauty in his work: 'Le vers se sent toûjours des bassesses du cœur' (*L'art poétique* IV 110). He too appears to assume that the pleasure afforded by art can be, indeed ought to be, a reasonable pleasure and that there is no difficulty in reconciling beauty with moral truth. Nicole and Bossuet diverge from the position of Chapelain and Boileau only in that they do not consider that the theatre is capable of producing this reasonable pleasure in the audience. Racine perhaps speaks from this same assumption that the beautiful is also the morally instructive when he says in the preface to *Phèdre* that Phèdre is his most reasonable character because she aspires to virtue and fears her own wickedness (*Oeuvres* III 299).[20]

Since the proportion and order required by reason can be a source of reasonable pleasure, the doctrine of reason in the seventeenth century is clearly not contrary to 'l'art de plaire' as Mornet has suggested.[21] Mornet speaks as if the demand that a work of art be in accord with reason means that it must be reducible to 'des règles méthodiques.' He concludes that since the art of pleasing cannot in this way be systematized, it conflicts with reason. This view is shared by a number of critics. Bray, for example, has suggested that for the classicist, the rules of art, like those of beauty and reason, are eternal.[22] Litman also identifies reason with the rules of art and treats it in opposition to the sublime.[23] It would seem however, that *raison* is not the same as 'règles méthodiques.' Since the object of art is an eternal model, the rules laid down by both ancient and modern are at best only an attempt to show the way by which the invisible order can be made visible. Although some authors, such as Chapelain whom Bray quotes, appear convinced that the rules by which beauty can be attained have been found, most authors, including Boileau, consider that the rules must never be allowed to take the place of the artist's reason, his ultimate guide and judge. Like God, the supreme architect, the artist must follow his vision, although, in being transferred to matter, it is likely to be disfigured to some degree; hence the emphasis given by many authors on a man knowing and creating, unhampered by the examples of others. Learning from others may be a necessary and even an essential prerequisite, but the rules, on their own, are regarded as always insufficient.

The thought is the same for Descartes, Balzac, La Rochefoucauld, and Félibien: one man using his reason can attain a good taste and a beauty and truth which are beyond the grasp of the multitude or of several men working together. Balzac writes to Méré (24 August 1646):

Le témoignage d'un seul qui voit clair, doit être préféré au soupçon et à l'ouïr-dire de tout un peuple d'Aveugles : Et vous avez bien plus de droit de juger des ouvrages de l'esprit, vous qui avez de l'esprit et du jugement, que ces Docteurs remarquables par le défaut de l'une et de l'autre pièce, qui se servent de la science contre la raison, et accusent Aristote de toutes leur mauvaises opinions. (*Les œuvres* I 702)

Descartes says that many hands cannot achieve the same perfect order in a work as can a single man 'usans de raison':

Il n'y a pas tant de perfection dans les ouvrages composez de plusieurs pieces, et faits de la main de divers maistres, qu'en ceux ausquels un seul a travaillé. Ainsi voit on que les bastimens qu'un seul Architecte a entrepris et achevez, ont coustume d'estre plus beaux et mieux ordonnez, que ceux que plusieurs ont taschè de raccommoder, en faisant servir de vieilles murailles qui avoient esté basties a d'autres fins... on diroit que c'est plutost la fortune, que la volonté de quelques hommes usans de raison, qui les a ainsi disposez. (*Discours de la méthode* 11–12)

In borrowing from others, who do not have the same conception and the same idea of a unified creation, the architect – and the philosopher – fail to give their works a harmonious form in which all parts tend towards the same end. Félibien says something very similar in the preface to volume I of his *Entretiens*: the architect must use his reason and must make it his principal guide. If he follows only the rules and the example of others, his work is likely to be 'un amas confus':

Aprés avoir fait voir qu'elle [la science d'un Architecte] tire ses principes de la raison, dont les lumieres doivent être l'unique guide et les seuls instrumens de celui qui travaille à de grandes entreprises, je tâche de montrer qu'un veritable Architecte n'agit pas simplement sur des exemples, et ne se conduit pas seulement par des regles que d'autres ayent pû inventer, mais qu'il se forme lui-même un modelle parfait qui n'est point composé d'un amas confus de diverses pieces prises de plusieurs autres Ouvrages, comme l'on en voit assez, son principal dessein étant toûjours de ne rien faire qui ne convienne à son sujet.

Like La Rochefoucauld, who remarks 'Il y a toujours quelque chose de faux et d'incertain dans toute imitation,' Félibien suggests that, in borrowing from others, something false and alien disrupts the unity of the artist's work. These passages from Descartes and Félibien, perhaps more than any others, speak for a close affiliation between Cartesian and classical aesthetics.

Reason is clearly separate and different from the rules of art. Brody agrees, but identifies reason with intuition: 'What else is *raison*, then, but a kind of intellectual 'sense', an eye of the mind? ... Each time Boileau enjoined in the name of Reason: *désillez les yeux, voyez, sentez ce que tous les hommes sentent d'abord*, he was appealing to intuition.'[24] The universalists' conception of reason does include an intuitive and feeling aspect enabling man to make contact with eternal truth. Méré and La Rochefoucauld hold that good taste is related to a sense or an awareness distinct from the capacity for argument or ratiocination. Méré says 'le bon goust se fonde toûjours sur des raisons tres-solides ; mais le plus souvent sans raisonner' and La Rochefoucauld implies that if explanations are found for good taste these are subsequent to immediate recognition – 'Ils trouvent raison de leur goût dans leur esprit et dans leur discernement.' Their views thus appear similar to that of M. de Roannez, as cited by Pascal: 'Les raisons me viennent après, mais d'abord la chose m'agrée ou me choque sans savoir la raison, et cependant cela me choque par cette raison que je ne découvre qu'ensuite.' Pascal, while agreeing, questions the validity of subsequent explanations and treats them as rationalizations: 'Je crois, non pas que cela choquait par ces raisons qu'on trouve après, mais qu'on ne trouve ces raisons que parce que cela choque' (*Pensées* §983). Although *raison*, for the universalists, is thus partly intuitive and, in this respect, resembles Pascal's *cœur*, it remains fundamentally a capacity for good judgment, an ability to distinguish the true from the false, true beauty from false beauty. Like eternal reason, it is connected with the capacity for ordering, for giving true proportion both to man's thought and feeling and to the materials with which he fashions a work of art. This capacity is not in fact separate from the intuitive aspect of reason. Man's innate knowledge consists in an awareness of order and proportion, for a sense of order is clearly the essence of knowing the true from the false and the whole from its parts. It is because reason is the source of order that it determines 'les bienséances' and it is because reason is also intuitive that it is able to adapt the order of a work to maximize its effect on the audience or public.

Some statements of Descartes, Méré, Pascal, and Boileau allow a closer examination of what might be termed the inner work of the artist. It would seem that the artist seeks within himself a relationship to his own idea – his thought or feeling – which is at once personal and universally available. It is by means of this inner relationship or understanding that he can give a perfect order and simplicity to his work and that this can be morally instructive. If the artist fully digests his idea and if he relates to it in the right way, he will be able to see all its ramifications and a simple and harmonious form will follow. To become simple in this sense is by no means easy and requires an honesty and integrity of unusual strength. Thus the reason of the artist represents a kind of inspiration: it is peculiar to the artist only in that he grasps his idea more fully than other men and achieves a detachment from the inconstancy of his own nature which enables him to weigh his idea and to give it suitable expression. In this sense, the artist must be 'reasonable' in order to provoke a 'reasonable' pleasure in his audience: unless he is upright and true he cannot convey an impression of truth to his public. Descartes, like Boileau, appears to associate this process with *raison*. Pascal does not stress the importance of reason in effecting this inner simplicity but his conception of the artist's inner work is nevertheless similar.

In the *Discours*, Descartes claims that the creativity of the poet depends on the natural talent – 'un don de l'esprit' – and not on learning or on knowledge of the rules of art:

J'estimois fort l'Eloquence, et j'estois amoureux de la Poësie : mais je pensois que l'une et l'autre estoient des dons de l'esprit, plutost que des fruits de l'estude. Ceux qui ont le raisonnement le plus fort, et qui digerent le mieux leurs pensées, affin de les rendre claires et intelligibles, peuvent toujours le mieux persuader ce qu'ils proposent, encore qu'ils ne parlassent que bas Breton, et qu'ils n'eussent jamais apris de Rhetorique. Et ceux qui ont les inventions les plus agreables, et qui les sçavent exprimer avec le plus d'ornement et de douceur, ne lairroient pas d'estre les meilleurs Poëtes, encore que l'art Poëtique leur fust inconnu.   (7)

Descartes is suggesting that if the poet fully digests his thought, he will excel whether or not he has been educated in the arts. He says the same of those who endeavour to understand his philosophy: they will be able to understand even if they have no learning because all men are equally endowed with *raison-bon sens*.[25] Consequently, it may be that this 'don de l'esprit' which Descartes attributes to the poet is not separate from *raison*. Descartes holds that the architect like the philosopher must use his reason and that reason rather than the opinions of others must be his guide. Now it appears that the poet's gift consists in a certain relationship to his own idea and depends on the degree to which he understands his idea: if he grasps it fully, he will excel in his art even if he has never received instruction. Descartes perhaps dismisses poetry in the *Discours* only because the poet, unlike the student of philosophy, does not require the deductive method and Descartes consequently has nothing to teach him: the inspiration of the poet's reason is sufficient to his task.

If this interpretation of Descartes's thought is correct, it correlates well with that of other classical writers. Poussin, Méré, Pascal, and Boileau claim that the writer must take his inspiration from within himself and they suggest that, if he does so in the right way, his thought will conform to universal truth. Like Pope, who says 'What oft was thought, but ne'er so well expressed,' they maintain that the impact of the artist's work depends on the way in which he possesses and formulates ideas which are accessible to all men. Poussin copied down these words from an unknown source: 'Si le peintre veut éveiller dans les âmes l'émerveillement, encore qu'il n'ait en mains un sujet habile à le faire naître, qu'il n'y introduise point de choses nouvelles, et étranges, et hors de raison, mais qu'il contraigne son esprit à rendre merveilleuse son œuvre par l'excellence de la manière, d'où se puisse dire : *materiam superbat opus*' (*Lettres et propos* 173). Blunt comments that this idea is common among Poussin's contemporaries and that it is found for example in Mascardi. He draws an interesting parallel with Racine's famous dictum in the preface of *Bérénice*: 'Toute l'invention consiste à faire quelque chose de rien.' Poussin's sentiment is more plainly echoed by Méré, Pascal, and Boileau. Méré writes: 'Il ne faut ni outrer, ni forcer, ni tirer de loin ce qu'on veut dire, cela reussît toûjours mal' (*Œuvres* I 105). Pascal remarks in *De l'art de persuader*: 'Il faut le plus souvent s'abaisser. Les meilleurs livres sont ceux que ceux qui les lisent croient qu'ils auraient pu faire. La nature, qui seule est bonne, est toute familière et commune' (358–9). And, in the *Pensées*, he says: 'Quand on voit le style naturel on est tout étonné et ravi, car on s'attendait de voir un auteur et on trouve un homme' (§675). Boileau advises the author:

Mais sans t'aller chercher des vertus dans les nuës,
Il faudroit peindre en toy des veritez connües :
Décrire ton esprit ami de la raison.   (*Epistre IX* 155–7)

He complains that few authors follow this precept. It is in this context that he describes the extreme difficulty of making reason one's guide:

La pluspart, emportez d'une fougue insensée
Toûjours loin du droit sens vont chercher leur pensée.
Ils croiroient s'abaisser, dans leurs vers monstrueux,
S'ils pensoient ce qu'un autre a pû penser comme eux.
Evitons ces excez. Laissons à l'Italie
De tous ces faux brillans l'éclatante folie.
Tout doit tendre au Bon sens : mais pour y parvenir
Le chemin est glissant et penible à tenir.
Pour peu qu'on s'en écarte ; aussi-tost l'on se noye.
La Raison, pour marcher, n'a souvent qu'une voye.   (*L'art poétique* I 39–48)

In *De l'art de persuader*, Pascal explains, like Descartes, that the force of eloquence springs from the depth of understanding with which the speaker grasps his thought and that it is this distinction in comprehension which marks the greater orator from his fellows: 'Tous ceux qui disent les mêmes choses ne les possèdent pas de la même sorte... Il faut donc sonder comme cette pensée est logée en son auteur ; comment, par où, jusqu'où il la possède' (357–8). He describes the difference between a truth superficially known and one which is deeply ingested with the metaphor Bossuet uses to distinguish false reason from true reason: the one is like 'un homme mort' and the other 'un homme plein de vie et de force.' Pascal maintains that through this deeper understanding an author is able to see all the ramifications of his ideas and so to give each its rightful place and emphasis: 'Tel dira une chose de soi-même sans en comprendre l'excellence, où un autre comprendra une suite merveilleuse de conséquences qui fait dire hardiment que ce n'est plus le même mot' (358).

While Pascal would not associate this comprehension with *raison*, his view appears very similar to that of Boileau. Like Descartes, Boileau makes no clear distinction between inspiration and reason. Venesoen has remarked on the surprising way in which Boileau moves directly from discussion of the importance of the artist's talent and inspiration to emphasis on the need for *raison-bon sens*[26] and Litman regards Boileau's thought on this matter as nothing short of muddled.[27] But Boileau seems unaware of any conflict between the following statements in *L'art poétique*:

C'est en vain qu'au Parnasse un temeraire Auteur
Pense de l'Art des Vers atteindre la hauteur.
S'il ne sent point du Ciel l'influence secrete,
Si son Astre en naissant ne l'a formé Poëte,
Dans son génie étroit il est toûjours captif.
Pour lui Phébus est sourd, et Pégaze est retif   (I 1–6)

and

Quelque sujet qu'on traite, ou plaisant, ou sublime,
Que toûjours le Bon sens s'accorde avec la Rime...
Aimez donc la Raison. Que toûjours vos écrits
Empruntent d'elle seule et leur lustre et leur prix.   (I 27–38)

In seeking to reconcile these two passages, Brody argues that *raison* for Boileau is a form of 'psychological energy,' that it is '*esprit* strengthened by the *influence secrète* of heaven.'[28] A *rapprochement* between judgment and inspiration which supports Brody's contention is suggested by some lines of Poussin, in a letter of 1 March 1665 to de Chambray: 'Il faut commencer par la disposition, puis par l'ornement, le décoré, la beauté, la grâce, la vivacité, le costume, la vraisemblance et le jugement partout. Ces dernières parties sont du peintre et ne se peuvent apprendre. C'est le rameau d'or de Virgile que nul ne peut trouver ni cueillier s'il n'est conduit par la fatalité' (*Lettres et propos* 165). It may be that Boileau, like Poussin and (I have suggested) like Descartes, regards the capacity to use reason to its full as a form of inspiration and as a sign of talent.

In *Epistre IX* where, as elsewhere, he says that the artist must be guided by reason, Boileau remarks that, in order to move his reader, the artist must speak from the heart and from an honest and full understanding of his conception:

Sçais-tu pourquoy mes vers sont lûs dans les Provinces...
Ce n'est pas que leurs sons agreables, nombreux,
Soient toujours à l'oreille également heureux...
Mais c'est qu'en eux le Vrai du Mensonge vainqueur
Par tout se montre aux yeux et va saisir le cœur :
Que le Bien et le Mal y sont prisez au juste...
Et que mon cœur toûjours conduisant mon esprit,
Ne dit rien aux Lecteurs, qu'à soy-mesme il n'ayt dit.   (47–58)

If a thought is recognized by the artist at its true value it will appear simple and natural but, just as the path to reason is slippery and arduous, so this simplicity is very difficult to achieve. In the following passage, Boileau uses *nature* in much the same sense as Pascal in the words 'la nature qui seule est bonne est toute familière':

Cessons de nous flatter. Il n'est Esprit si droit
Qui ne soit imposteur et faux par quelque endroit.
Sans cesse on prend le masque, et, quittant la Nature,
On craint de se montrer sous sa propre figure...
Le faux est toûjours fade ennuieux, languissant :
Mais la Nature est vraye, et d'abord on la sent.
C'est elle seule en tout qu'on admire et qu'on aime...
L'ignorance vaut mieux qu'un sçavoir affecté.
Rien n'est beau, je reviens, que par la verité.
C'est par elle qu'on plaist, et qu'on peut long-temps plaire.
L'esprit lasse aisément, si le cœur n'est sincere.   (ibid 69–104)

Thus, in terms of the artist's inner experience, *vérité*, *nature*, and *raison* all appear to refer to the quality of the artist's perception, to the way in which he possesses his idea and makes the universal his own. If he does so in a high degree his thought will appear simple and natural and will strike the heart of the reader, making him see a truth of which he was only dimly aware and a quality of being which he had forgotten or never fully discovered.

Consequently there would seem to be a marked similarity between Descartes's and Boileau's conception of reason as an aesthetic faculty, but this similarity does not rest, as Krantz maintains, on a rationalism devoid of Platonic elements.[29] On the contrary, the conception of the artist's reason in both Descartes and Boileau has markedly Platonic characteristics. For both, the universal is available only through the entirely personal – not through the individualistic and capricious but through that personal contact of the individual with the eternal and universal.

If *raison* itself represents a form of inspiration, and if, as Pascal and Félibien maintain, beauty cannot be finally explained, then *raison* is not opposed to the *je ne sais quoi* or the notions of *génie* and of *le sublime*. The *je ne sais quoi* by definition cannot be given methodical formulation. *Raison* too is sometimes presented as evading formulation. Chapelain, Méré, and Boileau on occasion describe it as defying the rules of art and as reaching beyond their restricting confines. In his discussion of *Le Cid*, Chapelain criticizes Corneille for following the rule of 24 hours at the expense of reason. He says that it is contrary to reason for Chimène to consent to marry her father's murderer within so short a time and that it would be better to break the rules than to commit such an offence against *raison*, *vraisemblance*, and *bienséance* (*Les sentimens* 168–9). Méré maintains that a work usually appears simple and natural when the rules are given a strictly subservient role (*Œuvres* III 104), and Boileau remarks that the critic – 'que la raison conduise, et la sçavoir éclaire' – will sometimes advise an author to abandon the rules and follow the force of his idea (*L'art poétique* IV 71–80). This does not mean that when reason defies the rules, it changes its nature and becomes haphazard emotion or imagination but rather that, through reason, the artist sees a new order more suited to the subject matter and to the effect desired than that provided by the rules.

Molière takes up a similar argument against his critics in *La critique de l'École des femmes*. Dorante, one of his characters, remarks that the reaction of the crowd is quite as valuable as that of the critics for 'le bon sens n'a point de place déterminée à la comédie' (*Œuvres* III 335). Dorante goes on to argue that if works made according to the rules fail to please, then the rules must be changed (358–9). The rules must serve the purposes of art; 'le bon sens' of the audience, not the prejudice of the critics, must assess a work. Molière's argument may not represent a protest against classical doctrine but rather an indictment of those who attempt to give a final definition to that which eludes rigid formulation.

If the order dictated by reason is in part inaccessible to the rules of art, this order itself represents a *je ne sais quoi*. Boileau attaches considerable value to the *je ne sais quoi* and he says that without it beauty itself is not beautiful. He praises the 'naïveté inimitable' of La Fontaine and comments: 'Ces sortes de beauté sont de celles qu'il faut sentir, et qui ne se prouvent point. C'est ce je ne sais quoi qui nous charme, et sans lequel la beauté même n'auroit ni grâce ni beauté' (*Dissertation sur la Joconde* 17–18). A remark by Félibien helps to explain this paradoxical statement. He considers that the *je ne sais quoi* depends on a subtle and hidden harmony and that it is not possible to formulate rules to show the artist how to give his painting an expression, a soul, suitable to the subject matter, how to make the movements of the body in a portrait express the sitter's inner state or quality of being. There can be beauty, he says, in the symmetry and proportion between the parts of the picture and this can largely be learned, but it is impossible to teach the artist to create a similar 'rapport' between the inner life and the external shape of his subject (*Entretiens* I 29–30). Thus there can be beauty, symmetry, and proportion in the lines of a work of art and yet it can still lack this additional dimension which gives greater pleasure.

This *je ne sais quoi* would seem also to be related to *génie*. Félibien, in the preface to his *Entretiens*, says that the discovery of the *je ne sais quoi* depends on 'l'excellence du genie du Peintre.' Then, like Boileau, he identifies this *génie* with *raison*: 'S'il y a un moyen pour faire davantage paroître les parties d'un Tableau, pour leur donner plus de force, plus de beauté et plus de grace ; c'est un moyen qui ne consiste pas en des règles qu'on puisse enseigner, mais qui se découvre par la lumiere de la raison, et où quelquefois il faut se conduire contre les règles ordinaires de l'Art.' Bouhours similarly identifies the source of the artist's inspiration with that which enlightens his reason:

C'est cette flâme [la plus vive et la plus ardente qui soit dans la nature] qui éclaire la raison, et qui échauffe l'imagination en mesme temps... C'est elle qui rend visibles à l'ame les especes des choses, et qui luy fait voir tous les objets dans leur jour : en un mot... c'est à la lueur de ce beau feu, que l'entendement découvre et contemple les veritez les plus obscures ; et c'est peut-estre ce feu qui brille dans les yeux des personnes spirituelles, et qui les distingue des gens stupides. (*Les entretiens* IV 123–4)

The *génie* of the poet is thus clearly related to his *raison*, but it appears to be capable of a more perfect order and harmony which are not available to the ordinary man and which elevate the genius above his fellow artists and poets.

La Bruyère and Bouhours associate genius with the capacity to combine order with enthusiasm and energy. La Bruyère expects from the preacher of genius a certain spontaneity, an impression of words flowing from a single source, an ability to hold together all the parts of his material – qualities which pertain also to reason. In addition, he emphasizes strength of feeling and the capacity to overpower an audience (*De la chaire* §29). Bouhours describes the genius of the statesman in similar terms: the genius has a fixed vision and he knows himself and his materials in such a way that he is able to master both. He is capable of order within fury, of creating or maintaining a balance and self-awareness despite apparent emotional abandon (*Les entretiens* IV 130).

Using *génie* in a rather different sense, Rapin asserts in *Les réflexions* that good judgment is an essential part of the genius of poetry: 'Quoiqu'en effet le discours du poète doive en quelque façon ressembler au discours d'un homme inspiré : il est bon toutefois d'avoir l'esprit fort serein, pour sçavoir s'emporter quand il le faut, et pour régler ses emportemens : et cette sérénité d'esprit, qui fait le sang froid et le jugement, est une des parties les plus essentielles du génie de la poésie, c'est par là qu'on se possède' (17). And he goes on to say: 'Un esprit médiocre peut imaginer un dessein vaste et grand : mais il faut un génie extraordinaire pour renfermer ce dessein dans la justesse et dans la proportion... C'est aussi la partie la plus difficile de l'art, parce que c'est l'effet d'un jugement consommé' (33). Bouhours praises the genius of the French language on the grounds that it retains an appropriate balance despite its sallies and resembles 'ces personnes raisonnables qui ne s'oublient jamais, et à qui rien n'échappe contre la bien-seance, quelque liberté qu'elles se donnent' (*Les entretiens* II 32). A sense of when and how much abandon is appropriate depends on reason and, while reason does not necessarily make the genius, there can be no genius without reason.

The two principles *génie* and *raison* are thus by no means antagonistic. Many authors stress the supreme beauty of order amid great enthusiasm and strength of feeling. Balzac exclaims on the beauty of 'la passion conduite et employée par le jugement.' This, he says, is the secret of great beauty, 'd'aymer et d'estre sage tout ensemble' (*Mélanges historiques* I 536). And in a letter to Richelieu (4 August 1630) he praises 'cette raisonnable fureur' beyond rule and precept 'qui pousse l'Orateur à des mouvemens si estranges, qu'ils paroissent plustost inspirez que naturels' (*Les œuvres* I 324). Chapelain admires Virgil as 'le seul poète qui conserve le jugement dans la fureur' and 'le seul peintre capable de bien imiter la nature' (*La pucelle* 275). Similarly, Bouhours maintains that 'le bel esprit' requires vivacity and fire as well as *bon sens*, in fact that *bon sens* is not necessarily separate from these qualities: 'Le vray bel esprit... est inseparable du bon sens ; et c'est se méprendre, que de le confondre avec je ne sçay quelle vivacité qui n'a rien de solide... Il y a une espece de bon sens sombre et morne, qui n'est gueres moins opposé à la beauté de l'esprit, que le faux brillant. Le bon sens dont je parle, est d'une espece toute differente : il est gay, vif, plein de feu' (*Les entretiens* IV 115). These arguments are of capital importance in explaining the aesthetic quality of classical rationalism. Far from being contrary to feeling or to the art of pleasing, *raison* and *bon sens* refer to a force of perception which controls and orders emotion and which itself springs, as it were, from the heart. In this sense *raison* incorporates inspiration and the modern *imagination*. While genius may go beyond the reason of the ordinary man, it is nevertheless in accord with reason. A comment of Balzac (in a letter of 25 February 1624 to de Bois Robert) perhaps sums up their relationship: 'Il y a force choses qui sont par dessus la raison, qui ne sont pas pour cela contre elle' (*Les œuvres* I 29–30).

Mille has described the relationship between reason and genius in terms of the conscious and subconscious mind. He identifies the conscious mind with reason but he suggests that the two eventually become one – the conscious effort of art is reabsorbed into the subconscious and, through the tuition of art and of study, the poet is eventually able to express himself freely and without conscious restraint: 'Cependant, la poésie n'exclut pas la raison, c'est-à-dire le conscient, mais elle a pour objet de faire monter l'inconscient jusqu'au conscient, et par un magnifique retour d'absorber le conscient dans l'inconscient.'[30] There is an element of feeling in the universalists' conception of reason and in Pascal's and Boileau's conception of the artist's internal preparation. The ideal of reason is recognized; it is not consciously appraised. The notion of *génie* extends this feeling element of reason and attains a *je ne sais quoi* or a perfection of order within enthusiasm and inspiration not accessible to conscious analysis.

The idea of the *sublime*, which is distinct from 'le stile sublime' (Boileau *Traité du sublime* 45), refers to that beauty which incorporates the *je ne sais quoi*. Boileau describes the *sublime* as simple and unpretentious and yet as striking: it appears 'libre' while being highly controlled (ibid 51). Also the *sublime*, like the ideal of reason and beauty, expresses the truth. According to La Bruyère it presents the whole truth – its cause and its effect – and it is 'l'expression ou l'image la plus digne de cette vérité.' He limits it to 'un sujet noble' (*Des ouvrages de l'esprit* 55) and says: 'Il n'a besoin que d'une noble simplicité, mais il faut l'atteindre, talent rare, et qui passe les forces du commun des hommes : ce qu'ils ont de génie, d'imagination, d'érudition et de mémoire ne leur sert souvent qu'à s'en éloigner' (*De la chaire* §26). La Bruyère describes the *sublime* in its simplicity and truth as beyond the reach of any specific human faculty or gift: yet such simplicity and truth are essential to the ideal of reason and beauty. Thus, provided reason is not regarded as necessarily 'dogmatique' and as referring solely to a logical faculty, there seems no cause to stress an opposition between *raison* and the *je ne sais quoi*, *génie*, or the *sublime*. All these terms blend to form a conception of art the ultimate aim of which is an ineffable ideal. Although this ideal is never quite realized by the artist, it is vivid and alive within his mind and he seeks through the intermediary of his art to render it equally vivid in the minds and hearts of his public.

While the universalists' conception of reason is dominant in the seventeenth century, the use of *raison* to refer to a 'bon sens sombre et morne' is found on occasion throughout the period and particularly in authors who treat reason as an empirical faculty. Thus Montaigne opposes reason to inspiration. Speaking of poetry, he says: 'La bonne, l'excessive, la suprême, la divine, est au-dessus des règles et de la raison. Quiconque en discerne la beauté d'une vue ferme et rassise, il ne la voit pas, non plus que la splendeur d'un éclair. Elle ne pratique point notre jugement ; elle le ravit et ravage' (*Essais* I 37). Montaigne's conception of human reason resembles that of Pascal. And if Pascal does not associate reason with good taste or with the perception of beauty, it is because, like Montaigne, he considers it as a cerebral and empirical faculty dissociated from feeling. In *De l'art de persuader*, Pascal distinguishes two aspects of eloquence: one which depends on 'agrément' and another which consists in clarity of definition and argument and which, he says, depends on reason and reasoning. While in his opinion the first cannot be taught, the second, deriving from reason, is capable of methodical formulation (356).

As the empirical approach gains increasing acceptance, the separation of reason from the inexpressible and its association with the rules of art become more common. Sometimes the narrow use of *raison* coexists with the universalists' conception. For example, Rapin speaks of reason as inseparable from the rules and as contrary to genius and to the art of pleasing. Praising the work of Lope de Vega, he says: 'Il avoit l'esprit trop vaste pour l'assujettir à des règles, et pour luy donner des bornes ; ce fut ce qui l'obligea de s'abandonner à son génie : parce qu'il en estoit toujours seur. Il ne consultoit point d'autre commentaire, quand il composoit, que le goust de ces auditeurs, et il se régloit plus sur le succès de ses pièces, que sur la raison' (*Les réflexions* 120).

This narrow conception of reason is more consistently presented in the aesthetic discussion of Charles Perrault and of Fontenelle. They retain the notion of an ideal and constant beauty but no longer associate the ineffable quality of beauty with reason. Alongside eternal or 'positive' beauty, Perrault introduces the notion of an 'arbitrary' beauty derived from custom and convention and similar in this respect to the relative norm *raison-raisonnement*. He borrows this conception of two kinds of beauty in literature from his brother Claude who applies the distinction to architecture[31] and whose empirical outlook resembles that of Fontenelle and Bayle.

Referring to eloquence, Charles Perrault says that examples of positive beauty 'ne sont point de pur goust ny de fantaisie, elles sont aimées et le seront éternellement de tout le monde.' Positive beauty consists, like Pascal's 'modèle naturel,' of more than demonstrable argument and definable rules. It includes some of the qualities which Pascal associates with 'l'agrément,' namely, the capacity to make contact with the feelings and sympathies of an audience (*Parallèle des anciens et des modernes* 192). But Perrault does not connect this indefinable aspect of beauty with reason. He uses *raison* only in the sense in which Montaigne and Pascal employ it – to refer to man's logical faculty. In the following passage, he stresses the inadequacy of human reason for the attainment of positive beauty and maintains that reason by itself can create only the dry scaffolding of eloquence. Criticizing Demosthenes, he says:

L'Eloquence de Demosthene est fort eloignée d'avoir du fard et des ajustemens superflus. Elle n'a pas mesme l'essentiel de la beauté ; ce qu'il dit est droit et de bon sens, mais ce n'est pas assés, il ne suffit pas pour estre belle de n'avoir pas la taille gastée et contrefaite, d'avoir deux yeux... La raison et le bon sens sont des conditions sans lesquelles il ne peut y avoir de veritable Eloquence, mais ils ne sont pas pour cela l'Eloquence, de mesme que les fondemens solides d'un bel édifice, ne sont point ce bel édifice.   (ibid 221)

Here *raison* is closely related to the rules of art and, while it is an essential element in a work, it is no guarantee of beauty.

Fontenelle's conception of the relationship between reason and beauty is similar. A work is reasonable if materials are used sparingly and subjugated to the end-design. In the preface to his edition of Corneille's works, he praises the economy of Corneille's dramatic art. He says that because *Mélite* was criticized by the public for being too simple, Corneille filled his next play, *Clitandre*, with a vicious profusion of incident. Thereafter, the public allowed him to return to his former style and consequently his later plays are 'raisonnables' (ii). According to Fontenelle, Corneille discovered the true rules for dramatic poetry: 'Il lui a donné [au théâtre] le premier une forme raisonnable ; il l'a porté à son plus haut point de perfection' (v). The word *raisonnable* continues to imply 'well-ordered' but it is associated with the economy and definable proportions of a work rather than with those qualities which elevate and stir the heart. *Raison* in art refers to an order like that which Fontenelle ascribes to personified nature.

Moreover, Fontenelle does not consider reason to be the artist's most distinctive faculty. He describes eloquence and poetry as dependent on imagination: 'L'éloquence et la poésie ne demandent qu'un certain nombre de vues assez borné, et elles dépendent principalement de la vivacité de l'imagination ; or les hommes peuvent avoir amassé en peu de siècles un petit nombre de vues, et la vivacité de l'imagination n'a pas besoin d'une longue suite d'expériences, ni d'une grande quantité de règles pour avoir toute la perfection dont elle est capable' (*Digression sur les anciens et les modernes* 166). This remark has been compared with Descartes's separation of poetry from other forms of intellectual endeavour in the *Discours de la méthode*.[32] Descartes indeed considers poetry relevant to his discussion of method but he nevertheless appears to associate artistic creativity with reason. Fontenelle, for his part, treats reason as a logical instrument dissociated from feeling and consequently he sees poetry as falling within the province of a less restricting faculty which he terms *imagination*. Thus, towards the end of the seventeenth century, both the inspiration of the artist and the indefinable qualities of beauty are sometimes separated from reason: while reason provides the necessary order of a work, it cannot in itself attain to beauty. Perrault's notion of arbitrary beauty and Fontenelle's association of beauty with imagination introduce a relativism into aesthetic theory which parallels the relativism of empirical reason.

Bray has suggested that in Fontenelle and Perrault reason is finally freed from the oppressive authority of the ancients which, he says, continually interferes with Boileau's and Chapelain's adherence to reason, preventing them from following their own precepts and from making reason their true guide.[33] But Bray does not consider the possibility that *raison* may not mean the same for Perrault as for Boileau and that the lessening of belief in the authority of the ancients is accompanied by the separation of human reason from the eternal and thus from a principle beyond the rules of art. French classical theory of art does not really become dogmatic until this separation has come about.

Conclusion

Une humanité vraiment grande n'est possible que le jour où l'intelligence n'est
pas seule intelligente, où les mœurs, où le goût, où la sensualité, où la
chair même et ses désordres participent à une même grâce, à un même
savoir.

Maulnier *Racine* 31

The dates and authors in this book were chosen so as to avoid a prejudgment
on the issue whether there is a characteristically classical reason and a
clearly definable classical period. Now, at the end of this study, some more
specific definition of classical reason and of classicism must be attempted in
the light of our investigations.

In the dictionaries and in the literature of the period *raison* has a wealth of
meanings and associations: it can refer to truth, order, good sense, prudence,
duty, right, vengeance; to explanation, cause, argument, justification; and to
a human faculty for judgment, perception, and discursive thought. Often
these senses are so closely linked that in a particular use several meanings
are conveyed. In the words of Corneille's Horace – 'Ma patience à la raison
fait place' – *raison* may refer to the reasoning faculty, to a standard which
justifies action, or simply to vengeance. Or it may refer to all of these. This
complexity of definition allows an author to compress his thought and so to
have a greater impact on his reader, but it also gives rise to vagueness and
lack of precision.

This vagueness can be useful. It would seem, as Bayet has remarked,[1] that
the most fundamental association of *raison* is with truth. Authors may sometimes use the word primarily because of this association which they can
assume is shared by their readers. By appealing to reason an author can
coerce the reader, he can assert the value of his words and demand attention.

As Peter France has noted, there is a rhetorical advantage in Descartes's assertion, at the beginning of the *Discours de la méthode*, that all men are equally endowed with reason and are therefore capable of knowing the same truths.[2] The association of reason with truth allows an author to develop poignant contrasts: the devaluation of *raison* in any of its acceptations contrasts sharply with its usual association and can be used in word-play (as in Molière's 'Le raisonnement en bannit la raison') or, more seriously, to evoke an awareness of the disparity between man's potential and his actual state, to remind the reader of the deceptiveness of appearances and to emphasize the distinction between opinion, fantasy, and true insight.

The association of reason with truth is also important in a more fundamental sense. The vagueness of this association is the key to understanding the sliding movement in the concept of reason during the seventeenth century. Two general conceptions of reason emerge in this study – that of the universalist and that of the empiricist. These are differentiated primarily by the different type of truth with which *raison* is connected. Consequently, the various seventeenth-century definitions of *raison* must all be seen in relation to this primary association. The descriptions of classical reason as 'prudence' and as 'common sense,' given by Fidao-Justiniani and by Wright, fail to differentiate classical reason from other seventeenth-century conceptions because they do not take account of the different types of truth with which these terms are connected. Both the universalists and the empiricists use *raison* in the sense of prudence and of common sense. But for the universalist prudence may represent the highest form of virtue linked with all perfection and common sense may represent the highest form of human awareness. For the empiricist, in contrast, prudence may refer merely to one of a number of tools at the disposal of the scientist or diplomat and common sense to the highest common factor of intelligence. These differences in the connotations and weight of the word *raison* are much more difficult to grasp than simple translations or definitions but they are also of central importance to an understanding of classicism and of classical reason. It would seem, as Michéa has remarked,[3] that an abstract word can express the strivings of an individual and of a period: *raison* is never once and for all defined but changes its complexion in response to underlying attitudes and aspirations. It is only by following these subtle shifts in the connotations of the word that a distinctively classical reason may be isolated and that the relative restrictiveness or freedom of classical reason can be appraised.

Classicism has often been seen as a moment of conscious order imposed on the disarray and crisis of the late sixteenth and early seventeenth centuries.[4]

Hazard describes it as a conscious striving for order which is eventually overtaken by the re-emergence of earlier trends and by a hardening of the classical conception of order: 'Dès que le classicisme cesse d'être un effort, une volonté, une adhésion réfléchie, pour se transformer en habitude et en contrainte, les tendances novatrices, toutes prêtes, reprennent-elles leur force et leur élan ; et la conscience européenne se remet a sa recherche éternelle. Commence une crise si rapide et si brusque, qu'elle surprend : alors que, longuement préparée par une tradition séculaire, elle n'est en réalité qu'une reprise, une continuation.'[5] This view of classicism as a vulnerable superstructure is shared by Borgerhoff: he describes it as a delicate equilibrium dependent on a balanced relationship between what he calls an 'intimate individuality' and 'forces which work too ardently for the establishment of obvious order and convention.' Like Hazard, Borgerhoff considers that this equilibrium eventually gives way to a more 'logicalistic' and 'totalitarian' outlook.[6]

This general pattern in seventeenth-century thought is reflected in the concept of reason. The conception of the early *libertins* is similar to that of Bayle and Fontenelle: for both, *raison* is on the whole narrowly defined and refers to a discursive faculty. However, this narrow conception is overlaid for a time by a striving for an eternal reason, order, and truth, and this aspiration is reflected in the use of *raison* to refer to a hypostatized standard and to an object of intellection. While this use long antedates the seventeenth century, it becomes temporarily highlighted during the period under study because it contrasts sharply with the scepticism which precedes and then, in a different form, eventually overtakes it.

In this way, the concept of reason reflects the pattern in seventeenth-century thought described by Hazard and by Borgerhoff. Reason does not counter and eventually defeat classicism and it does not represent solely a force for 'obvious order and convention' within classicism: rather, one might say that the concept of reason expands to meet the needs of the classical writer and that it contracts in response to the more pragmatic aspirations of the sceptic and the empiricist.

The belief in a universal reason has long been singled out as a central principle of classicism. But the effects of this belief on the concept of reason and on the use of the word *raison* have not been sufficiently explored: they emerge in this study as very extensive and of paramount importance. The belief in the universal gives rise to two levels of speech whereby *raison*, like *nature* and *vérité*, can refer to an eternal or to an inconstant reality; it links the ideal of reason with all other ideals and broadens the conception of human reason. Also it provides a clue to understanding the connection between many apparently contradictory tendencies in classical literature.

In some form, the narrow conception of reason is present throughout the period. The inquiring spirit, the analytical use of reason, and the rejection of the authority of books, systems, and the opinions of others, characteristic of Montaigne and of the early *libertins*, are in some degree shared by most seventeenth-century authors. Rational argument is used to question the value of reason and to demarcate its limitations and possibilities. It is used to analyse the nature of virtue and vice, of beauty and ugliness, to mock the convolutions and ineffectuality of human reasoning and to demonstrate the power of a reason correctly used. However, these analytical endeavours are not always based on a critical sense of philosophical doubt. In Descartes, Méré, Pascal, La Bruyère, Boileau, La Rochefoucauld, Bossuet, Malebranche, and many other authors, critical analysis is subjugated, to a greater or lesser extent, to an almost devout longing for closeness to an eternal centre and this focusing on one eternal truth helps to explain the apparent conservatism of many classical writers – a conservatism which has all too often been attributed simply to an excessive reverence for the ancients.

In many authors reasoning centres on an a priori truth known by means of an immediate experience. This experience provides the premise and ensures the validity of discursive thought. Thus the deductive reasonings of Cartesian philosophy are, in a sense, centrifugal: Descartes starts with an intuitive and immediate perception, which he expands and develops by means of reasoning, and by this process he breaks down the original perception into separate disciplines. But he hopes that eventually these disciplines will once again converge and that man will be able to attain an ultimate wisdom.[7] Many authors use reasoning in a similar, if less rigorous, way to explain and clarify an a priori truth. They are not concerned so much to discover new truths as to grasp in its fullness the eternal truth. The mass of critical commentary on aesthetics and on morals in the seventeenth century would seem to have this purpose. It is based on the assumption that there is a reason for *beauté* and a reason for *honnêteté*. If these commentaries seek to analyse and formalize eternal truth they nevertheless recognize that this truth is initially experienced rather than rationally perceived. Thus between the scepticism of the *libertins* and the empiricism of Bayle and Fontenelle we find a different kind of analytical endeavour, one which is bounded by a concentric movement of thought centred on an immediate and intuitive experience.

The desire to approach an eternal and a priori truth is simultaneously responsible for the aridity of many pedantic seventeenth-century treatises and for the vigour and force of the great works of literature. Rational analysis does not mix easily with the attempt to capture an eternal and constant truth: as in Cartesian philosophy, it quickly moves away from this centre or, if it does not do so, it easily becomes spurious and locked in circularity. The best seventeenth-century critics, such as Boileau and Bouhours, avoid this difficulty by using verse or dialogue for their exposition: by this method the eternal ideal can be both the critic's overture and his finale without leading him into unproductive reasoning. Indeed, the further the form of expression is from systematic analysis the better it may be suited to inspire an awareness of eternal truth. Pascal's *Pensées* and Bossuet's sermons approach from many different angles the truth on which they seek to focus the reader's attention. Much of the impact of the *Pensées* lies in the fact that Pascal never finally describes or defines this ultimate truth but leaves, as it were, a void in the centre of a spiral. The classicist's willingness to accept rigid rules, such as those taken from Aristotle's *Poetics*, may be partly explained by this striving for a single ideal: the constraining nature of the rules encourages and helps the dramatist to expand his themes around a single moment of experience. Thus the rules contribute to what Mourgues has called the 'triumph of relevance' in Racine's drama.[8]

Beneath the attempt to grasp a constant truth by means of analysis and exposition lies an acceptance of the reliability of a non-rational perception and an intuitive experience. This experience relates to an eternal reality and not to the external world. Yet it is, if anything, more direct and more immediate than the experience sought by the empiricist. The parallel deserves emphasis because it points to the underlying concreteness of the seventeenth-century mind, a quality which is as essential to the flowering of classicism as it is to the development of empiricism. Classicism has been admired as a perfect blend of form and content, of spontaneity and of rationality.[9] Such a blending of consciousness with feeling, with taste, and with sensibility is of the essence of the universalist's conception of human reason. By this conception *raison* can refer not only to discursive thought but also to something like the rational soul – the source of all that is reasonable in man – to a moral conscience, and to an aesthetic sense. This fusion of thought and feeling is seen in Balzac's notion of a 'raisonnable fureur,' in Bouhours's 'bon sens gay, vif et plein de feu,' and in Pascal's description of the language of Christ: 'J-C a dit les choses grandes si simplement qu'il semble qu'il ne les a pas pensées, et si nettement néanmoins qu'on voit bien ce qu'il en pensait. Cette clarté jointe à cette naïveté est admirable' (*Pensées* §309). Through the ideal of the *raisonnable*, the mathematical can be linked to the moral and the mechanics of a severe logic can be welded to a spontaneous creativity, and this even in authors who do not believe that the eternally reasonable is attainable specifically by means of human reason.

Just as universal truth has a tangential relationship with 'la raison raisonnante' and blurs the distinction between thought and feeling, so also it is not identical with any one moral code and overrules the distinction between virtue and vice as conventionally defined. Nadal has isolated in Corneille's plays three types of moral code which, he says, are often intertwined: one whereby the hero seeks glory in the eyes of others, one through which he strives to experience his own power, and one which requires him to obey an intimate inner law and conscience.[10] The contradictions implied in these concepts are not peculiar to Corneille: they are apparent in a different form in the theory of art. The artist is confronted with opposing standards: his work must not infringe convention yet it must be drawn solely from his inner vision and not from the imitation of others. The notion of the universal affords a reconciliation between these opposites: if the artist follows his reason rather than his fantasy or his self-interest, he will approach a truth available to all men and yet superior to custom and to convention. As with Pascal's Christ the universal truth of classicism stands between and above the extremes of individualism and of authoritarianism. *Raison* can be used to refer to the conventional and it can be used (usually derogatorily) to refer to the purely individual. It can also designate an equilibrium, a point of balance uniting the personal to the universal.

Thus, although the notion of a universal truth is not necessarily linked with belief in God, this notion in some ways resembles a religious aspiration. Like Christianity, it gives rise to a questioning of accepted standards, to an individualism, even a radicalism. At the same time, by insisting on a single and constant truth, it encourages authoritarianism. In Christianity these opposites are believed to be reconcilable. Similarly, the notion of a universal truth represents a link between the contradictory tendencies in classical literature: between the courageous unveiling of the springs of vice and virtue and the firm assertion of moral values, between the spontaneity and individuality of the great works of classical literature and the dogmatism of classical theory. It is in this notion of a possible binding of opposites that the distinctive quality of classicism is to be found. The word *raison*, more than any other word, is used to represent the ideal: this word has the great advantage that it can refer both to a discursive and logical faculty and to an ideal of proportion which is not limited to logic and can be applied even to the most intense emotion. In this way, the ideal of reason involves an element of the *je ne sais quoi* and evades complete formulation. It embraces the 'freedom' which Borgerhoff regards as essential to the creativity of the great classical writer[11] and it stands between the extremes of 'la Raison sans charme' and 'la Foi sans preuve' described by Busson.[12] Unlike the romantic, the classicist never succumbs to a complete individualism and, equally, he does not look solely to rules and precepts for guidance. He uses his gift for analytical reasoning and his gift for feeling in order to attain a reason and a reasonableness which can stir man in his totality.

If classicism is defined in terms of the presence of this ideal no author is constantly a classicist. The ideal cannot be relentlessly held in view or realized in a continuous way: it will be glimpsed, temporarily experienced, or recognized and then sought again in relation to changed circumstances, different ideas, and new materials. The classical conception of reason thus defined appears here and there, scattered through various authors, more frequent and more dominant in some than in others. It may be combined with different philosophies and attitudes and, although it is 'Platonic' and 'religious' in the loosest sense of these words, it is not peculiar to the Christian, the stoic or the epicurean, the Jansenist or the Jesuit. Thus only the period of its predominance and not the moment of its appearance or disappearance can be satisfactorily marked. It is apparent well before 1660 in Balzac, Descartes, Poussin, Chapelain, and Corneille. But in each of these authors *raison* is also used in a narrower sense, more typical of the empiricist, to refer to a faculty for discursive thought, to a standard based on human reasoning, or on the personal and social needs of the moment. Moreover, the classical conception of reason lingers on in an attenuated and somewhat jejune form in some of the uses of Saint-Evremond, Bayle, and Fontenelle who occasionally speak of reason as good judgment or expect that reasoning may eventually provide a moral direction.

But ideals of reason based on faith in the progress of human reasoning and in the accumulation of knowledge cannot fully replace the belief in constant and universal principles. As the classical awareness of a higher eternal truth is eroded, reason is increasingly identified with thought and is separated from feeling, from conscience, and from aesthetic sensibility. This division of the human mind is reflected in conceptions of history. For Bossuet all history is the unfolding of the eternal will; for the eighteenth-century historian it is divided into periods, into ages of reason and ages of sentiment or faith.[13] At the end of the seventeenth century this division is already marked. Reason and sentiment have different protagonists: Bayle and Fontenelle support reason while Béat de Muralt upholds instinct which he claims is man's only hope of true order and of moral direction.[14] Reason is no longer an eternal model and it cannot act as a law in man, uniting thought and sentiment. It has become simply a means to attain a knowledge from which, it is hoped, future generations may profit. While classicism may be admired for aspiring to order and to truth, the quality which gave it vigour and splendour is lost. Lenoble's words concerning the idea of nature after the seventeenth century may be applied to the concept of reason: 'L'homme a échangé son modèle, sa maîtresse, pour un outil.'[15]

Definitions of *raison* in three dictionaries

RAISON, s.f. Puissance de l'ame qui sépare le faux du vrai. C'est aussi une connoissance juste de la fin & des moiens que l'homme doit avoir dans sa conduite. [Le mot de *raison* en ce sens n'a point de pluriel, La droite raison. C'est une chose éloignée de la droite raison. *La Chamb.* C'est manquer de raison ou bien l'avoir blessée. N'avoir ne sens, ne raison. *Ablancourt, Luc.* Avoir l'usage de raison. *Ablancourt, Luc.* Gui Guillot a plus d'instinct que de raison.]

Raison. Sujet, cause, consideration. Ce mot de raison en ce sens à un pluriel. [Navoir aucune raison de se fâcher contre une personne. *Ablancourt, Luc.* Sans cela je vous demanderois raison de ce que vous m'acusez. *Voi. 1.35.* Ce n'est pas à vous que j'en veux rendre raison, *Moliere.* S'il a manqué à sa parole il a ses *raisons* pour cela. *Moliere.* Il a été contraint pour *quelques raisons* d'état de sortir de la Libre. *Voi. 1.41*].

Raison. Tout ce qu'on alégue, qu'on dit & qu'on aporte pour prouver, confirmer & persuader quelque chose. Le mot de *raison* en ce sens a un pluriel. [Une bonne, forte, solide, puissante, claire, invincible, foible, frivole, impertinente, ridicule, captieuse raison, une raison tirée du sujet. L'orateur doit prouver par de solides raisons ce qu'il avance. *Ablancourt, Lucien.* Détruire les raisons qu'on aporte contre nous].

Raison. Ce mot sert à marquer le ressentiment qu'on a d'une injure reçue, & il signifie une sorte de vengeance, une sorte de réparation & de satisfaction à cause de l'injure qu'on a reçüe. Le mot de *raison* en ce sens n'a point de pluriel. [Les loix du monde défendent de soufrir les injures sans en *tirer raison* soi-même & souvent par la mort de ses ennemis. *Pass. 1.7.* Venez me *faire raison* de l'insolence la plus grande du monde. *Moliere.*]

Raison. Ce mot se dit en parlant de gens qu'on range, ou qui se rangent à leur devoir, & viennent au point où l'on veut qu'ils viennent. Le mot de *raison* en ce sens n'a point de pluriel. [Ranger une personne à la raison. *Ablancourt, Luc.* Ah ! Monsieur, je suis ravi que vous vous mettez à la raison. *Moliere.*]

Raison. Ce mot se dit entre marchans & veut dire *sur le pié* d'une certaine somme. Le mot de *raison* en ce sens n'a point de pluriel. [J'ai acheté cela à *raison* de dix pour cent.]

Raison. Ce mot se dit entre gens qui boivent & qui se témoignent quelque amitié & il signifie boire à celui qui a bu à notre santé. Le mot de *raison* en ce sens a un pluriel. [Faire raison a un ami. *Ablancourt, Luc.* Souvent on perd la *raison* à force de faire des *raisons.*]

Raison. Termes de Mer. Voiez *ration.*

Raison. Terme de Matematiques. C'est le raport, ou la rélation d'un nombre à un autre nombre, & en général d'une quantité à une autre. La premiere se nomme *l'antecédent*, & la seconde *le conséquent*. La *raison* marque combien de fois l'antecedent contient le conséquent, ou est contenu dans son conséquent. [Il y a deux sortes de raison, *la raison éxacte*, ou de nombre à nombre, lors que les quantitez que l'on compare sont commensurables, & *la raison sourde*, lors que les quantitez sont incommensurables. *Port-Roial, Géometrie, 1.2.*]

Raisonnable, adj. Qui a de la raison, du sens, du jugement, qui peut raisonner. [L'homme est né raisonnable.]

Raisonnable. Sage, judicieux. [Imagination raisonnable. *Voi. 1.5.* Conseil raisonnable. *Voi. 1.8.* Gens heureux & raisonnables laissent dire les miserables. *Voit. Poës.*]

Raisonnable. Juste, qui agit raisonnablement. [C'est un homme fort raisonnable.]

Raisonnable. Qui est fait comme il faut, bien fait, bien proportionné. [Je ne lui voi rien de *raisonnable* que la taille & le souris. *Ablancourt, Lucien.* Un visage raisonnable. Une chambre raisonnable.]

Raisonnable. Ce mot se dit en parlant du prix & de la valeur d'une chose, & veut dire qui n'excéde pas, qui n'est pas exorbitant. [C'est un prix raisonnable.]

Raisonnablement, adverbe. Avec raison, de bon sens, d'une maniere raisonnable. [Il parle raisonnablement de tout. *Voi. Poës.*]

Raisonnablement. Bien, d'une maniere où il n'y a rien à dire, d'une maniere honnête & telle qu'il se pratique dans le monde entre honnêtes gens. [Un tel est logé fort raisonnablement pour un poëte.]

Raisonnement, s.m. Faculté de raisonner. [Il a le raisonnement fort bon.]

Raisonnement, s.m. Discours raisonné. Raison qu'on aporte pour persüader. [Le raisonnement doit être clair, fort, juste & solide. Détruire un raisonnement, afoiblir un raisonnement. *Ablancourt.*]

Raisonner, v.n. Parler, discourir de bon sens aporter & aléguer des raisons. [Nous alons *raisonner* sur votre afaire. *Moliere.* Enfant qui commence à raisonner. *La Chambre.* Raisonner parfaitement. *Voi. 1.8.*]

Raisonner. Voiez *résonner.*

Raisonner. Considerer, voir les suites d'une chose, faire reflexion. [Lors que l'on vient à voir vos celestes apas un cœur se laisse prendre & ne *raisonne* pas. *Mol.*]

Raisonner. Ce mot se dit d'un ton impérieux, & en parlant à une Personne sur qui nous avons quelque autorité, ou quelque avantage, & qui replique à ce que nous lui disons, au lieu de nous écouter avec soumission & avec respect. [Taisez-vous, Monsieur le sot, C'est bien à vous à faire à raisonner disoit un jour une Dame de qualité au bon homme du Clerat le plus irraisonnable de tous les animaux à deux piez.]

Raisonner à la patache. Raisonner à la chaloupe. Termes de Mer. Qui se disent des vaisseaux qui viennent mouiller. C'est montrer à la patache, ou chaloupe qui est de garde la permission qu'on a de mouiller dans le port, & rendre compte de la route qu'on veut faire.

Raisonné, raisonnée, adj. Chose, ou sujet sur lequel on a parlé, discouru, aporté des raisons, prouvé par raisons, examiné, & consideré à force de raisonnemens. [Discours raisonné. Grammaire raisonnée.]

Raisonneur, s.m. Celui qui replique trop à une personne à qui il doit du respect, celui qui pour excuser sa conduite répond à une personne qui lui est superieure & tâche de lui faire trouver bon quelque chose. Le mot de *raisonneur* se prononce d'un ton de maître. [Vous faites ici le *raisonneur*. Taisez-vous, vous n'étes qu'un animal.]

Raisonneuse, s.f. Celle qui pour s'excuser alégue quelques raisons qui ne valent pas grand chose, ou du moins que la personne à qui elle parle n'aprouve pas. Celle qui répond un peu trop à une personne de respect, où à qui elle est inférieure. [Mêle-toi de donner à téter à ton enfant sans faire tant la *raisonneuse. Moliere.*]

FURETIÈRE'S DICTIONNAIRE UNIVERSEL

RAISON. s.f. Entendement, premiere puissance de l'ame qui discerne le bien du mal, le vray d'avec le faux. Entre les corps sublunaires il n'y a que l'homme qui soit doüé de *raison*. La *raison* est souvent un guide trompeur. On appelle fous, ceux qui n'ont point de *raison*, ou de qui la *raison* est perduë & égarée. La droite *raison*, c'est la lumiere naturelle. Un enfant au dessous de sept ans ne peche point, parce qu'il n'a pas l'âge de *raison*. Il n'y a point de *raison* de s'amuser à luy. C'est un homme de bien, qui vit selon Dieu & *raison*.

Raison, se dit quelquefois de la seule faculté imaginative. Les chimeres sont des estres de *raison*, qui ne subsistent que dans nostre imagination.

Raison, signifie aussi, Cause, motif, fondement de quelque chose. Les Philosophes ignorent la *raison*, la cause de la plus-part des effets de la nature. Ce Prince a eu des *raisons* secretes, de bons motifs pour faire une telle entreprise. Quand on veut croire une chose, il faut voir s'il y a de la *raison*, du fondement, de l'apparence.

Raison, signifie aussi, Argumentation, preuve. Les mysteres de la foy ne se peuvent prouver par *raison*, ils sont au dessus de la raison, & non pas contre la *raison*. Il faut captiver sa *raison*, deferer plus à l'autorité qu'à la *raison*. Les *raisons* des Geometres sont demonstratives, convaincantes ; celles des autres sciences sont seulement probables, vraisemblables. En Jurisprudence, quand on pose l'espece d'une Loy, on adjouste toûjours la *raison* de douter & de decider.

Raison, en termes de Palais, se dit du droit qu'on a de poursuivre quelque chose en Justice, du titre d'une possession. Un donateur ou cedant subroge un cessionaire en tous ses droits, noms, *raisons*, & actions. Il ne joüit de cette ferme qu'à *raison* de ce qu'elle dépend de sa Seigneurie, de son Benefice. Cette demande est fondée en droit & *raison*. La *raison* d'Estat prevaut souvent sur les *raisons* de famille, l'emporte sur l'interest des particuliers. Les Grands fort peu souvent se rendent à la *raison*, se payent de *raison*, veulent écouter la *raison*.

Raison, en termes de Geometrie, d'Arithmetique, & d'Algebre, signifie, Proportion, rapport d'une quantité à une autre. Il y a des *raisons* doubles, triples, multiples, sesquialteres, & superpartientes. Voyez à leur ordre. Comme, deux est à quatre, ainsi que quatre est à huit : c'est la *raison* ou proportion geometrique. Les lignes ou nombres qui ont *raison* ou proportion entre elles s'appellent *rationelles* ; & celles qui n'en ont point, *irrationelles* : & quand on compare des superficies ensemble, on les appelle *rationelles en puissance*. Voyez le VI. & le X. Livre d'Euclide. On dit en ce sens, Il y a *raison* par tout, c'est à dire, qu'il faut qu'il y ait une certaine égalité ou proportion entre les choses. Il ne demande l'interest qu'à *raison* de l'Ordonnance au taux du Roy.

Raison, en termes de Marchands, se dit des livres qu'ils tiennent, qu'ils appellent livres de *raison*, qui servent à rendre *raison* de l'estat de leur negoce, tant à eux, qu'à leurs associez. Ils disent souvent, que la marchandise est hors de *raison*, quand elle est portée à un prix excessif.

Raison, se dit aussi de la justice qu'on fait, ou qu'on demande à quelqu'un, de l'esclaircissement de quelque doute, de la reparation de quelque injure receuë. Je ne sçaurois tirer *raison* de ce debiteur, estre payé de ce qu'il me doit. Un Procureur dit à son confrere, Faites moy *raison* sur cette affaire, faites moy l'expedition que je vous demande. On dit aussi, Faites moy *raison* de l'absence d'un tel, éclaircissez moy pourquoy il vous a quitté. Les braves se font eux-mêmes *raison* des affronts qu'on leur a fait, ils en tirent *raison* l'espée à la main. Les bourgeois taschent d'en avoir *raison* ou reparation en Justice.

Raison, est quelquefois un compte qu'on rend à son superieur : On a mandé en Cour cet Officier pour rendre *raison* de sa conduite, pour rendre compte de ses actions. On appelle cela, *donner un veniat* contre luy. Autrefois les Juges estoient obligez de venir rendre *raison* de leurs jugements, dés qu'il y en avoit appel.

Raison, se dit en débauche des verres de vin qu'un homme boit pour satisfaire aux santez qu'on luy a portées. Les Allemans s'offensent beaucoup, lors qu'on ne leur fait pas *raison* en beuvant, qu'on ne boit pas autant qu'eux.

Raison, en termes de Marine, est la mesure du biscuit, pitance & boisson qui se distribuë à chacun dans le vaisseau. A Dieppe on l'appelle *l'ordinaire* ; dans les armées de terre, *ration*.

Raison, se dit proverbialement en ces phrases. C'est la *raison* que chacun soit maistre en sa maison. On dit ironiquement, La beste a *raison*, quand on se rend au sentiment d'une personne qu'on témoigne mespriser. On dit aussi d'un coq à l'asne, d'un galimathias, qu'il n'y a ni rime ni *raison*.

Raisonnable. adj. m. & f. Qui est pourveu de raison. L'homme est defini, Animal *raisonnable* ; il a une ame *raisonnable* & immaterielle. Ce garçon est devenu grand, il est maintenant fort *raisonnable*. Vous n'estes pas *raisonnable* de faire cette extravagance.

Raisonnable, signifie aussi, Juste & traitable, qui se paye de raison, qui entend raison. Ce Marchand est fort *raisonnable*, il ne vend point trop cher sa marchandise. Je ne trouve personne plus *raisonnable* que cet homme-là, il fait bon avoir à faire avec luy ; il ne propose que des conditions *raisonnables*.

Raisonnable, se dit aussi de ce qui est mediocre, convenable, suffisant. Cet appartement n'est pas magnifique, mais il est bien *raisonnable*, il y en a assez pour vous. On vit dans la Province à un prix fort *raisonnable*, fort mediocre.

Raisonnablement. adv. D'une maniere raisonnable, suffisante, convenable. Cet homme parle fort *raisonnablement*, de fort bon sens. Il y avoit à ce repas raisonnablement à manger. Cet homme n'est pas fort riche, mais il a du bien *raisonnablement* pour vivre.

Raisonnement. s.m. Action de l'entendement par laquelle on connoist le bien ou le mal, la verité ou la fausseté des choses. Toutes les sciences & les arts sont les enfans du *raisonnement.* Tout le *raisonnement* consiste à tirer d'un principe connu une consequence qui n'estoit pas connuë. L'homme seul est doüé de *raisonnement.*

Raisonnement, se dit aussi de l'argumentation formée par la puissance qui raisonne. Voilà un *raisonnement* demonstratif ; un *raisonnement* captieux, un *raisonnement* sophistique.

Raisonnement, se dit aussi des repliques, des excuses, des difficultez qu'on apporte à faire quelque chose. Un superieur qui commande absolument, dit, Obeïssez, je ne veux point tant de *raisonnements.*

Raisonner. v. neut. Exercer son entendement, sa faculté raisonnable. Un Geometre *raisonne* juste. En la plus-part des sciences on ne *raisonne* qu'à tastons. La Logique apprend l'art de bien *raisonner,* de *raisonner* en forme.

Raisonner, signifie aussi, Examiner, discuter une affaire, une question. *Raisonnons* un peu sur cette matiere. A force de *raisonner,* d'examiner une chose, on trouve la verité. Il faut donner un placet *raisonné* à vos Juges, qui contienne succinctement vos raisons.

Raisonner, signifie aussi, Faire des difficultez, des objections, des repliques pour se dispenser d'obeïr. En matiere de foy, il faut croire, & ne pas *raisonner.* Il faut obeïr à un maistre, & non pas *raisonner* avec luy. Un brutal dit aussi, Si vous *raisonnez,* je vous casseray la teste.

Raisonner, en termes de Marine signifie aussi, Parlementer pour avoir permission d'entrer dans un port : ce qu'on fait, en monstrant à l'Officier de la chalouppe ou vaisseau qui est de garde, les pouvois & permissions qu'on a d'y entrer, & en faisant avec luy les autres raisonnements necessaires pour la seurté des uns & des autres.

Raisonné, ée. adj. Qui est bien fondé en raison. Voilà une requeste bien *raisonnée.*

Raisonneur, euse. s.m. & f. Qui fait des difficultez, des repliques, de mauvais raisonnements. Quand les superieurs commandent, ils ne veulent point de *raisonneurs*, de gens qui murmurent, qui obeïssent à regret. Cet homme est un *raisonneur* avec lequel on ne conclud rien.

DICTIONNAIRE DE L'ACADÉMIE FRANÇOISE

RAISON. s.f. Puissance de l'ame, par laquelle l'homme discourt, & est distingué des bestes. *Dieu a donné la raison à l'homme. de tous les animaux l'homme seul est capable de raison, est doüé, pourvû de raison. l'usage de la raison ne vient aux enfants qu'à un certain âge. il n'a pas encore l'usage de raison, il n'est pas encore en âge de raison. il n'a pas encore l'age de raison. la raison humaine est bornée. les mysteres ne sont pas contre la raison, mais au dessus de la raison. la raison humaine ne sçauroit atteindre jusques-là. la raison nous est donnée pour nous conduire. il faut que les passions soient soumises à la raison. s'il avoit consulté sa raison.*

Raison, se prend aussi quelquefois pour Le bon sens, le droit usage de la raison. Ainsi on dit qu'*Un homme n'a point de raison*, qu'*il n'y a pas de raison à ce qu'il fait, à ce qu'il dit*, pour dire, qu'Il n'y a point de bon sens à ce qu'il fait, à ce qu'il dit, qu'il ne fait pas un droit usage de sa raison.

On dit aussi dans le mesme sens, qu'*Un homme a perdu la raison*, qu'*il n'y a point de raison à luy*. Et la mesme chose se dit encore d'Un homme qui a entierement perdu le bon sens, & qui est tombé en demence.

On dit prov. & fig. d'Un raisonnement, d'un discours de travers, d'un ouvrage d'esprit mal fait, d'un ouvrage de l'art mal entendu, &c. qu'*Il n'y a ni rime ni raison. il n'y a ni rime ni raison à tout ce qu'il dit. cet Autheur a fait une piece où il n'y a ni rime ni raison. cet Architecte a fait un bastiment où il n'y a ni rime ni raison.*

On appelle en termes de Logique *Estre de raison*, Un Estre qui n'est point réel, & qui ne subsiste que dans l'imagination. *Les universels sont des estres de raison.*

Raison, signifie aussi, Preuve par discours, par argument. *Grande, forte, puissante raison, raison probable. raison demonstrative, decisive, peremptoire. raison valable. raison convaincante, invincible. foible raison. raison frivole, fausse, plausible, specieuse. chercher, trouver, apporter des raisons. donnez-nous de meilleures raisons. il n'y a pas apparence de raison. il n'y a pas ombre de raison. il appuye son opinion de bonnes raisons, d'authoritez & de raisons, je me rends à vos raisons, il vous accablera de raisons. il m'a payé de bonnes raisons, de mauvaises raisons. alleguer de bonnes raisons.* On dit, *Point tant de raisons,* Et c'est une façon de parler dont un superieur se sert envers un inferieur pour luy marquer que ses objections, ses repliques ne luy plaisent pas.

Raison, signifie aussi, Sujet, cause, motif. *Juste raison. grande raison. bonne raison. quelle raison avez-vous d'en user comme vous faites ? il a fait cela sans raison. je ne sçay pas les raisons qu'il a euës d'entreprendre cette affaire. chacun a sa raison, ses raisons. il a quelque raison. il y a raison de douter. avez-vous raison de vous en plaindre ? la raison de douter est que.*

Pour raison de quoy. Façon de parler dont on se sert en stile d'affaires, pour dire, A cause de quoy.

On dit fig. *Conter ses raisons à quelqu'un,* pour dire, L'entretenir de ses affaires, de ses interests, du sujet qu'on a eu d'en user comme on a fait, luy justifier la conduite qu'on a tenuë. *Je luy ay conté mes raisons, & il a approuvé tout ce que j'avois fait.*

On dit aussi d'Un homme qui s'attache auprés d'une femme, & qui l'entretient de sa passion, qu'*Il luy conte ses raisons.*

On appelle, *Raison d'estat, raison de famille,* Les considerations d'interest par lesquelles on se conduit dans un estat, dans une famille.

A telle fin que de raison. Façon de parler dont on se sert pour exprimer qu'on fait une chose dans la pensée qu'elle pourra estre utile, sans sçavoir pourtant precisément à quoy. *Il fit faire un procés verbal des lieux à telle fin que de raison.* On se sert aussi de la mesme phrase, pour dire, A tout evenement, & par precaution. *Nous ne sçavons pas si nous trouverons à manger où nous allons : il sera bon de porter quelques provisions à telle fin que de raison.*

Raison, se prend aussi quelquefois pour tout ce qui est de devoir, de droit, d'équité, de justice. *Se rendre à la raison. se mettre à la raison. reduire, ranger, amener à la raison. la droite raison veut. il a raison. ils pretendent tous deux avoir raison. s'il vous doit, c'est la raison qu'il vous paye.*

il n'entend pas raison. c'est un homme qui se paye de raison. vous n'avez pas raison de l'inquieter. cela est contre tout droit & raison.

On dit prov. *Où force domine, raison n'a point de lieu.*

On dit aussi prov. *Comme de raison*, pour dire, Comme il est juste qu'on fasse. Et on dit encore prov. & dans le mesme sens, *Selon Dieu & raison.* Et dans le stile de Pratique on dit *Pour valoir ce que de raison*, pour dire, Ce qui sera de justice, d'équité.

On dit, *Faire valoir ses raisons*, pour dire, Faire valoir ses pretensions. Et en stile de Contract on dit, *Droits, noms, raisons & actions* ; & sous ces noms on comprend tous les droits & toutes les pretensions d'une personne.

On dit, d'Une marchandise qu'*Elle est hors de raison*, pour dire, qu'Elle est à un prix excessif.

Raison, signifie encore, Satisfaction, contentement sur quelque chose qu'on demande, qu'on pretend.

Il m'a offensé, j'en auray raison, j'en auray ma raison. il a tiré raison de cet affront. je vous feray avoir raison de vos pretensions. faites-moy raison de la succession. s'il se plaint, je luy feray raison par les voyes d'honneur.

On dit, *Se faire raison*, pour dire, Se faire rendre justice par force, par authorité. *S'il ne me fait raison, je me la feray moy-mesme. il n'est pas permis de se faire raison soy-mesme.*

Lors qu'Un homme boit une santé qu'on luy a portée, on dit qu'*Il en fait raison. je vous fais raison de la santé que vous m'avez portée. je vous porte la santé d'un tel, faites-moy raison.*

On dit aussi dans le stile familier, *Faites-moy raison d'un tel*, pour dire, Rendez-moy compte pourquoy il en use comme il fait.

On dit, *Demander raison d'une chose*, pour dire, En demander satisfaction. *Je viens vous demander raison de l'insolence de vos gens.*

On dit aussi, *Demander raison*, pour dire, Demander à quelqu'un qu'il rende compte de quelque chose. *On luy a demandé raison de sa conduite.*

On dit aussi, *Rendre raison de quelque chose*, pour dire, En rendre compte. *On luy a fait rendre raison de son administration. il rendra bonne raison de sa conduite.*

On appelle, *Livre de raison*, Un livre de compte.

Raison, signifie aussi, Rapport d'une quantité, soit estendüe, soit numerique à une autre. *Il y a mesme raison entre trois & six qu'entre six & douze. raison multiple, raison double, triple.*

A raison. Façon de parler adv. A proportion, sur le pié. *Je vous payeray cette estoffe à raison de dix livres l'aune, il luy doit le change de dix mille livres à raison de dix pour cent.*

Raisonner. v.n. Discourir, se servir de la raison pour connoistre, pour juger. *C'est le propre de l'homme de raisonner. les bestes ne raisonnent point. raisonner juste. raisonner faux, raisonner de travers. raisonner consequemment. il raisonne bien. il raisonne mal. raisonner sur de mauvais principes, sur de faux principes, sur de bons principes. il ne faut pas raisonner sur les choses de la Foy.*

Il signifie aussi, Chercher & alleguer des raisons pour examiner une affaire, une question, pour appuyer une opinion, &c. *Nous avons fort raisonné sur cette affaire. la loy ne doit pas raisonner, mais commander. les maistres ne veulent pas qu'on raisonne, mais qu'on obeïsse. il faut obeïr sans raisonner.*

Lors qu'on se sent offensé ou importuné des discours, des repliques d'une personne fort inferieure, on dit, *Ne raisonnez pas tant. si vous me raisonnez davantage.*

On dit prov. & bass. *Raisonner pantoufle, raisonner comme un cheval de carrosse*, pour dire, Raisonner de travers.

Raisonné, ée, part. Qui est appuyé de raisons. *Un placet raisonné. une requeste raisonnée, bien raisonnée.*

Raisonneur, euse. s.v. Qui raisonne. Il ne se prend ordinairement qu'en mauvaise part, & ne se dit que d'une personne qui fatigue, qui importune par de longs, par de mauvais raisonnemens. *C'est un raisonneur ennuyeux, un raisonneur perpetuel.*

Raisonnement. s.m.v. La faculté ou l'action de raisonner. *C'est un homme qui a le raisonnement bon. c'est un homme d'un raisonnement profond, solide.*

Il se prend aussi pour, Argument, Syllogisme, pour les raisons dont on se sert dans une question, dans une affaire. *Raisonnement solide, juste, droit, faux, clair & net. raisonnement obscur. c'est un homme qui est fort, qui est puissant en raisonnement. ce raisonnement là est trop profond pour moy, trop eslevé pour moy. tous ces raisonnemens là sont superflus.*

Raisonnable. adj. de tout genre. Qui est doué de raison, qui a la faculté de raisonner. *L'homme est un animal raisonnable. l'ame raisonnable.*

Il signifie aussi, Equitable, qui agit, qui se gouverne suivant la raison, selon le droit & l'équité ; qui est conforme à l'équité, à la raison. *Vous n'estes pas raisonnable d'en user comme vous faites. vous estes trop raisonnable pour exiger de moy que... il n'est pas raisonnable là-dessus. c'est un homme tres-raisonnable, une femme tres-raisonnable. les conditions qu'on luy a imposées sont assez raisonnables. des prétensions raisonnables.*

Il signifie encore, Convenable. *On luy a donné une pension raisonnable. c'est un homme qui joüit d'un revenu raisonnable. le bled est à prix raisonnable, à un prix raisonnable.*

Il signifie aussi, Qui est au dessus du mediocre. *Il a la taille raisonnable. il fait une chere assez raisonnable. ce stile est fort raisonnable. il a un appartement raisonnable, assez raisonnable.*

Raisonnablement. adv. Avec raison, conformément à la raison, à l'équité. *C'est parler raisonnablement, vous en usez trop raisonnablement pour... il a répondu fort raisonnablement.*

Il signifie aussi, Convenablement. *Il a du bien raisonnablement. vous avez travaillé raisonnablement, reposez-vous.*

Il signifie encore, Passablement, ou d'une maniere au dessus du mediocre. *Il escrit raisonnablement bien. il a raisonnablement de l'esprit. elle est raisonnablement belle.*

Desraisonnable. adj. de tout genre. Injuste, qui n'entend point raison, qui n'est pas équitable. *C'est un homme tout-à-fait desraisonnable, des conditions, des propositions desraisonnables.*

Desraisonnablement. adv. Sans raison. *Je n'ay jamais oüy parler si desraisonnablement.*

Irraisonnable. adj. de tout genre. Qui n'est pas doüé de raison. *Animal irraisonnable.*

Rationnel, le. adj. Terme de Mathematique qui se dit de toute quantité qui se peut exprimer par nombre. *Le nombre de six est la racine rationnelle quarrée de trente-six.*

Irrationnel, le. adj. Terme de Mathematique qui se dit de ce qui ne se peut exprimer par nombre. Ainsi on dit, que *La racine quarrée de trente-neuf est irrationnelle,* parce qu'elle ne se peut exprimer par nombre.

Ratiociner. v.n. Raisonner. Il n'a d'usage que dans le dogmatique.

Ratiocination. s.f. Raisonnement.

Ration. s.f. La portion soit du pain, soit d'autres vivres, soit de fourrage, qui se distribuë aux troupes. *Distribuer les rations aux soldats, les rations de foin & d'avoine aux cavaliers.* Il se dit aussi sur mer de la quantité de pain, de viande, de boisson, qui se distribuë à chacun pour sa portion.

Notes

INTRODUCTION

1 Bush 'Two Roads to Truth: Science and Religion in the Early Seventeenth Century' *Journal of English Literary History* VIII (1941) 95–8

2 Bethell *The Cultural Revolution of the Seventeenth Century* (London 1951) 57–64

3 Hoopes *Right Reason in the English Renaissance* (Cambridge, Mass. 1962) 161

4 Lewis *The Discarded Image* (Cambridge 1970) 155–8

5 Fidao-Justiniani *Discours sur la raison classique* (Paris 1937)

6 Michéa 'Les variations de la raison au XVIIe siècle: essai sur la valeur du langage employé en histoire littéraire' *Revue de l'histoire de la philosophie en France et à l'étranger* (1938) 183–201; also pub in Jules Brody ed *French Classicism: A Critical Miscellany* introduction by Jules Brody (Princeton, NJ, 1966) 94–103

7 Taine 'L'esprit classique' in Brody ed *French Classicism: A Critical Miscellany* 34–48

8 See, for example, Brunetière *L'évolution des genres dans l'histoire de la littérature* (Paris 1890) I 87–110 and Saintsbury *A History of Criticism and Literary Taste in Europe* II (Edinburgh 1949) 240–321 (first pub 1900–4).

9 Bray *La formation de la doctrine classique en France* (Paris 1927)

10 Lanson *Boileau* (Paris 1892) 93–5; Wright *French Classicism* (Cambridge 1920) 96–7; Mornet *Histoire de la littérature française classique 1660–1700 ; ses caractères véritables, ses aspects inconnus* first edn 1940 (Paris 1942) 97; Soreil *Introduction à l'histoire de l'esthétique française* (Brussels 1955) 38; Borgerhoff *The Freedom of French Classicism* (Princeton, NJ, 1950) 236; and Peyre *Qu'est-ce que le classicisme ?* (Paris 1965) 86–93

11 Michéa 'Les variations de la raison'; Brody *Boileau and Longinus* (Geneva 1958) 54–87. See also Brody and Cabeen *A Critical Bibliography of French Literature: The Seventeenth Century* (Syracuse, NY, 1961) §780.

12 Brunetière *Histoire de la littérature française classique (1515–1830)* II (Paris 1912–13) 583–5; Lanson 'L'influence de la philosophie cartésienne sur la littérature française' *Études d'histoire littéraire*, réunies et publiés par ses collègues, ses élèves, et ses amis, first pub 1896 (Paris 1929) 77–81; Bray *La formation de la doctrine classique* 127

13 Mornet *Histoire de la littérature française classique* 375

14 Brody 'Platonisme et classicisme' Brody ed *French Classicism: A Critical Miscellany* 207

15 Borgerhoff *The Freedom of French Classicism* 236. See also Peyre *Qu'est-ce que le classicisme ?* 89, 101.

16 Brody *Boileau and Longinus* 84–7

17 Mornet *Histoire de la littérature française classique* 62ff; Borgerhoff *The Freedom of French Classicism* vii; Jasinski *Histoire de la littérature française* (Paris 1947) 255–9; Peyre *Qu'est-ce que le classicisme ?* 40

18 Some of the highlights of this discussion are found in: Krantz *Essai sur l'esthétique de Descartes : rapports de la doctrine cartésienne avec la littérature classique française au XVIIe siècle* first edn 1882 (Paris 1898); Lanson 'L'influence de la philosophie cartésienne' *Études d'histoire littéraire* 58–96; Brunetière 'Descartes et la littérature classique' *Études critiques sur l'histoire de la littérature française*, troisième série (Paris 1887); Abercrombie 'Cartesianism and Classicism' *Modern Language Review* XXXI (1936) 358–76; Tatarkiewicz 'L'esthétique du grand siècle' *XVIIe siècle* LXXVIII (1968) 21–39

19 Wright *French Classicism* 102

20 Fidao-Justiniani *Discours sur la raison classique* 30–2

21 Michéa 'Les variations de la raison' Brody ed *French Classicism : A Critical Miscellany* 102

22 Bayet *Qu'est-ce que le rationalisme ?* (Paris 1939) 10

23 Hazard *La crise de la conscience européenne, 1680–1715* first pub 1935 (Paris 1961) 109–41

24 Borgerhoff *The Freedom of French Classicism* 199

25 Wright has observed this dual use of *raison*. See his *French Classicism* 21.

26 This is suggested by Peyre; see his *Qu'est-ce que le classicisme ?* 80–2.

27 Bénichou *Morales du grand siècle* (Paris 1948) 231

28 Allonnes 'L'esthétique de Descartes' *Revue des sciences humaines* LXI (1951) 50–5

29 Brody *Boileau and Longinus* 84–7

CHAPTER ONE: RAISON AND RELATED WORDS

1 Estienne's *Dictionnaire françois-latin* of 1539, edited numerous times by
Jacques du Puys and enlarged by Nicot, provides the basis for most seventeenth-century compilations. Aymard de Ranconnet (1606), Voultier (1612),
Buon (1614), Pajot (1643), and also Monet and Pomey (whose dictionaries
appeared in several editions from 1620 to 1645 and from 1664 to 1681
respectively) continued Nicot's work. In 1640 Antoine Oudin produced a
'supplément aux dictionaires,' entitled *Curiositez françoises*, in which he
collected a large number of popular terms. Other bilingual dictionaries giving
increased emphasis to contemporary words are Cotgrave's *A Dictionaire of the
French and English Tongues* (1611), Duillier's *Dictionnaire françois-italien*
(1677) and Guy Miège's *Nouveau dictionnaire françois et anglois* (1679).
Despite some advances, these dictionaries tend to be highly repetitive and to
rely heavily on Estienne for their inventories and translations. Some other
dictionaires consulted include the *Glossarium ad scriptores mediæ et infimæ
Latinitatis* (1678) by Du Cange, the Trévous dictionary of 1704, and La
Curne de Sainte-Palaye's *Dictionnaire historique de l'ancien language français*
of 1756. Trévoux relies on the Academy and particularly on Furetière for
definitions and adds some elaboration and clarification; Sainte Palaye cites
early examples and comments on semantic development.

2 In brief the definition reads: '*Raison*. f.f. Puissance de l'ame par laquelle
l'homme discourt, et est distingué des bestes. *Dieu a donné* la raison à
l'homme... *l'usage de la raison ne vient aux enfants qu'à un certain âge... la
raison humaine est bornée.* les mystères *ne sont pas contre la raison, mais au
dessus de la raison... la raison nous est donnée pour nous conduire. il faut que les
passions soient soumises à la raison... Raison,* se prend aussi quelquefois pour
Le bon sens, le droit usage de la raison. Ainsi on dit qu'*Un homme n'a point
de raison, qu'il n'y a pas de raison à ce qu'il fait, à ce qu'il dit* pour dire, qu'Il
n'y a point de bon sens à ce qu'il fait, à ce qu'il dit, qu'il ne fait pas un droit
usage de sa raison... On dit aussi dans le mesme sens, qu'*Un homme a perdu la
raison,* qu'*il n'y a point de raison à luy.* Et la mesme chose se dit encore d'Un
homme qui a entierement perdu le bon sens, et qui est tombé en demence.'

3 *Discourir* is defined as 'raisonner, discourir en soi-même' and as 'parler de
quelque chose.'

4 Richelet's definition, again in brief, reads: '*Raison*. f.f. Puissance de l'ame qui
sépare le faux du vrai. C'est aussi connoissance juste de la fin et des moiens
que l'homme doit avoir dans sa conduite. [Le mot de raison en ce sens n'a
point de pluriel, La droite raison. C'est une chose éloignée de la droite
raison... N'avoir ni sens, ni raison...] '

5 '*Raison*. f.f. Entendement, premiere puissance de l'ame qui discerne le bien
du mal, le vray d'avec le faux. Entre les corps sublunaires il n'y a que
l'homme qui soit doüé de *raison*. La *raison* est souvent un guide trompeur.
On appelle fous, ceux qui n'ont point de *raison*, ou de qui la *raison* est
perdüe et égarée. La droite *raison*, c'est la lumiere naturelle. Un enfant
au dessous de sept ans ne peche point parce qu'il n'a pas l'âge de *raison*...
C'est un homme de bien, qui vit selon Dieu et *raison*.'

6 Furetière refers to the idea that from the age of seven a child has the use of
reason and is therefore responsible for his actions. According to *The Oxford
Dictionary of the Christian Church* (1957) 'Age of reason' can signify 'the
normal age at which a child may be supposed to become wholly responsible
for his conduct, and therefore capable of mortal sin.' The dictionary adds
that 'in R.C. moral theology this age is held to be reached at about seven
years.' The *Dictionnaire de théologie catholique* (1930–50) explains that
according to Thomas Aquinas man, like the angels, was in his original state
of innocence incapable of mortal or venial sin and that this same innocence
pertains to the child during 'le temps qui précède l'usage de la raison.'
This view was sometimes disputed, but the dictionary says: 'La pensée de
St Thomas est demeurée commune'; s.v. 'Péché véniel considéré en
lui-même.'

7 Furetière says of *entendement*: 'C'est la partie dominante de l'ame, où
reside la raison et le jugement. L'Astronomie est le plus grand effort de
l'*entendement* humain. Il faut avoir perdu l'*entendement* pour nier la Divinité.
C'est un homme d'entendement, c'est à dire, qui raisonne bien.'

8 See Jacques du Puys, Pomey, and Pajot.

9 Richelet defines *entendement*: 'Faculté de l'ame pour comprendre les choses
intelligibles, Jugement, Esprit'; and *esprit*: 'Substance qui pense, Partie de
l'ame qui juge, comprend, raisonne, et invente.' For *esprit*, both Furetière
and the Academy give some dozen definitions and they include the reasonable soul and the reasoning faculty. Furetière says: 'Esprit se dit... de l'ame
raisonnable... des raisonnements... du jugement, de l'imagination et de la
mémoire... du genie particulier de chaque personne... du sens, de l'intelligence d'une chose, du dessein, du motif qui la fait agir' and the Academy:
'*Esprit*... se dit... de l'ame de l'homme... se prend quelquefois pour la facultez
de l'ame raisonnable... signifie quelquefois, La facilité de l'imagination et de
la conception... L'imagination seule... La conception seule... L'humeur... La
disposition, l'aptitude qu'on a à quelque chose.'

10 See Jacques du Puys.

11 See definition of *droit*.

12 See for example, Robert *Dictionnaire de la langue française* (1970).

13 Lalande *Vocabulaire technique et critique de la philosophie* (Paris 1960) 537–8
14 *Oxford English Dictionary* (hereinafter *OED*) and *The Oxford Dictionary of English Etymology*
15 Bethel *The Cultural Revolution of the Seventeenth Century* (London 1951) 57
16 See definition of *œil* in the *Dictionnaire de l'Académie*.
17 Brody *Boileau and Longinus* (Geneva 1958) 85
18 On this point it would be interesting to see seventeenth-century French translations of the *Regulae*, but the work was not published until the eighteenth century and no seventeenth-century translations exist. *La logique* of Port-Royal paraphrases passages from *Regulae* xiii and xiv in translation (300ff) but these do not contain forms of *intuitio* or of *intuitus*.
19 There may be no final answer to this question. In their definitions of *universaux*, the Academy and Furetière mention a discussion about whether universals have an objective reality or exist only in the mind. They are probably referring to the medieval argument between realists and nominalists about the nature of abstract concepts – whether these reflect truth shrouded from man's vision or are simply human inventions. The ambivalent meaning of *imagination* may be related to this unresolved discussion.
20 Robert *Dictionnaire de la langue française*
21 Castor *Pléiade Poetics : A Study in Sixteenth-Century Thought and Terminology* (Cambridge 1964) 127–36
22 Yon *Ratio et les mots de la famille de reor : contribution à l'étude historique du vocabulaire latin* (Paris 1933) 107
23 See Lalande *Vocabulaire technique* 877.
24 Bayet *Qu'est-ce que le rationalisme ?* (Paris 1939) 16
25 Ibid 14
26 Littré *Dictionnaire de la langue française* (1863)
27 *OED*: see *revenge*.
28 Bayet *Qu'est-ce que le rationalisme ?* 15
29 See Lalande *Vocabulaire technique* 887–8.
30 Ibid 878n
31 Lewis and Short *A Latin Dictionary*
32 Bayet *Qu'est-ce que le rationalisme ?* 10

CHAPTER TWO: REASON, GOD, AND NATURE

1 Published in *Revue de métaphysique et de morale* LXIX (1964) 118
2 Vernay *Les divers sens du mot 'raison' : autour de l'œuvre de Marguerite d'Angoulême, reine de Navarre (1492–1549)* (Heidelberg 1962) 63

3 Crocker *Nature and Culture: Ethical Thought in the French Enlightenment* (Baltimore, Md, 1963) 3–5

4 Hoopes *Right Reason in the English Renaissance* (Cambridge, Mass, 1962) 4, 163

5 Lovejoy *The Great Chain of Being: A Study of the History of an Idea* (Cambridge, Mass, 1950) 315

6 Spink *French Free Thought from Gassendi to Voltaire* (London 1960) 243

7 Busson *La religion des classiques, 1660–1685* (Paris 1948) 362; Borgerhoff *The Freedom of French Classicism* (Princeton, NJ, 1950) 130–1

8 Ramsey *Religious Language: An Empirical Placing of Theological Phrases* (London 1957) 59

9 Busson *La religion des classiques* 205

10 Vereker *Eighteenth-Century Optimism: A Study of the Interrelations of Moral and Social Theory in English and French Thought between 1689 and 1789* (Liverpool 1967) 4

11 See, for example, Lenoble *Esquisse d'une histoire de l'idée de Nature* (Paris 1969) 324.

12 Keefe 'Descartes's "Morale Définitive" and the Autonomy of Ethics' *Romanic Review* LXIV (1973) 85–98

13 Gilson *Étude de philosophie médiévale* (Strasbourg 1921) 188–90

14 Lenoble *Esquisse d'une histoire de l'idée de Nature* 332

15 Busson *La religion des classiques* 205

16 While this treatise was first published in 1713, it has been included in this study because it is thought to have been written prior to 1690. Indeed, some critics have suggested that passages from this work may have been composed in Fénelon's youth, before his encounter with Mme de Guyon in 1678. Referring to this *Traité*, Carcassonne commented in 1939: 'Il serait capital de savoir si l'on doit dater de la jeunesse de Fénelon certaines pages où la ferveur contemplative fait songer aux enivrements du panthéisme oriental. Selon un de ses commentateurs les plus attentifs, M. Rivière, ces passages trahiraient l'action de l'influence quiétiste. N'y pourrait-on voir aussi bien l'effet d'un "tempérament philosophique" qui le prédispose à recevoir les "communications de grâce" de Mme Guyon : mysticisme métaphysique, qu'une femme devait attendrir et surexciter à la fois ? Pour répondre, il faudrait être mieux renseignés que nous ne sommes sur la chronologie des traités de Fénelon'; *État présent des travaux sur Fénelon* 23. The question which Carcassonne here raises is echoed by Varillon in his introduction of 1954 to Fénelon's *Œuvres spirituelles*: 'Le vrai, c'est qu'au cours de ces dix années qui précédent la rencontre avec Mme Guyon (1678–88), l'âme de Fénelon nous demeure encore très obscure. Si l'on pouvait dater la compo-

sition du *Traité de l'existence de Dieu*, si l'on était sûr que certaines de ses pages au moins, comme l'affirme Ramsey, ont été écrites à cette époque, il serait peut-être possible de découvrir, dans la genèse même de sa vie religieuse, le progrès et les vicissitudes de son inquiétude spirituelle'; 19.

17 Abercrombie *Saint Augustine and French Classical Thought* (Oxford 1938) 73
18 Busson *La religion des classiques* 425–6
19 Gouhier *La philosophie de Malebranche et son expérience religieuse* (Paris 1926) 43
20 Lalande *Vocabulaire technique et critique de la philosophie* (Paris 1960): see definition of *raison*.

CHAPTER THREE: REASON AS NORM

1 Thuau *Raison d'état et pensée politique à l'époque de Richelieu* (Paris 1966) 385
2 Brimo claims that Pascal himself allows for the notion of judicial progress: 'C'est dans l'union du droit et d'une morale, la morale chrétienne que se traduit l'idée du progrès juridique'; *Pascal et le droit* (Paris 1942) 44. Pascal, however, never makes this explicit, and Brimo's conclusion would seem to rest heavily on extrapolation from Pascal's scientific work.
3 Lalande *La raison et les normes* (Paris 1948) 10–11
4 Brody *Boileau and Longinus* (Geneva 1958) 65
5 Edelman 'L'art poétique : "Long-temps plaire, et jamais ne lasser"' J.J. Demorest ed *Studies in Seventeenth-Century French Literature Presented to Morris Bishop* (Ithaca, NY, 1962) 235
6 Lalande *La raison et les normes* 82–3
7 Nadal remarks: 'La vertu recherche la gloire, qui peut avoir un objet moral, honnête, juste, raisonnable mais aussi injuste, insensé, criminel'; *Le sentiment de l'amour dans l'œuvre de P. Corneille* (Paris 1948) 296–7.
8 Bénichou *Morales du grand siécle* (Paris 1948) 23
9 See Forsyth 'The Tragic Dilemma in *Horace' Australian Journal of French Studies* IV (1967) 174n. Godefroy cites an example from Corneille where 'faire raison' is used to mean 'rendre justice.' He points out also that the definite article is sometimes included in the phrases *faire raison* and *tirer raison*, which become *faire la raison* and *tirer la raison*; *Lexique comparé de la langue de Corneille et de la langue du XVIIe siècle en général* (Paris 1862) 243–4.
10 Herland concludes: 'Mais qu'est-ce que la *vertu* pour un héros cornélien, sinon le courage de passer par-dessus les affections les plus chères ? '; *Horace ou naissance de l'homme* (Paris 1952) 186.

11 See Lawrence *Molière: The Comedy of Unreason* (New Orleans 1968) 10; Burgess 'Molière and the Pursuit of Criteria' *Symposium* XXIII (1969) 11; Danson 'Molière: The Spectrum of Reason,' thesis, Oxford University, 1972, preface.

12 Moore 'Molière's Theory of Comedy' *L'esprit créateur* VI (1966) 137. See also his 'Raison et structure dans la comédie de Molière' *Revue d'histoire littéraire de la France* LXXII (1972) 803.

13 Lanson *Boileau* (Paris 1892) 95

14 Thibaudet 'Boileau' *Tableau de la littérature française de Corneille à Chénier* préface par André Gide (Paris 1939) 129

15 Thibaudet says: 'Heureusement, ce refus de surfaire ne se ramène pas chez Boileau à une négation'; ibid 130.

16 Culler claims that La Rochefoucauld's use of qualifiers such as 'souvent' and 'presque toujours' leaves open at least the possibility of uncorrupted values; 'Paradox and the Language of Morals in La Rochefoucauld' *Modern Language Review* LXVIII (1973) 37. Starobinski remarks that despite the scepticism of the *Maximes* a sense of true values would seem to persist: 'L'échelle idéale des valeurs morales persiste et règne dérisoirement, sans trouver nulle part d'application réelle... Le bien et le mal existent, mais dans un monde à part des concepts'; 'La Rochefoucauld et les morales substitutives' *La nouvelle revue française* XIV (1966) 24.

17 See below, 124ff.

18 Lalande says: 'Une fois l'idée de causalité naturelle entrée dans la science, et utilisée de plus en plus systématiquement, elle revient sur l'ordre moral par une sorte de récurrence. L'idée d'une régularité prévisible *ex lege* dans la conduite humaine n'a pas été étrangère à Aristote ou aux stoïciens, mais elle se développe surtout au XVIIe siècle avec les *Essays* de Bacon, le *Traité des Passions* de Descartes, l'*éthique* de Spinoza'; *La raison et les normes* 79.

19 Sutcliffe has examined some of the variations in meaning of *prudence*. He concludes that, although *raison* and *prudence* are sometimes synonymous, on the whole 'la raison dépasse la prudence'; *Guez de Balzac et son temps : littérature et politique* (Paris 1959) 225.

20 Clarke 'Heroic Prudence and Reason in the Seventeenth Century: Auguste's Pardon of Cinna' *Forum of Modern Language Studies* I (1965) 335

21 Sutcliffe, speaking in general terms about the ideal of reason in early seventeenth-century political thought, remarks: 'La raison des sujets diffère totalement de la raison du roi : elle s'appelle obéissance'; *Guez de Balzac et son temps* 235.

22 See for example:
   satisfaction, vengeance: *Le Cid*, I, vi, 331; *Nicomède*, IV, ii, 1257–8; V, iv, 1375;
   explanation, motive: *Horace* V, iii, 1732; *Nicomède*, II, i, 370–2; V, i, 1504;
   cause: *Horace*, III, iii, 847; *Cinna*, V, ii, 1587–8; *Nicomède*, III, ii, 846;
   argument: *Horace*, III, iv, 896; *Nicomède*, III, iv, 985.

23 In a footnote to this passage, Régnier remarks that while the edition of 1679
   gives *raison* in the plural, many later editions give the singular.

24 Machiavelli *The Prince* in *The Chief Works and Others* trans Allan Gilbert, I
   (Durham, NC, 1965) 58

25 Baudin calls the reason of La Fontaine's fables 'la raison utilitariste,' owing
   to La Fontaine's insistence on practical precept; *La philosophie morale des
   Fables de la Fontaine* (Neuchâtel 1951) 17, 22. Couton goes further and
   says: 'Sans faire de profession de foi politique, les rois ou les animaux-rois des
   Fables, par leur seule insouciance à l'égard de la moralité, y font régner
   un climat machiavélique'; *La politique de La Fontaine* (Paris 1959) 67.

26 Sutcliffe *Guez de Balzac et son temps* 183

27 Harrington here uses Brunschvicg's edition, fragment 324. Lafuma gives a
   different syntax: 'Les demis-savant triomphent à montrer là-dessus la folie
   du monde, mais par une raison qu'ils ne pénètrent pas. On a raison';
   Pensées §101.

28 Harrington *Vérité et méthode dans les 'Pensées' de Pascal* (Paris 1972) 35

29 Gouhier *Blaise Pascal : commentaires* (Paris 1966) 287–8

30 Topliss *The Rhetoric of Pascal: A Study of His Art of Persuasion in the Provinciales and the Pensées* (Leicester 1966) 205

31 See: *Bérénice*, IV, v, 1075–8 and *Britannicus*, III, vi, 939–40. For other
   examples of *raison(s)* as cause, explanation, argument and motive, see *Andromaque*, II, ii, 577–9; *Iphigénie*, III, i, 811; IV, ii, 1151; *Britannicus*, I, i, 126; II
   ii, 521; IV, ii, 1208; *Bajazet*, III, vi, 1060; *Mithridate*, I, iii, 284; II, vi,
   705–6; IV, iv, 1271–2.

32 Orgel 'What is Tragic in Racine?' *Modern Language Review* XIV (1950)
   312–18

33 Fernandez 'Molière' *Tableau de la littérature française* 86

34 According to the *Dictionnaire de l'Académie*, *science* means knowledge or a
   body of knowledge. It is listed under *sçavoir* and defined as: 'Connoissance
   qu'on a de quelque chose. Je sçay cela de science certaine... Connoissance
   certaine et évidente des choses par leurs causes... La connoissance de toutes
   les choses dans lesquelles on est bien instruit. la science du monde. la science
   de la cour. la science du salut.' Furetière defines it: 'Connoissance des
   choses, acquise par une grande lecture, ou une longue meditation... se dit

plus specifiquement d'un art particulier, de l'application qu'on a euë à approfondir la connoissance d'une matière, de la réduire en regle et en methode pour la perfectionner... se dit aussi de la Morale, de ce qui sert à la conduite de la vie... se dit aussi de la connoissance de quelque fait particulier.' The principal distinction between *science* and *art* (in so far as they are distinct) would seem to be that of knowledge versus method. The Academy defines *art*: 'la regle et la méthode de bien faire un ouvrage,' 'la méthode de bien faire quelque chose que ce soit.' Furetière says that *art* can mean 'Prudence, sage conduite' and can refer to practical knowledge, 'une connoissance reduite en pratique.' But he also remarks that *art* may be used of 'science' and 'philosophie': 'Art se pousse quelquefois par extension jusqu'à la science, à la Philosophie.' In literature, *science* is given a variety of senses, all indeed referring to knowledge, but to different forms of knowledge. Balzac uses it to mean acquired knowledge and contrasts it with *raison*, a natural good sense; see 75 above. *La logique* of Port-Royal insists that *science* should only be used of particularly 'evident' knowledge: 'Si cette raison n'est pas seulement apparente, mais solide et veritable, ce qui se reconnoît par une attention plus longue et plus exacte, par une persuasion plus ferme, et par la qualité de la clarté, qui est plus vive et plus penetrante, alors la conviction que cette raison produit s'appelle *science*'; 292. Bossuet speaks of the *science* of God as if *science* meant not so much factual knowledge as wisdom: 'la pure science du Christianisme,' 'les lumières de la science de Dieu'; *Panégyrique de Sainte Catherine* in *Œuvres oratoires* III 569, 571. Pascal, in the above passage, would seem to mean by *science* 'disciplines,' 'sujets.' He says that geometry, arithmetic, medicine, music, and so on represent sciences in which reasoning and experiment prevail but he does not say that they alone are sciences. On the contrary, the implication is that theology and history are also sciences, although of a different kind. Fragment 720 of the *Pensées* supports this conclusion: 'Morale et langage sont des sciences particulières mais universelles.' It will be seen in chapter 5 that Fontenelle's use of *science* is considerably more precise: he considers that the word should be used to refer to forms of knowledge which allow accumulation of evidence and progress of knowledge.

35 Potts 'Saint-Evremond and Seventeenth-Century "Libertinage"', thesis, Oxford University, 1961, 406

CHAPTER FOUR: HUMAN REASON AS UNIVERSAL REASON

1 In the seventeenth century, both in England and in France, *common sense* could be used in a more specialized sense to mean 'an "internal" sense which

was regarded as the common bond or centre of the five senses, in which the various impressions received were reduced to the unity of a common consciousness'; *O.E.D.* Littré cites Bossuet's words: 'Cette faculté de l'ame, qui réunit les sensations... en tant qu'elle ne fait qu'un seul objet de tout ce qui frappe ensemble nos sens, est appelée le sens commun : terme qui se transporte aux opérations de l'esprit, mais dont la propre signification est celle que nous venons de remarquer'; *De la connoissance de Dieu et de soi-même* in *Œuvres complètes* XXIII 41.

2 Wright *French Classicism* (Cambridge 1920) 102

3 Frankfurt claims that Descartes's purpose in the first of the meditations is 'to reduce common sense to absurdity'; *Demons, Dreamers and Madmen: The Defense of Reason in Descartes's 'Méditations'* (New York 1970) 15

4 Bush *Paradise Lost in Our Time: Some Comments* (Ithaca, NY, 1945) 37–8

5 Before Descartes, Montaigne had said: 'Je ne crois pas... que la science est mère de toute vertu, et que tout vice est produit par l'ignorance'; *Essais* II 12.

6 Equally, Bossuet who divides the intellect into three parts – *esprit, raison,* and *conscience* – indicates no distinction in value between these functions and says that all three have been given to man by God to be his guide: 'L'entendement est la lumière que Dieu nous a donnée pour nous conduire. On lui donne divers norms : en tant qu'il invente et qu'il pénètre, il s'appelle *esprit* ; en tant qu'il juge et qu'il dirige au vrai et au bien, il s'appelle *raison* et *jugement*... La raison, en tant qu'elle nous détourne du vrai mal de l'homme, qui est le péché, s'appelle la *conscience*'; *De la connoissance de Dieu* in *Œuvres complètes* XXIII 49.

7 Lewis gives this rendering in *The Discarded Image* (Cambridge 1970) 157.

8 Gilson *Études de philosophie médiévale* (Strasbourg 1921) 183

9 Ibid 172

10 Kenny *Descartes: A Study of His Philosophy* (Oxford 1968) 100

11 Gilson *Études de philosophie médiévale* 172ff

12 Laporte *Le cœur et la raison selon Pascal* (Paris 1950) 107–11

13 Cruickshank 'Knowledge and Belief in Pascal's Apology' J.C. Ireson, I.D. McFarlane, and G. Rees ed *Studies in French Classical Literature Presented to W.H. Lawton* (Manchester 1968) 97

14 Keefe 'Descartes's "Morale Définitive" and the Autonomy of Ethics' *Romanic Review* LXIV (1973) 95

15 Brody *Boileau and Longinus* (Geneva 1958) 87

16 For example, in *Réflexions critiques*, he says that if the greatness of Homer, Plato, Cicero, and Virgil is not apparent to you, you may safely conclude 'que vous n'avez ni goust, ni génie, puisque vous ne sentez point ce qu'ont senti tous les hommes'; 95.

17 Brody has said that Boileau's *raison* represents a form of 'psychological energy'; *Boileau and Longinus* 62.

18 These words are cited by Fidao-Justiniani *Discours sur la raison classique* (Paris 1937) 3.

19 Gilson *Discours de la méthode : texte et commentaire* (Paris 1925) 82

20 Rodis-Lewis *L'individualité selon Descartes* (Paris 1950) 155

21 Maritain *Le songe de Descartes, suivis de quelques essais* (Paris 1932) 92–6; Laporte *Le rationalisme de Descartes* (Paris 1945) 123, 323

22 The comparison of reason with instinct can have a very different import. See below, 107–8.

23 Bloomberg claims to find five different senses of *raison* in the *Pensées*: *raison-prétention, esprit, bon sens, justice,* and *raison* (in the modern sense); 'Étude sémantique du mot "raison" chez Pascal' *Orbis litterarum* XXVIII (1973) 124–37.

24 Laporte describes this fallible reason (which is also the constructive reason of the *Pensées* and of Pascal's scientific work) as follows: 'La raison, quoi qu'elle prétende, ne peut servir de règle, étant "ployable à tous sens". Simple instrument, faculté purement formelle et sans contenu propre, elle démontrera tout ce qu'on voudra, selon les principes qu'on lui fournira pour point de départ. Quant à trouver elle-même ces principes elle en est bien incapable'; *Le cœur et la raison* 68.

25 These words are used by the English translators of *La logique* in the introduction to *Logic; or, the Art of Thinking* (London 1685) A3v. See Howell *Logic and Rhetoric in England, 1500–1700* (New York 1961) 352.

26 Laporte *Le rationalisme de Descartes* 172

CHAPTER FIVE: HUMAN REASON AS EMPIRICAL REASON

1 'Empirical' is here used in its broadest English sense as meaning 'based, acting, on observation and experience, not on theory'; *OED*.

2 'Il n'a guere d'usage qu'en cette phrase *Medecin empirique*'; *Dictionnaire de l'Académie* (1694). Furetière suggests that *empyrique* often refers to a medical charlatan 'qui s'attache plus à quelques experiences particulieres dans la Medicine, qu'à la methode ordinaire de l'Art... Les Medecins de la Faculté de Paris traitent tous les autres d'*Empyriques*, de Charlatans'; *Dictionnaire universel* (1690). This is the sense Guy Patin gives to the adjective: 'les rèmedes mystiques des médecins chimiques, empiriques, charlatans'; lettre à M. Spon, 24 décembre 1649, *Lettres du temps de la Fronde* 174.

3 Robert *Dictionnaire de la langue française*

4 Moore 'Montaigne's Notion of Experience' Will Moore, Rhoda Sutherland, and Enid Starkie ed *The French Mind* (Oxford 1952) 42–3

5 Busson cites other passages from various authors including Lamy, Mme de Sablé, Chapelain, and La Fontaine, illustrating an awareness of the need for collaboration between *raison* and *expérience*, *raisonnement* and *faits*; *La religion des classiques 1660–1685* (Paris 1948) 82.

6 Busson, for example, says 'Le plus cartésien des cartésiens... c'est Fontenelle'; *La religion des classiques* 79.

7 Labrousse *Pierre Bayle* II (The Hague 1964) 39

8 Prat: introduction and notes to Pierre Bayle *Pensées diverses sur la comète* I (Paris 1912) 39

9 Delbos *La philosophie française* V (Paris 1919) 133

10 Pintard *Le libertinage érudit dans la première moitié du XVIIe siècle* I (Paris 1943) 576

11 Ibid 484–5

12 Ibid 489

13 Ibid 488

14 Tisserand: introduction and notes to François La Mothe Le Vayer *Deux dialogues faits à l'imitation des anciens* (Paris 1922) 49

15 Lamy says something very similar in his *Traitez de méchanique*: 'Comme en fait de Religion on doit se régler sur la Sainte Ecriture, sans prendre garde au nombre de sectateurs, en fait de philosophie, on doit se régler sur la raison et sur l'expérience, sans compter les partisans de chaque secte'; 251.

16 Boulainviller *L'idée d'un système général de la nature* (1683) published in Simon 'Raison, imagination, entendement : Henry de Boulainviller (1658–1722)' *XVIIe siècle* XXI (1956) 391–6

17 Spink *French Free Thought from Gassendi to Voltaire* (London 1960) 171

18 Ibid 216

19 See Busson *La religion des classiques* 121–36 and 165–96; Rosenfield *From Beast-Machine to Man-Machine: Animal Soul in French Letters from Descartes to La Mettrie* (New York 1941) xix–xxviii.

20 Barber regards Bayle's Protestantism as the key to understanding his attitude to faith and reason; 'Pierre Bayle: Faith and Reason' Moore et al ed *The French Mind* 109–25. Bayle's view of the relationship between faith and reason is, however, substantially the same as that of Fontenelle, although the latter is a Catholic.

21 Hippeau *Essai sur la morale de La Rochefoucauld* (Paris 1967) 162

22 The date of this fragment and of *De la connaissance de l'esprit humain* (first published together by Trublet in 1724) does not appear to have received

much attention. Marsak, without any explanation, gives 'ca. 1720' – *Bernard de Fontenelle: The Idea of Science in the French Enlightenment*, (Philadelphia 1959) 31 – a date which would appear to be surmised from the date of publication. In his *La philosophie de Fontenelle ou la sourire de la raison* (Paris 1932) chapter 5, J.-R. Carré discusses these fragments in some detail, but makes no attempt to date them. In his introduction to *De l'origine des fables* (Paris 1932) he attributes the ideas for *De l'origine* and *Sur l'histoire* (both of which were first published at the same time as the *Fragmens*) to the 1670s: 'Les idées de *Sur l'histoire*, et donc de l'*Origine des fables*, seraient antérieures à 1680'; 5. Even if the *Fragmens* and *De la connaissance* were not written before the publication in 1690 of Locke's *Essay on Human Understanding*, Fontenelle's rejection of innate ideas and his emphasis on the importance of experiment are stressed in his work prior to that date. Shackleton comments in 107n of his edition of *Entretiens sur la pluralité des mondes* (Oxford 1955): 'Fontenelle's claim that reasoning is based entirely on experience is surprising so early as 1686, four years before Locke's *Essay on Human Understanding*. The influence of Locke was not extensively felt in France until the eighteenth century, and the most important exponent of empiricism in France, before Locke, was Montaigne.' Shackleton says also: 'From the claim made by Locke, that knowledge was in fact derived from experience, arose the scientific precept, that investigations must be based on experiment.' This claim, however, can be seen taking form in France in Pascal and the *libertins* well before 1690.

23 Labrousse *Pierre Bayle* II 64
24 Carré *La philosophie de Fontenelle* 206
25 Fontenelle's use of *science* in this passage is considerably more precise than the uses seen in chapter 3, n 34. It does not refer simply to knowledge or to wisdom but to a form of knowledge which allows cumulative development: this seems to be the distinction between knowing the myths of the Greeks versus understanding why they adopted them and their significance.
26 Marsak *Bernard de Fontenelle* 51

CHAPTER SIX: REASON AND BEAUTY

1 Soreil *Introduction à l'histoire de l'esthétique française* (Brussels 1955) 56. Soreil later qualifies this remark; 138–9.
2 See 26.
3 Blunt has found a trace of the Platonic attitude in Poussin's notebook and suggests that Poussin copied these words from Albert Dürer's treatise on proportion: 'La peinture n'est autre qu'une idée des choses incorporelles...

Elle est plus attentive à l'idée du beau qu'à toute autre'; editor, Nicolas Poussin *Lettres et propos sur l'art* (Paris 1964) 172.

4 Brody 'Platonisme et classicisme' Brody ed *French Classicism: A Critical Miscellany* (Princeton, NJ, 1966) 192

5 See above, 86ff.

6 Bray *La formation de la doctrine classique en France* (Paris 1927) 133–5

7 Marin 'Réflexions sur la notion de modèle chez Pascal' *Revue de métaphysique et de morale* LXXII (1967) 91

8 Topliss *The Rhetoric of Pascal: A Study of His Art of Persuasion in the Provinciales and the Pensées* (Leicester 1966) 290–4

9 Tourneur *'Beauté poëtique' : histoire critique d'une 'pensée' de Pascal et de ses annexes* (Melun 1933) 114

10 Lanson *Boileau* (Paris 1892) 107

11 Ibid 95

12 Haley *Racine and the 'Art poetique' of Boileau* (Baltimore, Md, and London 1938) 141

13 Barnwell 'Some Reflections on Corneille's Theory of *Vraisemblance* as Formulated in the *Discours' Forum for Modern Language Studies* I (1965) 297

14 Butcher *Aristotle's Theory of Poetry and Fine Art with a Critical Text and Translation* (London 1898) 116–22

15 Saint-Girons 'L'idée de nature dans l'esthétique de Pascal' *XVIIe siècle* XLIX (1960) 1–4

16 Fontaine *Les doctrines d'art en France : peintres, amateurs, critiques de Poussin à Diderot* (Paris 1909) 12

17 See above, 88.

18 Allonnes 'L'esthétique de Descartes' *Revue des sciences humaines* LXI (1951) 55

19 Tatarkiewicz 'L'esthétique du grand siècle' *XVIIe siècle* LXXVIII (1968) 30

20 However, when Racine wrote the preface in which this remark appears he had already decided to give up the theatre in favour of religion and was no doubt concerned to present his work in a light acceptable to the church.

21 Mornet *Histoire de la littérature française classique 1660–1700 ; ses caractères véritables, ses aspects inconnus* (Paris 1942) 97

22 Bray *La formation de la doctrine classique* 127

23 Litman *Le sublime en France 1660–1714* (Paris 1971) 19

24 Brody *Boileau and Longinus* (Geneva 1958) 84–7

25 See above, 85.

26 Venesoen '"L'entretien sur le bel esprit" de Bouhours : source de "L'art poétique" de Nicolas Boileau' *XVIIe siècle* LXXXIX (1970) 23–45

27 Litman *Le sublime en France* 69–70

28 Brody *Boileau and Longinus* 62
29 Krantz *Essai sur l'esthétique de Descartes : rapports de la doctrine cartésienne avec la littérature classique française au XVIIe siècle* (Paris 1898) 117
30 Mille 'La fille de Minos et de Pasiphaé' *Nouvelles littéraires* 7 novembre 1925
31 Sayce claims that this represents the most direct influence of architectural theory on literature: 'Sans doute le cas le plus frappant d'une influence directe de la théorie architecturale sur la littérature'; 'Littérature et architecture au XVIIe siècle' *Cahiers de l'association internationale des études françaises* XXIV (1972) 239
32 Saisselin *The Rule of Reason and the Ruses of the Heart: A Philosophical Dictionary of Classical French Criticism, Critics and Aesthetic Issues* (London 1970) 269
33 Bray *La formation de la doctrine classique* 125

CONCLUSION

1 Bayet *Qu'est-ce que le rationalisme ?* (Paris 1939) 16ff
2 France *Rhetoric and Truth in France: Descartes to Diderot* (Oxford 1972) 56–7
3 Michéa 'Les variations de la raison au XVIIe siècle : essai sur la valeur du langage employé en histoire littéraire' Brody ed *French Classicism: A Critical Miscellany* (Princeton, NJ, 1966) 95
4 Peyre *Qu'est-ce que le classicisme ?* (Paris 1965) 46; Jasinski *Histoire de la littérature française* I (Paris 1965) 156
5 Hazard *La crise de la conscience européenne 1680–1715* (Paris 1961) 418
6 Borgerhoff *The Freedom of French Classicism* (Princeton 1950) 240
7 This pattern in Descartes's thought has led Corte to compare the Cartesian method with the process of artistic creativity, namely with the artist's repeated and alternating consultation of his inner conception and of his model; 'La dialectique poétique de Descartes' *Archives de philosophie* XIII (1937) 136.
8 Mourgues *Racine, or the Triumph of Relevance* (Cambridge 1967). She claims: 'Everything in his [Racine's] tragedies is directed towards one single aim: to bring the tragic emotion to the highest degree of intensity'; 6–7.
9 Maulnier *Racine* (Paris 1947) 26
10 Nadal *La sentiment de l'amour dans l'œuvre de Pierre Corneille* (Paris 1948) 307
11 Borgerhoff *The Freedom of French Classicism* 235–45
12 Busson *Les sources et le développement du rationalisme dans la littérature française de la renaissance 1533–1601* (Paris 1922) 634

13 Gay *The Enlightenment: An Interpretation* (London 1966) 72–8

14 In *La crise de la conscience européenne*, Hazard quotes a lengthy passage from Béat de Muralt's *Lettre sur les voyages*, written between 1698 and 1700; 374. He remarks that at the end of the seventeenth century the main trends of the eighteenth are already apparent: 'De cette période si dense et si chargée qu'elle paraît confuse partent clairement les deux grands fleuves qui traverseront tout le siècle : l'un, le courant rationaliste ; l'autre, menu dans ses commencements, mais qui plus tard débordera ses rives, le courant sentimental'; 419.

15 Lenoble *Esquisse d'une histoire de l'idée de Nature* (Paris 1969) 337

Works cited

Many other books bearing on this subject are listed in the bibliography of my thesis, Bodleian Library, Oxford.

TEXTS BEFORE 1800

ACADÉMIE FRANÇAISE *Le dictionnaire de l'Académie françoise* Paris 1694
- *Le grand dictionnaire des arts et des sciences par MM. de l'Académie françoise* Paris 1696
ARNAULD, ANTOINE *Œuvres philosophiques d'Arnauld, comprenant les objections contre les Méditations de Descartes, la Logique de Port-Royal, le Traité des vraies et des fausses idées*, et publiées avec des notes et une introduction par C. Jourdain, Paris 1843
ARNAULD, ANTOINE et PIERRE NICOLE *La logique ou l'art de penser*, édition critique par Pierre Clair et François Girbal, Paris 1965
AUBIGNAC, FRANÇOIS HÉDELIN, ABBÉ D' *La pratique du théâtre*, nouvelle édition avec des corrections et des additions inédites de l'auteur, par P. Martino, Alger 1927
BALZAC, JEAN-LOUIS GUEZ DE *Les entretiens (1657)*, édition critique avec introduction, notes et documents inédits, établie par B. Beugnot, 2 vols., Paris 1972
- *Lettres de Jean-Louis Guez de Balzac*, publiées par Philippe Tamizey de Larroque [in] *Mélanges historiques : choix de documents*, 2 vols., Paris 1873
- *Les œuvres de monsieur de Balzac*, divisées en deux tomes, Paris 1665
- *Le prince de Balzac*, revu, corrigé, et augmenté de nouveau par l'autheur avec les sommaires sur les chapitres, Paris 1660 (first published 1631)
- *Le Socrate chrestien* Arnhem 1675 (first published 1652)
BAYLE, PIERRE *Dictionnaire historique et critique*, 4 vols., Rotterdam 1697

- *Pensées diverses sur la comète*, édition critique avec une introduction et des notes publiée par A. Prat, 2 vols., Paris 1912

BLONDEL, FRANÇOIS *Cours d'architecture enseigné dans l'Académie royale d'architecture*, seconde édition, augmentée et corrigée, 2 vols., Paris 1698 (first published 1675)

BOILEAU-DESPRÉAUX, NICOLAS [*Œuvres complètes*], texte établi et présenté par Charles-H. Boudhors, 7 vols., Paris 1934–43

BOSSUET, JACQUES-BÉNIGNE *L'église et le théâtre : maximes et réflections sur la comédie*, précédées d'une introduction historique et accompagnées de documents contemporains et de notes critiques par Ch. Urbain et E. Levesque, Paris 1930

- *Œuvres complètes de Bossuet*, par F. Lachat, 31 vols., Paris 1875
- *Œuvres oratoires de Bossuet*, édition critique de l'abbé J. Lebarq, revue et augmentée par Ch. Urbain et E. Levesque, 7 vols., Paris 1914–26
- *Traité de la concupiscence*, texte établi et présenté par Ch. Urbain et E. Levesque, Paris 1930

BOUHOURS, DOMINIQUE *Les entretiens d'Ariste et d'Eugène*, présentation de F. Brunot, Paris 1962

- *La maniére de bien penser dans les ouvrages d'esprit, dialogues*, seconde édition, Paris 1691 (first edition 1687)

BOULAINVILLER, HENRY DE: 'Raison, imagination, entendement : Henry de Boulainviller (1658–1722)' *XVIIe siècle* XXI (1956) 391–6

CHAPELAIN, JEAN *Lettres de Jean Chapelain de l'Académie française*, publiées par Ph. Tamizey de Larroque, 2 vols., Paris 1880–3

- *Opuscules critiques*, avec une introduction par Alfred C. Hunter, Paris 1936
- *La querelle du Cid : pièces et pamphlets publiés d'après les originaux*, avec une introduction par Amand Gasté, Paris 1898
- *Les sentimens de l'Académie françoise sur la tragi-comédie du Cid*, d'après le manuscrit de la main de Chapelain conservé à la Bibliothèque nationale avec les corrections, une introduction, et des notes par Georges Collas, Paris 1912

CORNEILLE, PIERRE *Œuvres de P. Corneille*, nouvelle édition, revue sur les plus anciennes impressions et les autographes et augmentée de morceaux inédits par M. Ch. Marty-Laveaux, 12 vols. et un album, Les grands écrivains de la France, Paris 1862–8

COTGRAVE, RANDLE *A Dictionarie of the French and English Tongues* London 1611

DESCARTES, RENÉ *Œuvres*, publiées par Ch. Adam et P. Tannery, 13 vols., Paris 1897–1913

- *Regulae ad directionem ingenii : Règles pour la direction de l'esprit*, texte revu et traduit par Georges Le Roy, Paris 1933

DU CANGE, CHARLES DU FRESNE, SEIGNEUR *Glossarium ad scriptores mediæ et infimae latinitatis*, 3 vols., Paris 1678

DU PUYS, JACQUES *Dictionnaire françois-latin, augmenté outre les precedentes impressions d'infinies dictions françoises, specialement des mots de marine, venerie et faulconnerie : recueilli des observations de plusieurs hommes doctes : entre autres de M. Nicot [...]* Paris 1573

ESTIENNE, ROBERT *Dictionnaire françois-latin, autrement dict les mots françois, avec les manières d'user d'iceulx, tournez en latin,* corrigé et augmenté, Paris 1549

FÉLIBIEN, ANDRÉ *Des principes de l'architecture, de la sculpture, de la peinture, et des autres arts qui en dépendent, avec un dictionnaire des termes propres à chacun de ces arts,* 4 vols., Paris 1676

– *Entretiens sur les vies et sur les ouvrages des plus excellens peintres anciens et modernes,* nouvelle édition revue, corrigée et augmentée [...] , 4 vols., Londres 1705 (first published 1666)

FÉNELON, FRANÇOIS DE SALIGNAC DE LA MOTHE *Dialogues sur l'éloquence* édité par le cardinal de Bausset, Paris 1925

– *Lettre à l'Académie (1713),* édition critique par E. Caldarini, Genève 1970

– *Œuvres spirituelles,* introduction et notes par François Varillon, Paris 1954

– *Traité de l'existence et des attributs de Dieu, Entretiens sur la religion [...]* Paris 1891

FONTENELLE, BERNARD LE BOUVIER DE *De l'origine des fables (1724),* édition critique avec une introduction, des notes et un commentaire par J.-R. Carré, Paris 1932

– *Entretiens sur la pluralité des mondes ;* [et] *Digression sur les anciens et les modernes,* edited by Robert Shackleton, Oxford 1955

– *Histoire des oracles,* édition critique publiée par Louis Maigron, Paris 1908

– *Œuvres choisies de Fontenelle* publiées avec une préface par J.-F. Thénard, 2 vols., Paris 1883

– *Œuvres de Fontenelle,* nouvelle édition, augmentée de plusieurs pièces relatives à l'auteur [...] , 8 vols., Paris 1790–2

– *Œuvres de P. Corneille,* précédées d'une notice sur la vie et ses ouvrages par Fontenelle, Paris 1858

FURETIÈRE, ANTOINE *Dictionnaire universel, contenant generalement tous les mots françois, tant vieux que modernes, et les termes de toutes les sciences et des arts,* 3 vols., La Haye 1690

LA BRUYÈRE, JEAN DE *Œuvres de La Bruyère,* nouvelle édition, revue sur les plus anciennes éditions et les autographes et augmentée de morceaux inédits [...] , par G. Servois, 4 vols., Les grands écrivains de la France, Paris 1865–78 ; nouvelle édition, notes et commentaires par G. Servois, 6 vols. et album, Paris 1920–3

LA CURNE DE SAINTE-PALAYE *Dictionnaire historique de l'ancienne langue françoise ou glossaire de la langue françoise depuis son origine jusqu'au siècle de Louis XIV suivi des Curiositez françoises, pour supplément aux dictionnaires par Antonin Oudin* Paris 1898

LA FAYETTE, MARIE-MADELEINE, COMTESSE DE *Romans et nouvelles*, textes revus par Émile Magne, introduction et bibliographie par Alain Niderst, Paris 1970

LA FONTAINE, JEAN DE *Œuvres de Jean de La Fontaine*, nouvelle édition, revue sur les plus anciennes impressions et les autographes et augmentée de morceaux inédits [...] par M. Henri Regnier, 12 vols., Les grands écrivains de la France, Paris 1883–97

LA MOTHE LE VAYER, FRANÇOIS DE *Deux dialogues faits à l'imitation des anciens*, introduction et notes par Ernest Tisserand, Paris 1922

– *Œuvres de François de La Mothe Le Vayer*, nouvelle édition revue et augmentée, 14 vols., Dresden 1756–9

– *Soliloques sceptiques*, réimprimés sur l'édition de 1670, Paris 1875

LAMY, BERNARD *Traitez de méchanique : de l'équilibre des solides et des liqueurs*, nouvelle édition, où l'on ajoute une nouvelle manière de démontrer les principaux théorèmes de cette science, Paris 1687 (first edition 1679)

LA ROCHEFOUCAULD, FRANÇOIS, DUC DE *Œuvres de La Rochefoucauld*, nouvelle édition, revue sur les plus anciennes impressions et les autographes et augmentée de morceaux inédits [...] par D.L. Gilbert et J. Goudault, 4 vols., Les grands écrivains de la France, Paris 1868–83

MACHIAVELLI, NICCOLÒ *The Prince* in *The Chief Works and Others*, translated by Allan Gilbert, 3 vols., Durham, NC, 1965

MALEBRANCHE, NICOLAS *Recherche de la vérité*, édité par Geneviève Rodis-Lewis, 3 vols., Paris, 1962–4 in *Œuvres de Malebranche*, publiées par André Robinet, 21 vols., Paris 1962–70

MÉRÉ, ANTOINE GOMBAULT, CHEVALIER DE *Lettres de Monsieur le chevalier de Méré*, 2 vols., Paris 1689

– *Œuvres complètes du chevalier de Méré*, texte établi et présenté par Ch.-H. Boudhors, 3 vols., Paris 1930

MIÈGE, GUY *A New Dictionary French and English with another English and French; According to the Present Use, and Modern Orthography of the French* London 1679 (first published 1677)

MOLIÈRE, JEAN-BAPTISTE POQUELIN DE *Œuvres de Molière*, nouvelle édition, revue sur les plus anciennes impressions et augmentée des variantes, de notices, de notes [...] par Eug. Despois et P. Mesnard, 11 vols., Paris 1873–93

MONTAIGNE, MICHEL EYQUEM DE *Œuvres complètes*, texte établi et annoté par Robert Barral en collaboration avec Pierre Michel, Paris 1967

NAUDÉ, GABRIEL *Apologie pour tous les grands personnages qui ont esté faussement soupçonnez de magie* Paris 1625
- *Instruction à la France sur la vérité de l'histoire des Frères de la Roze-Croix [...]* Paris 1623
NICOLE, PIERRE *Essais de morale, contenus en divers traités sur plusieurs devoirs importans, et instructions théologiques,* réimpression de l'édition de Paris 1733–51, 4 vols., Genève 1971 (Slatkine reprints)
- *La logique ou l'art de penser:* see Arnauld.
- *Traité de la comédie,* présenté par Georges Couton, Paris 1961
- *Traité de la vraie et de la fausse beauté dans les ouvrages d'esprit et particulierement dans l'Epigrame,* translated from the Latin by Richelet and published in *Nouveau recueil des epigramistes françois, anciens et modernes,* par Mr. Bruzen de la Martinière, 2 vols., Amsterdam 1720 (Latin version first published 1650)
NICOT, JEAN: see Du Puys; Ranconnet.
OUDIN, ANTOINE *Curiositez françoises, pour supplement aux dictionnaires* Paris 1640
PAJOT, CHARLES *Dictionnaire nouveau, françois-latin, enrichi de quantité de mots,* dernière édition, Rouen 1658 (first edition 1643)
PASCAL, BLAISE *Œuvres complètes,* préface d'Henri Gouhier, présentation et notes de Louis Lafuma, Paris 1963
PATIN, GUI *Lettres du temps de la Fronde,* introduction et notes de André Thérive, Paris 1921
PERRAULT, CHARLES *Parallèle des anciens et des modernes en ce qui regarde les arts et les sciences* Munich 1964 (facsimile reprint of 1688–97 edition)
POMEY, FRANÇOIS-ANTOINE *Le dictionnaire royal,* augmenté de nouveau et enrichi d'un grand nombre d'expressions, Lyon 1684 (first edition 1667)
POUSSIN, NICOLAS *Lettres et propos sur l'art,* textes réunis et présentés par Anthony Blunt, Paris 1964
RACINE, JEAN *Œuvres de J. Racine,* nouvelle édition, revue sur les plus anciennes éditions et les autographes, et augmentée de morceaux inédits [...] par Paul Mesnard, 9 vols., Les grands écrivains de la France, Paris 1865–73
RANCONNET, AIMAR DE *Thrésor de la langue françoyse, tant ancienne que moderne [...] ,* revue et augmenté [...] de plus de la moitié par J. Nicot, Paris 1606
RAPIN, RENÉ, SJ *Les réflexions sur la poétique de ce temps et sur les ouvrages des poètes anciens et modernes,* édition critique publiée par E.T. Dubois, Genève 1970
RICHELET, PIERRE-CÉSAR *Dictionnaire françois, contenant les mots et les choses, plusieurs nouvelles remarques sur la langue françoise [...] ,* nouvelle édition, revue, corrigée, 2 vols., Genève 1680 (facsimile reprint, Tokyo 1969)

RICHELIEU, ARMAND-JEAN DU PLESSIS, CARDINAL DUC DE *Testament politique*, édition critique publiée avec une introduction et des notes par Louis André, et une préface de Léon Noel, Paris 1947

ST AUGUSTINE: Peter Brown *St Augustine of Hippo: A Biography* London 1967

SAINT-EVREMOND, CHARLES DE MARGUETEL DE SAINT-DENIS, SEIGNEUR DE *Mélange curieux des meilleures pièces attribuées à M. de Saint-Evremond, et de quelques autres ouvrages rares ou nouveaux*, nouvelle édition, 2 vols., Paris 1740

– *Œuvres en prose*, textes publiés avec introduction, notices et notes par R. Ternois, 4 vols., Paris 1962–9

THEVET, ANDRÉ *La cosmologie universelle* Paris 1575

[TRÉVOUX] *Dictionnaire universel françois et latin*, imprimé à Trévoux, et se vend à Paris, 1721

VAUVENARGUES, LUC DE CLAPIERS, MARQUIS DE *Œuvres de Vauvenargues*, publiées, avec une introduction et des notices par Pierre Varillon, 3 vols., Paris 1929

CRITICAL WORKS AND GENERAL STUDIES

ABERCROMBIE, NIGEL 'Cartesianism and Classicism' *Modern Language Review* XXXI (1936) 358–76

– *St. Augustine and French Classical Thought* Oxford 1938

ALLONNES, O. RAVAULT D' 'L'esthétique de Descartes' *Revue des sciences humaines* LXI (1951) 50–5

BARBER, W.H. 'Pierre Bayle: Faith and Reason' Will Moore, Rhoda Sutherland, and Enid Starkie ed *The French Mind* Oxford 1952, 109–25

BARNWELL, H.T. 'Some Reflections on Corneille's Theory of *Vraisemblance* as Formulated in the *Discours*' *Forum for Modern Language Studies* I (1965) 296–310

BAUDIN, E. *La philosophie morale des Fables de La Fontaine* Neuchâtel 1951

BAYET, ALBERT *Qu'est-ce que le rationalisme ?* Paris 1939

BÉNICHOU, PAUL *Morales du grand siècle* Paris 1948

BETHELL, SAMUEL LESLIE *The Cultural Revolution of the Seventeenth Century* London 1951

BLOOMBERG, EDWARD 'Étude sémantique du mot "raison" chez Pascal' *Orbis Litterarum* XXVIII (1973) 124–37

BLUNT, ANTHONY editor, Nicolas Poussin *Lettres et propos sur l'art* Paris 1964

BORGERHOFF, E.B.O. *The Freedom of French Classicism* Princeton, NJ, 1950

BRAY, RENÉ *La formation de la doctrine classique en France* Paris 1927 (reprinted 1966)

BRIMO, ALBERT *Pascal et le droit : essai sur la pensée pascalienne, le problème juridique et les grandes théories du droit et de l'état* Paris 1942

BRODY, JULES *Boileau and Longinus* Geneva 1958

BRODY, JULES ed *French Classicism: A Critical Miscellany*, intro by Jules Brody, Princeton, NJ, 1966

BROWN, PETER *St Augustine of Hippo: A Biography* London 1967

BRUNETIÈRE, FERDINAND *Études critiques sur l'histoire de la littérature française*, 9 séries, Paris 1886–1925

– *L'évolution des genres dans l'histoire de la littérature* Paris 1890

– *Histoire de la littérature française classique (1515–1830)*, 3 vols., Paris 1912–13

BURGESS, G.S. 'Molière and the Pursuit of Criteria' *Symposium* XXIII (1969) 5–15

BUSH, DOUGLAS *Paradise Lost in Our Time: Some Comments* Ithaca, NY, 1945

– 'Two Roads to Truth: Science and Religion in the Early Seventeenth Century' *Journal of English Literary History* VIII (1941) 81–102

BUSSON, HENRI *La religion des classiques, 1660–1685* Paris 1948

– *Les sources et le développement du rationalisme dans la littérature française de la renaissance (1533–1601)* Paris 1922

BUTCHER, S.H. *Aristotle's Theory of Poetry and Fine Art with a Critical Text and Translation* London 1898

CABEEN, D.C. and J BRODY *A Critical Bibliography of French Literature* vol. III: *The Seventeenth Century* Syracuse, NY, 1961

CARCASSONNE, ELY *État présent des travaux sur Fénelon* Paris 1939

CARRÉ, J.-R. critical edition with intro, notes, and commentary to Bernard Le Bouvier de Fontenelle *De l'origine des fables (1724)* Paris 1932

– *La philosophie de Fontenelle ou le sourire de la raison* Paris 1932

CASTOR, G. *Pléiade Poetics: A Study in Sixteenth-Century Thought and Terminology* Cambridge 1964

CLARKE, D.R. 'Heroic Prudence and Reason in the Seventeenth Century: Auguste's Pardon of Cinna' *Forum for Modern Language Studies* I (1965) 328–38

CORTE, M. DE 'La dialectique poétique de Descartes' *Archives de philosophie* XIII (1937) 101–58

COUTON, GEORGES *La politique de La Fontaine* Paris 1959

CROCKER, L.G. *Nature and Culture: Ethical Thought in the French Enlightenment* Baltimore, Md, 1963

CRUICKSHANK, JOHN 'Knowledge and Belief in Pascal's Apology' J.C. Ireson, I.D. McFarlane, and G. Rees ed *Studies in French Literature Presented to W.H. Lawton* Manchester 1968, 89–103

CULLER, JONATHAN 'Paradox and the Language of Morals in La Rochefoucauld' *Modern Language Review* LXVIII (1973) 28–39

DANSON, BARBARA E. 'Molière: The Spectrum of Reason,' thesis, Oxford University, 1972

DELBOS, V. *La philosophie française* Paris 1919

DEMOREST, JEAN-JACQUES ed *Studies in Seventeenth-Century French Literature Presented to Morris Bishop* Ithaca, NY, 1962

DERRIDA, JACQUES 'A propos de "cogito et histoire de la folie"' *Revue de métaphysique et de morale* LXIX (1964) 116–19

EDELMAN, NATHAN 'L'art poétique : "Long-temps plaire, et jamais ne lasser"' in J.J. Demorest ed *Studies in Seventeenth-Century French Literature Presented to Morris Bishop* Ithaca, NY, 1962, 231–46

FERNANDEZ, R. 'Molière' in *Tableau de la littérature française, de Corneille à Chénier*, préface par André Gide, Paris 1939, 68–88

FIDAO-JUSTINIANI, J.E. *Discours sur la raison classique* Paris 1937

FONTAINE, ANDRÉ *Les doctrines d'art en France : peintres, amateurs, critiques de Poussin à Diderot* Paris 1909

FORSYTH, ELLIOTT 'The Tragic Dilemma in *Horace*' *Australian Journal of French Studies* IV (1967) 162–76

FRANCE, PETER *Rhetoric and Truth in France: Descartes to Diderot* Oxford 1972

FRANKFURT, HARRY G. *Demons, Dreamers and Madmen: The Defense of Reason in Descartes's 'Méditations'* New York 1970

GAY, PETER *The Enlightenment: An Interpretation*, 2 vols., London 1966

GILSON, ÉTIENNE *Discours de la méthode : texte et commentaire* Paris 1925

– *Études de philosophie médiévale* Strasburg 1921

GODEFROY, FRÉDÉRIC *Lexique comparé de la langue de Corneille et de la langue du XVIIe siècle en général*, 2 vols., Paris 1862

GOUHIER, HENRI *Blaise Pascal : commentaires* Paris 1966

– *La philosophie de Malebranche et son expérience religieuse* Paris 1926

HALEY, MARIE PHILIP, SISTER *Racine and the 'Art poétique' of Boileau* Baltimore, Md, and London 1938

HARRINGTON, THOMAS MORE *Vérité et méthode dans les 'Pensées' de Pascal* Paris 1972

HAZARD, PAUL *La crise de la conscience européenne, 1680–1715* Paris 1935 (reprinted 1961)

HERLAND, LOUIS *Horace, ou naissance de l'homme* Paris 1952

HIPPEAU, LOUIS *Essai sur la morale de La Rochefoucauld* Paris 1967

HOOPES, ROBERT *Right Reason in the English Renaissance* Cambridge, Mass, 1962

HOWELL, WILBUR SAMUEL *Logic and Rhetoric in England 1500–1700* New York 1961

IRESON, J.C., I.D. MCFARLANE, AND G. REES ED *Studies in French Literature Presented to H.W. Lawton* Manchester 1968

JASINSKI, RENÉ *Histoire de la littérature française*, 2 vols., Paris 1947

KEEFE, T. 'Descartes's "Morale Définitive" and the Autonomy of Ethics' *Romanic Review* LXIV (1973) 85–98

KENNY, ANTHONY *Descartes: A Study of His Philosophy* Oxford 1968

KRANTZ, ÉMILE *Essai sur l'esthétique de Descartes : rapports de la doctrine cartésienne avec la littérature classique française au XVIIe siècle*, deuxième édition, Paris 1898 (first edition 1882)

LABROUSSE, ÉLISABETH *Pierre Bayle*, 2 vols., The Hague 1963–4

LALANDE, ANDRÉ *La raison et les normes* Paris 1948

– *Vocabulaire technique et critique de la philosophie* Paris 1960

LANSON, GUSTAVE *Boileau* Paris 1892

– *Études d'histoire littéraire*, réunies et publiées par ses collègues, ses élèves, et ses amis, Paris 1929 (first published 1896)

LAPORTE, JEAN *Le cœur et la raison selon Pascal* Paris 1950

– *Le rationalisme de Descartes* Paris 1945

LAWRENCE, FRANCIS L. *Molière: The Comedy of Unreason*, Tulane Studies, New Orleans, Louisiana, 1968

LENOBLE, ROBERT *Esquisse d'une histoire de l'idée de Nature* Paris 1969

LEWIS, C.S. *The Discarded Image* Cambridge 1970

LEWIS, GENEVIÈVE: see Rodis-Lewis.

LITMAN, THÉODORE A. *Le sublime en France (1660–1714)* Paris 1971

LOVEJOY, ARTHUR O. *The Great Chain of Being: A Study of the History of an Idea* Cambridge, Mass, 1950

MARIN, L. 'Réflexions sur la notion de modèle chez Pascal' *Revue de métaphysique et de morale* LXXII (1967) 89–108

MARITAIN, JACQUES *Le songe de Descartes, suivis de quelques essais* Paris 1932

MARSAK, LEONARD M. *Bernard de Fontenelle: The Idea of Science in the French Enlightenment* Philadelphia, Penn, 1959

MAULNIER, THIERRY *Racine* Paris 1947

MICHÉA, R., 'Les variations de la raison au XVIIe siècle : essai sur la valeur du langage employé en histoire littéraire' *Revue de l'histoire de la philosophie en France et à l'étranger* (1938) 183–201; also published in Jules Brody ed *French Classicism: A Critical Miscellany*, intro by Jules Brody, Princeton, NJ, 1966, 94–113

MILLE, P. 'La fille de Minos et de Pasiphaé' *Nouvelles littéraires* 7 novembre 1925

MOORE, W.G. 'Molière's Theory of Comedy' *L'esprit créateur* VI (1966) 137–44

– 'Montaigne's Notion of Experience' Will Moore, Rhoda Sutherland, and Enid Starkie ed *The French Mind*, Oxford 1952, 34–52

– 'Raison et structure dans la comédie de Molière' *Revue d'histoire littéraire de la France* LXXII (1972) 800–5

MORNET, DANIEL *Histoire de la littérature française classique 1660–1700 ; ses caractères véritables, ses aspects inconnus* Paris 1942 (first edition 1940)

MOURGUES, ODETTE DE *Racine, or the Triumph of Relevance* Cambridge 1967

NADEL, OCTAVE *Le sentiment de l'amour dans l'œuvre de Pierre Corneille* Paris 1948

ORGEL, VERA 'What is tragic in Racine?' *Modern Language Review* XIV (1950) 312–18

PEYRE, HENRI *Qu'est-ce que le classicisme ?* , revue et augmentée, Paris 1965

PINTARD, RENÉ *Le libertinage érudit dans la première moitié du XVIIe siècle* 2 vols., Paris 1943

POTTS, DENYS C. 'Saint Evremond and Seventeenth-Century "Libertinage"', thesis, Oxford, 1961

PRAT, A. critical edition with introduction and notes to Pierre Bayle *Pensées diverses sur la comète*, 2 vols., Paris 1912

RAMSEY, IAN T. *Religious Language: An Empirical Placing of Theological Phrases* London 1957

RAMSEY, IAN T. ed *Words about God: The Philosophy of Religion* London 1971

[RODIS-] LEWIS, GENEVIÈVE *L'individualité selon Descartes* Paris 1950

ROSENFIELD, LEONORA COHEN *From Beast-Machine to Man-Machine: Animal Soul in French Letters from Descartes to La Mettrie* New York 1941

SAINT-GIRONS, C. 'L'idée de nature dans l'esthétique de Pascal' *XVIIe siècle* XLIX (1960) 1–10

SAINTSBURY, GEORGE *A History of Criticism and Literary Taste in Europe from the Earliest Texts to the Present Day*, 3 vols., Edinburgh 1949

SAISSELIN, REMY G. *The Rule of Reason and the Ruses of the Heart: A Philosophical Dictionary of Classical French Criticism, Critics and Aesthetic Issues* London 1970

SAYCE, R.A. 'Littérature et architecture au XVIIe siècle' *Cahiers de l'association internationale des études françaises* XXIV (1972) 233–50

SHACKLETON, ROBERT editor, Bernard Le Bouvier de Fontenelle *Entretiens sur la pluralité des mondes* [and] *Digression sur les anciens et les modernes* Oxford 1955

SIMON, RENÉE 'Raison, imagination, entendement : Henry de Boulainviller (1658–1722)' *XVIIe siècle* XXI (1956) 391–6

SOREIL, ARSÈNE *Introduction à l'histoire de l'esthétique française* Brussels 1955

SPINK, J.S. *French Free Thought from Gassendi to Voltaire* London 1960

STAROBINSKI, J. 'La Rochefoucauld et les morales substitutives' *La nouvelle revue française* XIV (1966) 16–34 and 211–29

SUTCLIFFE, F.E. *Guez de Balzac et son temps : littérature et politique* Paris 1959

TAINE, HIPPOLYTE 'L'esprit classique' Jules Brody ed *French Classicism: A Critical Miscellany*, intro by Jules Brody, Princeton, NJ, 1966, 34–48

TATARKIEWICZ, LADISLAS 'L'esthétique du grand siècle' *XVIIe siècle* LXXVIII (1968) 21–39

THIBAUDET, A. 'Boileau' *Tableau de la littérature française, de Corneille à Chénier*, préface par André Gide, Paris 1939, 119–33

THUAU, ÉTIENNE *Raison d'état et pensée politique à l'époque de Richelieu* Paris 1966

TISSERAND, ERNEST introduction and notes to François de La Mothe Le Vayer
Deux dialogues faits à l'imitation des anciens Paris 1922

TOPLISS, PATRICIA *The Rhetoric of Pascal: A Study of His Art of Persuasion in the
Provinciales and the Pensées* Leicester 1966

TOURNEUR, Z. *'Beauté poétique' : histoire critique d'une 'pensée' de Pascal et de ses
annexes* Melun 1933

VARILLON, FRANÇOIS intro and notes to François de Salignac de la Mothe Fénelon
Œuvres spirituelles Paris 1954

VENESOEN, CONSTANT ' "L'entretien sur le bel esprit" de Bouhours : source de
l' "art poétique" de Nicolas Boileau' *XVIIe siècle* LXXXIX (1970) 23–45

VEREKER, CHARLES *Eighteenth-Century Optimism: A Study of the Interrelations of
Moral and Social Theory in English and French Thought between 1689 and 1789*
Liverpool 1967

VERNAY, HENRI *Les divers sens du mot 'raison' ; autour de l'œuvre de Marguerite
d'Angoulême, reine de Navarre (1492–1549)* Heidelberg 1962

WRIGHT, CHARLES C. *French Classicism* Cambridge 1920

YON, ALBERT *Ratio et les mots de la famille reor : contribution à l'étude historique
du vocabulaire latin* Paris 1933

DATES OF FIRST PUBLICATION

BOSSUET *Discours sur l'histoire universelle* 1681; *Oraison funèbre de Henriette Marie
de France* 1669; *Oraison funèbre de Marie-Thérèse d'Autriche* 1683

BOUHOURS *Les entretiens d'Ariste et d'Eugène* 1671

CHAPELAIN *La pucelle* 1656; *Les sentiments de l'Académie française sur la tragi-
comédie du Cid* 1638

CORNEILLE *Agésilas* 1666; *Le Cid* 1637; *Cinna* 1643; *Horace* 1641; *Nicomède*
1651; *Polyeucte* 1643; *Pompée* 1644

D'AUBIGNAC *La pratique du théâtre* 1657

DESCARTES *Compendium musicae* 1650; *Discours de la méthode* 1637; *Méditations*
1641; *Les passions de l'âme* 1649; *Principes* 1644; *Regulae ad directionem
ingenii* 1650

FÉLIBIEN *Des principes de l'architecture, de la sculpture, de la peinture et des autres
arts* 1676

FONTENELLE *Dialogues des morts* 1683; *Digression sur les anciens et les modernes*
1688; *Entretiens sur la pluralité des mondes* 1686; *Histoires des oracles* 1687

LA BRUYÈRE All these are part of *Les caractères*, first published in 1688: *De la
chaire*; *De la société*; *De l'homme*; *De quelques usages*; *Des esprits forts*; *Des jugements*; *Des ouvrages de l'esprit*; *Du cœur*.

LA FAYETTE *La princesse de Clèves* 1687; *Zaïde* 1670–1

LA FONTAINE *Les fables* 1688 (*Le loup et l'agneau, Un animal dans la lune, Daphné,* and so on are all fables contained in *Les fables.*)

LA ROCHEFOUCAULD *Sentences et maximes de morale* 1664 (*Refléxions diverses, Réflexions ou sentences,* and *Maximes supprimées* may all be contained in this original publication. However, since La Rochefoucauld's works consist in a collection of thoughts and adages, it is also possible that the original publication was not complete.)

MALEBRANCHE *Recherche de la vérité* 1674–5

MOLIÈRE *La critique de l'école des femmes* 1663; *Dom Juan* 1665; *Les femmes savantes* 1672; *George Dandin* 1669; *Le misanthrope* 1667; *Monsieur de Pourceaugnac* 1670; *Tartuffe* 1669

MONTAIGNE *Essais* 1580 (*De la coutume* is one of the *Essais.*)

NICOLE et ARNAULD *La logique ou l'art de penser* 1662

PASCAL *Lettres provinciales* 1656–7; *Pensées* 1669

RACINE *Andromaque* 1668; *Bérénice* 1671; *Iphigénie* 1675; *Phèdre* 1677

RAPIN *Les réflexions sur la poétique de ce temps* 1674

Index

UNIVERSITY OF TORONTO
ROMANCE SERIES